Entrepreneurship in Post-Communist Countries

Jovo Ateljević • Jelena Budak
Editors

Entrepreneurship in Post-Communist Countries

New Drivers Towards a Market Economy

Editors
Jovo Ateljević
Faculty of Economics
University of Banja Luka
Banja Luka, Bosnia and Herzegovina

Jelena Budak
The Institute of Economics
Zagreb, Croatia

ISBN 978-3-319-75906-7   ISBN 978-3-319-75907-4 (eBook)
https://doi.org/10.1007/978-3-319-75907-4

Library of Congress Control Number: 2018941544

© Springer International Publishing AG, part of Springer Nature 2018
This work is subject to copyright. All rights are reserved by the Publisher, whether the whole or part of the material is concerned, specifically the rights of translation, reprinting, reuse of illustrations, recitation, broadcasting, reproduction on microfilms or in any other physical way, and transmission or information storage and retrieval, electronic adaptation, computer software, or by similar or dissimilar methodology now known or hereafter developed.
The use of general descriptive names, registered names, trademarks, service marks, etc. in this publication does not imply, even in the absence of a specific statement, that such names are exempt from the relevant protective laws and regulations and therefore free for general use.
The publisher, the authors and the editors are safe to assume that the advice and information in this book are believed to be true and accurate at the date of publication. Neither the publisher nor the authors or the editors give a warranty, express or implied, with respect to the material contained herein or for any errors or omissions that may have been made. The publisher remains neutral with regard to jurisdictional claims in published maps and institutional affiliations.

Printed on acid-free paper

This Springer imprint is published by the registered company Springer International Publishing AG part of Springer Nature.
The registered company address is: Gewerbestrasse 11, 6330 Cham, Switzerland

Foreword

The entrepreneur is at the same time one of the most intriguing and one of the most elusive characters in the cast that constitutes the subject of economic analysis (Baumol 1968, p. 64).

For market-oriented economies, understanding the elusive ways of the entrepreneur is key for fueling sustainable economic growth. The goal is clear but the challenge lies in the details: how to cultivate and support innovative and job creating entrepreneurship development?

This challenge becomes even greater in post-conflict environments such as in Southeast Europe (SEE) where the political and policy landscape is undergoing significant changes. There is little doubt that in the SEE countries, entrepreneurship will play a critical role in rejuvenating economic development and growth. Already, a significant share of small and medium-sized enterprises (SMEs) positively contributes to economic growth in the SEE region.

It is important to remember that entrepreneurship is conditional: Economically productive entrepreneurial ventures only emerge and grow under certain conditions that cannot be taken for granted. Developing countries need to reach a certain development threshold so that entrepreneurship can fully contribute to economic growth. And globally, countries need to ensure that their institutional environments provide a supportive ecosystem and formal regulatory environment that allows entrepreneurs to fully contribute to economic growth.

In order to do this, it is necessary to understand the specific entrepreneurial context. This book serves that important role for transition countries in Southeast Europe.

Developing effective institutional arrangements for the governance and support of SMEs in the economy is a challenge shared by all transition countries. The state has an important role to play in fostering entrepreneurship by developing a strategy for removing obstacles to enterprise creation, for establishing facilitating environment for private sector development, and for contributing to the development of appropriate market supportive institutions which are an important part of the business environment.

The lack of rigorous analysis on key issues affecting entrepreneurs in the SEE countries has interfered with the development of a deeper understanding of the size and scope of entrepreneurial activities. This chapter in this book fills this critical knowledge gap by providing insights into key areas such as entrepreneurial behavior and intentions, networking, and access to tangible and intangible resources.

Even as we gain a better understanding of the country-specific context, we need to also understand the variations that exist within countries. Not all entrepreneurs have the same access to resources, knowledge, and networks needed to grow a business from the innovative idea to a profitable enterprise. To unleash the full entrepreneurial potential of the SEE region, the gender dimension needs to be addressed since women entrepreneurs have traditionally been considered "less entrepreneurial" and have limited access to the resources, knowledge, and networks they need to succeed.

By providing both the contextual framework of entrepreneurship in post-transition SEE countries and a focused look into SME entrepreneurship in the Balkans, this book gives us a useful roadmap of where we are now and what is likely to happen in the future. It provides a significant contribution to the evidence base on entrepreneurship in the SEE countries with some important implications for policy development.

Schar School of Policy and Government   Ruta Aidis
George Mason University, Arlington, VA,
USA

Reference

Baumol, W. J. (1968). Entrepreneurship in economic theory. *American Economic Review, 58*(2), 64–71.

Contents

Introduction to "Entrepreneurship in Post-Communist Countries: New Drivers Towards a Market Economy" 1
Jovo Ateljević and Jelena Budak

Part I Entrepreneurship in Post-Transition Context

The Influence of the Motives of Entrepreneurial Activity on Economic Growth of Developing Countries in Southeast Europe 11
Suzana Stefanović, Maja Ivanović-Đukić, Vinko Lepojević, and Jovo Ateljević

Financial Instruments for Boosting Entrepreneurship in Selected Post-Communist EU Countries 29
Mihaela Grubišić Šeba

FDI Flows and Regional Development: Lessons for Transition Countries 47
Kurt A. Hafner and Jörn Kleinert

Sources of Financing in the Process of Enterprise Restructuring Focusing on Transitional Countries 61
Dragan Milovanović, Saša Vučenović, and Igor Mišić

Dominant Motives of Entrepreneurial Behaviour in Transitional Countries 77
Božidar Leković and Slobodan Marić

The Distinctiveness of Female Entrepreneurship in Post-Transition Countries: The Case of Central Europe and the Baltic States 99
Jelena Petrović and Snežana Radukić

The Local Economic Impact of Universities: An International Comparative Analysis (France and Hungary) 115
Balázs Kotosz, Marie-France Gaunard-Anderson, and Miklós Lukovics

Part II Small and Medium-Sized Entrepreneurship in the Balkans Region

The Impact of Tangible and Intangible Assets on the SMEs' Success: The Albanian Case 135
Ylvije Boriçi Kraja

The Role of Networking in the Company's Growth Process 147
Anamarija Delić, Julia Perić, and Tihana Koprivnjak

The Effect of EU Membership on Public Procurement for SMEs in Post-Transition Countries 163
Sunčana Slijepčević, Jelena Budak, and Edo Rajh

The Effect of Market Liquidity on the Company Value 183
Tajana Serdar Raković

Assessing Entrepreneurial Intentions, Motivations and Barriers Amongst WBC Students Through Developing a Network of Co-Creative Centers–iDEA Labs 197
Petar Vrgović, Danijela Ćirić, and Vladimir Todorović

Ethical Behavior in the Context of Managerial Decision Making and Satisfaction of Employees: Lessons from the Experience of the Post-Transition Country 211
Ivana Bulog, Dženan Kulović, and Ivan Grančić

Editors and Contributors

Jovo Ateljević is professor of strategic management at the Faculty of Economics, University of Banja Luka, Bosnia and Herzegovina, and has research interests in local/regional development, institutional framework for entrepreneurship and SME development, and entrepreneurial behavior in different sociopolitical contexts including countries in transition. His chapters appear in a number of international journals including *Entrepreneurship and Innovation Management*, *Europe-Asia Studies*, *Journal of Entrepreneurial Behaviour and Research*, *Journal of the Balkan and Near East Studies*, and *Tourism Management*. Dr Ateljevic has also been involved in a number of consultancy/research projects related to capacity building in entrepreneurship, business strategy, and tourism development in a number of countries. He is the founder and chair of the REDETE conference. Contact: Faculty of Economics, University of Banja Luka, Majke Jugovića 4, 78000 Banja Luka, Republic of Srpska, Bosnia and Herzegovina, jovo.ateljevic@efbl.org

Jelena Budak is senior research fellow with the Institute of Economics, Zagreb. She had participated in research projects on various aspects of Croatia's accession to the EU, such as institutional convergence, public sector policies, and regional development issues. Her research interests are institutions and applied institutional analysis and socioeconomic assessments of transition, and her most recent publications are in economics of corruption and privacy issues. She is a lead researcher of the PRICON project. Contact: Institute of Economics, Zagreb, Trg J.F. Kennedyja 7, 10000 Zagreb, Croatia, jbudak@eizg.hr

Ivana Bulog works as assistant professor at the Faculty of Economics, University of Split, Croatia. She has published, both independently and as coauthor, a number of scientific papers and books. For the purpose of her personal and professional development, she participated at numerous national and international conferences, seminars, and trainings. Her scientific and professional interests are focused on the areas of managerial decision making, managerial skills, business leadership, and family businesses. Contact: Faculty of Economics University of Split, Croatia ivana. bulog@efst.hr

Danijela Ćirić is a final year PhD student at the Faculty of Technical Sciences, University of Novi Sad, at the Department of Industrial Engineering and Management with specialization in agile management in innovation projects. She holds an MSc in economics. Through Erasmus Mundus Programme of European Commission, she was a scholar and a visiting researcher at the Faculty of Economics, University of Split, Croatia. Her research fields of interest are agile management, innovative project management approaches, innovation management, and entrepreneurship. She has been involved in a number of HEI capacity building projects. Currently, she is involved in project team of 3-year TEMPUS project at the University of Novi Sad called iDEAlab which aims to foster student entrepreneurship and innovation, and she is leading the project management package on the Erasmus+ KA2 Capacity building project K-FORCE coordinated by the University of Novi Sad. Contact: Faculty of Technical Sciences, Trg Dositeja Obradovica 6, 21000 Novi Sad, Republic of Serbia.

Anamarija Delić is assistant professor at Josip Juraj Strossmayer University, Faculty of Economics in Osijek. Her research interests are focused on business ecosystem, business models, finance for SMEs, and capital structure of SMEs. She is a researcher in the project "Development and application of growth potential prediction models for small and medium enterprises in Croatia," focused on SME companies in the manufacturing industry (2014–2018). She is also researcher and adviser in CEPOR (SMEs and Entrepreneurship Policy Centre). Contact: Josip Juraj Strossmayer University, Faculty of Economics in Osijek, Osijek, Trg Ljudevita Gaja 7, 31000 Osijek, Croatia, adelic@efos.hr

Marie France Gaunard-Anderson is associate professor at the Department of Geography, University of Lorraine. She is a member of LOTERR, geographical research center of Lorraine, and the "UniGR—Center for Border Studies." She was the director of a master's degree in territorial planning and defense (1997–2009). She works as an expert for local and regional authorities (e.g., for the Economic, Social and Environmental Council of Lorraine), above all in territorial planning and economic development. Her research interests are local and regional development and cross-border cooperation (analysis of Euroregions development process) in a comparative approach at the European level. She has been involved in different European programs (INTERREG IIIC e-Bird "MOSAME" project, TACIS CBC-ENACT—a project between France, Poland, and Ukraine, INTERREG IVA Greater Region, etc.). Contact: University of Lorraine, UFR Human Sciences and Arts, Department of Geography, Ile du Saulcy, 57000 Metz, France. marie-france.gaunard@univ-lorraine.fr

Ivan Grančić graduated at the Faculty of Economics, University of Split, Croatia, on ethical behavior of managers and employee satisfaction. His thesis was based on the case study of Croatian enterprise, and ethics in business is his main area of interest. Ivan Grančić is also interested in management and managerial decision-making issues. Contact: ivan.grancic@hotmail.com

Mihaela Grubišić Šeba is an independent senior research associate, Zagreb, Croatia. She has obtained her PhD degree from the University of Zagreb, Faculty of Business and Economics, in 2011 and worked at the Institute of Economics, Zagreb, till 2017. In her 15+ years career, she has published about 50 academic and professional chapters. She has also (co-)authored many project studies of importance for national economy and advised a number of public and corporate clients on various issues. Her professional interests include, but are not limited to, financing entrepreneurship, determining suitable financial options for enterprises and projects, estimating financial feasibility of projects and corporate decisions, and other financial management and strategic management issues. Contact: mihaela.g.seba@gmail.com

Kurt Hafner is professor of economics and quantitative methods at the Faculty of International Business, Heilbronn University, Germany, and has been working on several projects regarding firm heterogeneity, agglomeration economies, and the clustering of firms. He recently worked with Jörn Kleinert on a joint project of intra-firm service trade assessing empirically the effect of IT intensive service imports on German affiliates' productivity. The chapter (as a co-work with Jörn Kleinert, University of Graz) is part of an extensive study regarding the role of multinational firms on regional economic development using micro and macro data at different aggregated levels. His work is published in a number of international journals including *Applied Economics*, *Review of Regional Research*, *Review of International Economics*, *Review of Development Economics*, and *Journal of Macroeconomics*. Contact: Heilbronn University, Faculty of International Business, Max-Planck-Straße 39, 74081 Heilbronn, Germany. Tel: +49-7131-504516, E-mail: kurt.hafner@hs-heilbronn

Maja Ivanović-Đukić is associate professor of management at the Faculty of Economics, University of Nis, Serbia. She holds an MSc from the Faculty of Economics, Belgrade University, and a PhD from the Faculty of Economics, University of Nis, Serbia. Her research interests are entrepreneurial and managerial behavior, social responsibility of companies, social entrepreneurship institutional framework, entrepreneurship, and SME development in different sociopolitical contexts including countries in transition with a particular focus on Serbia and all the regions of the Western Balkans. Her articles have been published in international journals such as *Journal of Balkan and the Near East Studies* and *Engineering Economics* as well as in the leading national journals and international conference proceedings. Contact: Faculty of Economics, University of Nis, Trg kralja Aleksandra Ujedinitelja 11, 18000 Nis, Serbia, maja.djukic@eknfak.ni.ac.rs

Jörn Kleinert is professor of international economics at the Department of Economics, Karl-Franzens-University of Graz, Austria, and has been working on several projects harnessing firm-level data of cross-border activities. Several of his former projects are close to his work at the Kiel Institute of World Economics and his study of "The Role of Multinational Enterprises in Globalization." He has been using firm-level data from German affiliates of foreign MNEs and foreign affiliates of German firms abroad in several projects and recently works, among other projects, on the impact of MNEs on German affiliates' productivity. His work is published in a number of international journals including *Review of World Economics*, *American Economic Journal: Macroeconomics*, *The World Economy*, *Review of World Economics*, *Review of International Economies*, *European Economic Review*, *Economic Policy*, *Economic Letters*, and *German Economic Review*. Contact: Universität Graz, Institut für Volkswirtschaftslehre, Universtitätsstraße 15/F4, 8010 Graz, Austria. Tel: +43-316380-3443, E-mail: joern.kleinert@uni-graz.at

Tihana Koprivnjak works at Josip Juraj Strossmayer University of Osijek, Faculty of Economics, in Osijek as teaching and research assistant. Currently, she is enrolled in the international interuniversity postgraduate interdisciplinary doctoral program "Entrepreneurship and Innovativeness." She works on courses entrepreneurship, introduction to entrepreneurship research, entrepreneurial skills, new venture creation, and strategies for SME growth, as these are also her research interests. Contact: Josip Juraj Strossmayer University, Faculty of Economics in Osijek, Osijek, Trg Ljudevita Gaja 7, 31000 Osijek, Croatia, tihana@efos.hr

Balázs Kotosz is associate Professor at the University of Szeged (Hungary), Faculty of Economics and Business Administration, and is a member of the Department of Economics and Management at Methodologica Universitas in Paris (France). He got his MSc (1999—economist, finance, and accounting specialization) at the University of Miskolc and (1999—financial management) at Business School of Rouen (France) and PhD (2006—economics) at the Corvinus University of Budapest. His main research fields are fiscal policy and spatial analysis including the combination of these fields in public policy evaluation. He is author of 2 books, more than 30 journal papers, and 20 book chapters. Contact: University of Szeged, Faculty of Economics and Business Administration. H-6722 Szeged, Kálvária sgt. 1, Hungary. kotosz@eco.u-szeged.hu

Ylvije Boriçi Kraja is lecturer at the Faculty of Economy, University "Luigj Gurakuqi" in Shkodër, Albania. She graduated in mathematics and physics and also in business administration. She completed her master's degree in business administration at the Faculty of Economics, Tirana University, in collaboration with the University of Nebraska Lincoln, USA. She is Doctor of Science in Business Administration. She trained at the University of Illinois, Carbondale, USA, and also at Sandhills Community College and Pembroke University, North Carolina, USA, and at Varna University of Management, VUM, in Bulgaria. Her field of expertise is economics, SME management, corporate governance, and decision making. In Northern Regional Business Agency, she offered consultancy, training, and research for SMEs for several years. The author has published several research papers in well-known international journals such as *European Scientific Journal* and *Academic Journal of Interdisciplinary Studies*, Rome, Italy, and has held several presentations in international conferences such as in Graz, Austria. Dr. Kraja is a scientific collaborator of "Institute for Research and Development." She is four times chess champion of Albania. Contact: Faculty of Economy, University "Luigj Gurakuqi," Shkoder, Albania; ykraja@unishk.edu.al

Dženan Kulović is an assistant professor of strategic management and entrepreneurship at the Faculty of Economics, University of Zenica, Bosnia and Herzegovina. During his academic career, he was an author/coauthor of numerous books published in Sarajevo, Belgrade (SRB), Split (CRO), and Zenica out of which the most notable one is *Vatican: Organization and Functioning*. His research up to now is mainly based on areas of management competency, strategic management of human resources, due diligence, and SME management. Contact: Faculty of Economics, University of Zenica, Bosnia and Herzegovina. dzenan.kulovic@ef.unze.ba

Božidar Leković, PhD, is a full professor at the Department of Management, Faculty of Economics Subotica, University of Novi Sad, Republic of Serbia, where he teaches bachelor courses in principles of management, master courses performance management and contemporary management, and PhD courses management theory and technologies. Her research interests include leadership, communication, human resources, and entrepreneurship. Besides her work at the faculty, he has been engaged in the various national and international projects and activities in the field of research, education, and development of curricula and syllabus for management study. He authored numerous scientific research articles in various kinds of publications. Contact: University of Novi Sad, The Faculty of Economics Subotica, Republic of Serbia, bolesu@ef.uns.ac.rs

Vinko Lepojević is associate professor of statistics at the Faculty of Economics, University of Nis, Serbia. He holds an MSc degree in statistics from the Faculty of Economics, Belgrade University, and a PhD from the Faculty of Economics, University of Nis, Serbia. His research interests are application of mathematical and statistical methods in economic research and application of statistical methods in market research. His research works have been published in international journals such as *Engineering Economics* and also in the highly regarded national journals. He has presented his research works at many international conferences. Contact: Faculty of Economics, University of Nis, Trg kralja Aleksandra Ujedinitelja 11, 18000 Nis, Serbia, vinko.lepojevic@eknfak.ni.ac.rs

Miklós Lukovics is associate professor at the University of Szeged, Faculty of Economics and Business Administration, and possesses a "courtesy appointment" affiliation at Arizona State University (ASU). He got his MSc (2003—economist in enterprise development, marketing specialization) and PhD (2007—regional economics) at the University of Szeged, Faculty of Economics and Business Administration. He worked as director for strategy and development (2011–2014) and as head of tender office at the University of Szeged (2011–2012), as PCM branch manager at the Innogrant Consulting Ltd. His main research fields are responsible innovation, economic development, and regional competitiveness. He has published 37 English and more than 100 Hungarian articles and book chapters in these fields. He was the project leader of the FaRInn (Facilitating Responsible Innovation in South-East European Countries) project at the University of Szeged. Miklós Lukovics spent two months at Arizona State University where the STIR (Socio-Technical Integration Research) research group is working and got in touch with key experts in the topic. Since then, he has annually visited the ASU to consult with the American experts. Contact: University of Szeged, Faculty of Economics and Business Administration. H-6722 Szeged, Kálvária sgt. 1, Hungary. miki@eco.u-szeged.hu

Slobodan Marić PhD, is an assistant professor at the Department of Management, Faculty of Economics Subotica, University of Novi Sad, Republic of Serbia, where he teaches bachelor courses in principles of management and master courses performance management and contemporary management. He has taken part in many national and international scientific and research projects. In addition, he is the author and coauthor of numerous scientific and professional works in the fields of management, entrepreneurship, and project management. Contact: University of Novi Sad, The Faculty of Economics Subotica, Republic of Serbia, marics@ef.uns.ac.rs

Dragan Milovanović is professor in the scientific field management at the Faculty of Economics, University of Banja Luka, in crisis management and commercial operations. His research interest is related to corporate restructuring, financial restructuring of companies, crisis management, and risk management. His papers appear in several international and domestic journals and conferences including Annals, *International Journal of Economics and Statistics*, *Acta Economica*, Redete, Strategic Management—determinants of development and business efficiency, etc. He had participated in several research projects and scientific meetings on the subject "Corporate restructuring." Contact: Faculty of Economics, University of Banja Luka, the Mother Jugovic 4, 78000 Banja Luka, Republic of Srpska, Bosnia and Herzegovina, dragan.milovanovic@efbl.org

Igor Mišić is internal actuary in "Aura Insurance" Inc. Banja Luka, Bosnia and Herzegovina. He has research interest in company finance, particularly finance insurance companies, company valuation, and investment projects. He had participated in several research projects and scientific meetings on the subject "Development insurance market in countries in transition." His papers appear in a few domestic journals. Contact: Aura Insurance Inc., Veljka Mlađenovića 7d 78000 Banja Luka, Republic of Srpska, Bosnia and Herzegovina, igor.misic@auraosiguranje.com

Julia Perić, PhD, is employed at J. J. Strossmayer University of Osijek, Faculty of Economics in Osijek, where she works as assistant professor on courses: entrepreneurship, entrepreneurial skills, and business ethics. Besides regular education, Julia Perić had intensive additional education but always focused on the issue of entrepreneurship, social entrepreneurship, social responsibility, and volunteering at many European, American, and Croatian institutions. Julia Perić is a member of research team of SMEs and Entrepreneurship Policy Centre CEPOR and a member of expert group in iPRESENT project (Installation Project for REsearch about Social ENTrepreneurship). Field of interest: entrepreneurship, social entrepreneurship, corporate and university social responsibility, business ethics, and volunteering. Contacts: Josip Juraj Strossmayer University, Faculty of Economics in Osijek, Osijek, Trg Ljudevita Gaja 7, 31000 Osijek, Croatia, julia@efos.hr

Jelena Petrović is an associate professor of economics at the Department of Geography, Faculty of Science and Mathematics, University of Nis, Republic of Serbia. She has published monographs and numerous research articles in national and international journals. She participates in research project supported by the Ministry of Education, Science and Technological Development of the Republic of Serbia. Her current research interests are focused on tourism management and marketing. Contact: Faculty of Science and Mathematics, University of Niš, Visegradska 33, 18000 Niš, Republic of Serbia, jelena25@pmf.ni.ac.rs

Snežana Radukić is associate professor of microeconomics at the Faculty of Economics, University of Niš, Republic of Serbia. She has published a textbook, three monographs, and a number of papers in journals and international and national conference proceedings. She participates in research project supported by the Ministry of Education, Science and Technological Development of the Republic of Serbia. Her research interests are microeconomic issues and sustainable development. Contact: Faculty of Economics, University of Niš, Trg kralja Aleksandra ujedinitelja 11, 18000 Niš, Republic of Serbia, snezana.radukic@eknfak.ni.ac.rs

Edo Rajh is senior research fellow with the Institute of Economics, Zagreb, Croatia, the Department for Innovation, Business Economics and Business Sectors. He is a researcher in the extended model of online privacy concern (PRICON) project. He received his PhD at the University of Zagreb, Faculty of Economics and Business. His primary research areas are consumer behavior, market research methodology, and measurement scales development. Recent publications are related to his work on the survey-based research projects. Contact: Institute of Economics, Zagreb, Trg J.F. Kennedyja 7, 10000 Zagreb, Croatia, erajh@eizg.hr

Tajana Serdar Raković PhD, is a senior assistant at the Faculty of Economics, University of Banja Luka, Republic of Srpska, Bosnia and Herzegovina. She had participated in several scientific and research projects regarding intangible assets and investments, firm behavior, corporate restructuring, instruments for business frauds prevention, etc. She is coauthor of monograph *Intangible Assets as a Potential for Growth in Republic of Srpska* and author of a number of scientific papers. She was a member of the organizational committee of several international conferences and coordinator deputy for international cooperation of the Faculty of Economics in Banja Luka. Her main area of research interests are finance, investments, business valuation, and international finance. Contact: Faculty of Economics, University of Banja Luka, Majke Jugovića 4, 78000 Banja Luka, Republic of Srpska, Bosnia and Herzegovina, tajana.serdar@efbl.org

Sunčana Slijepčević is senior research associate with the Institute of Economics, Zagreb, Croatia, the Department for Regional Development. She received her PhD at the University of Zagreb, Faculty of Economics and Business. Her primary research area is economics of public sector and in particular focuses on analysis of public finances, effectiveness and efficiency of public sector policies, and local and regional development. Her most recent scientific articles are related to local and regional finances, local economic development, and energy efficiency. She is also author of two books. Contact: Institute of Economics, Zagreb, Trg J.F. Kennedyja 7, 10000 Zagreb, Croatia, sslijepcevic@eizg.hr

Suzana Stefanović is professor of strategic management and business planning and policy at the Faculty of Economics, University of Nis, Serbia. She holds an MSc from the Faculty of Economics, University of Belgrade, and a PhD from the Faculty of Economics, University of Nis, Serbia. Dr. Stefanovic has research interests in strategic management of SMEs and companies, namely, strategies of cooperation and networking between firms, as well as institutional framework for entrepreneurship development, business planning, etc. Her research works have been published in international journals such as *Journal of Balkan and the Near East Studies* and also in the highly regarded national journals such as *Themes* and *Industry*. Also, she has presented her research works in various international conferences such as REDETE. Contact: Faculty of Economics, University of Nis, Trg kralja Aleksandra Ujedinitelja 11, 18000 Nis, Serbia, suzana.stefanovic@eknfak.ni.ac.rs

Vladimir Todorović is working in International and Project Office at the Faculty of Technical Sciences, University of Novi Sad. Currently, he is at the final year of PhD studies at the Department of Industrial Engineering and Management at the University of Novi Sad with specialization in the integration of IT in the production process. He holds MSc in power, electronics, and telecommunication. He was a scholar of the European Commission for two years through Erasmus Mundus Programme at Technical University Cluj-Napoca, Romania. He was part of project management team in FP7, TEMPUS, HORIZON 2020, and IPA cross-border projects. Currently, is leading three-year TEMPUS project at the University of Novi Sad called iDEAlab. As a youth activist and director of Creative Educational Center (NGO), he was involved and responsible for many projects in the field of nonformal education for preuniversity and university students. Contact: Faculty of Technical Sciences, Trg Dositeja Obradovica 6, 21000 Novi Sad, Republic of Serbia. vladimir.todorovic@uns.ac.rs

Petar Vrgović is an assistant professor at the Faculty of Technical Sciences, University of Novi Sad, Serbia. With a basic degree in psychology and a PhD in engineering management, he has a multidisciplinary approach for topics of human aspects of managerial processes. His main fields of interest are business communication and creativity in industrial context, with focus on designing creative networks that influence employees and customers to make significant contributions in industry. He has collaborated in a number of international projects that foster student entrepreneurship and innovation management. Contact: Faculty of Technical Sciences, University of Novi Sad, Trg Dositeja Obradovica 7, 21000 Novi Sad, Republic of Serbia. vrgovic@uns.ac.rs

Saša Vučenović is professor of investment management at the Faculty of Economics, University of Banja Luka, Bosnia and Herzegovina. He has research interests in investment projects, company valuation, international project management, and project management in the public sector. His papers appear in several international and domestic journals and conferences including *Industry*, *Acta Economica*, Redete, etc. He had participated in several research projects and scientific meetings on the subject "Feasibility projects." Contact: Faculty of Economics, University of Banja Luka, Majke Jugovića 4, 78000 Banja Luka, Republic of Srpska, Bosnia and Herzegovina, sasa.vucenovic@efbl.org

Introduction to "Entrepreneurship in Post-Communist Countries: New Drivers Towards a Market Economy"

Jovo Ateljević and Jelena Budak

The volume is a collection of 14 interconnected chapters that address and analyse the most current issues in the field of entrepreneurship in post-communist countries. There are certainly an increasing number of scholarly monographs, textbooks and edited volumes written by researchers or practitioners on the subject. There is also a significant amount of material on small business/entrepreneurial development in the transition economies held by the European Commission, who have been the major providers and sponsors of programmes to develop the enterprise sector since the early 1990s. In addition, there is published material from organisations like EBRD, GTZ and the banks active in the region—especially ProCredit Bank; added to that is data from a number of NGOs—e.g. CARE—as well as Western European development agencies which were active in SME development—e.g. Shannon Development in Ireland. Some of these titles and available material give researchers, practitioners and students a reasonable understanding of entrepreneurship in those countries, but serious scholars, policymakers and students would require additional empirically proven material to gain a complete understanding of the phenomenon in specific countries.

The book title suggests that the transition period by definition has come to an end, even though the process has never been completed in a number of countries for various reasons. Some of the factors that affect the transitional process are outlined below. Entrepreneurship, the focus of the book, was seen to be clearly located in "free market" ideology, and this has tended to provide negative reactions concerning the potential for cooperative actions with other entrepreneurs, the idea of planning

J. Ateljević (✉)
University of Banja Luka, Banja Luka, Bosnia and Herzegovina
e-mail: jovo.ateljevic@efbl.org

J. Budak
The Institute of Economics, Zagreb, Zagreb, Croatia
e-mail: jbudak@eizg.hr

© Springer International Publishing AG, part of Springer Nature 2018
J. Ateljević, J. Budak (eds.), *Entrepreneurship in Post-Communist Countries*,
https://doi.org/10.1007/978-3-319-75907-4_1

and strategic formulation and the level of willingness to liaise with state organisations. The cult of individualism has thus been seen as the antidote to the decades of socialism but at the risk of undermining any concept of cooperation between entrepreneurs. Previous structures of socialist economy tended to marginalise entrepreneurial activity, and thus, models of enterprise activity post-1990 were drawn from the USA or UK, which were not necessarily coherent or sympathetic with local environment and culture. Ownership of the enterprise has also taken a rather consuming role; individuals are often unwilling to consider involving financial partners who may seek a share of the equity and thus a degree of involvement in the management of the enterprise. Therefore, state structures in transition economies have tended to take a bureaucratic approach to the problems associated with the SME sector. Generally, they have taken a more favourable view of the medium-sized enterprises (due to their employment generating profile) rather than to the micro and small enterprise sector. Public intervention and support of entrepreneurial growth has been patchy and not always clearly focused. The managers of state SME development organisations are frequently bureaucrats with no solid understanding of the problems of the entrepreneur. Equally, entrepreneurs are frequently secretive and unwilling to disclose important strategic information. Their closeness to the invisible line between the formal and informal economies tends to underline this secretive element. The ultimate aim of the volume is to unravel the most critical barriers, from both external and internal environment to the process of entrepreneurship and enterprise development in different socioeconomic contexts.

1 The Book Background

The manuscript is a part of a book series in entrepreneurship in transition countries, largely based on the REDETE conference. This particular one is the outcome of the fifth REDETE conference titled "Is free trade working for transitional and developing economies" and tends to address an increasing number of issues facing transition economies. From the 1960s towards 1980s, a number of countries pursued a neo-liberal economic development strategy. Some of the examples are South Korea, Taiwan, New Zealand and even China to some extent. The reality, however, was very different indeed. For instance, what Korea actually did during those periods was to foster certain new industries, selected by the government in consultation with the private sector, through tariff protection, subsidies and other forms of government support until they "grew up" enough to withstand international competition. It's very important to mention that the government owned all the banks, able to support businesses through credit. Outward-oriented policies brought dynamism and greater prosperity to most of the East Asia region, one of the poorest areas of the world 40–50 years ago (IMF 2000).

By contrast, in the 1970s and 1980s many countries in Latin America and Africa pursued inward-oriented policies, facing stagnation and decline of their economies. In many cases, especially in Africa, adverse external developments made the problems worse. Today is a bit different: the world economy has become increasingly open, interdependently underpinned by "globalisation" the concept that has acquired considerable controversial force. Some view it as a process that is beneficial—a key to future world economic development—and also inevitable and irreversible. Others see it as hostility, even fear, believing that it increases inequality within and between nations, affecting domestic firms, labour market affecting overall social progress. Indeed, globalisation offers many opportunities for development but it is not progressing evenly. Economic "globalisation" is a historical process, the result of human innovation and technological progress. Due to this, some countries are becoming integrated into the global economy more quickly than others. Countries that have been able to integrate are experiencing faster growth and reduced poverty (IMF 2008).

When it comes to Europe the past two to three decades have seen a dramatic transformation in former communist countries, resulting in their reintegration into the global economy, for better in most cases. But the task of building full market economies has been difficult and prolonged. Liberalisation of trade and prices came fast, but institutional reforms—in areas such as governance, competition policy, labour markets, privatisation and enterprise restructuring—often faced opposition from various sides. The results of the first years of transition were uneven. Initial conditions and external factors played a role, but policies were critical too. Countries that undertook radical reforms were rewarded with faster recovery and income convergence. Others were less resistant to the crises. In contrast to the turbulence of the first decade of transition, the early and mid-2000s saw uniformly strong growth. With macroeconomic stability established, the region experienced large capital inflows, supported by a friendly global environment and increasing confidence in rapid convergence with Western Europe—especially for those countries that joined the EU during this period. Many factors can help or hinder global/transitional processes. The experience of the countries that have increased output most rapidly shows the importance of creating conditions that are conducive to long-run per capita income growth. Economic stability, institution building and structural reform are at least as important for long-term development as financial transfers. What matters is the whole package of policies, financial and technical assistance and debt relief if necessary, this might include:

- Macroeconomic stability to create the right conditions for investment and saving
- Outward-oriented policies to promote efficiency through increased trade and investment
- Structural reform to encourage domestic competition
- Strong institutions and an effective government to foster good governance
- Education, training and R&D to promote productivity
- External debt management to ensure adequate resources for sustainable development

It is clear that macro environment plays a big role in creating conditions for entrepreneurial activities, developed in general. Therefore, questioning the existing economic model is not really being addressed by policymakers, yet if we are to retain and improve entrepreneurial activity and make an economy working, we need to analyse a number of questions. The central one is how to formulate fine-tuning strategies for economic development and rejuvenation. In this book are presented some of these topics that required further scholarly investigation.

2 Structure of the Book

The book material is divided into two interrelated parts: the Part I, consisting of eight chapters, provides analyses of entrepreneurship in post-transition context, and the second part, encompassing the remaining five chapters, deals with various issues related to entrepreneurship, SMEs and economic development in the selected countries of the Western Balkans region. The following provides a short outline of each chapter.

Chapter 2 Economic growth is one of the most extensively studied macroeconomic phenomena in the economic literature. How to stir economic growth and what are the drivers of growth are the issues that a number of economists are trying to answer. In this chapter the authors analyse economic growth by looking at the gross domestic product rate (GDPR), but also through the unemployment rate (UR), which we believe can have a significant impact on the achievement of the objectives of economic growth and development in developing countries.

Chapter 3 The role of this chapter is to research the contribution of the EU funds to boosting the entrepreneurship in the new EU member states of the CEE and SEE region. Even though there are some less developed areas, i.e. below the 75% of EU average GDP per citizen in the old member states (Portugal, Malta, southern Italy and east Great Britain), this research focuses on the continental EU member countries.

Chapter 4 One of the topics that is increasingly relevant in the context of transition economies is FDI. Indeed, multinational enterprises (MNEs) are important players on many goods and factor markets worldwide, while their foreign affiliates and FDI flows play an increasing role in spurring economic development. However, FDI flows do not necessarily increase the welfare of regions or push regional economic development if there is no match between the profile (and therefore the needs) of the region and the activities of MNEs. In the advance of their research project, the authors add to the literature a fundamentally microeconomic view of an optimal location choice of a firm amongst heterogeneous regions. They take into account macroeconomic and regional characteristics and combine firm-specific characteristics with regional data to model the match between firms and locations.

Chapter 5 The need to restructure the company during a turbulent business environment is critical as a large number of companies faced a crisis of business, a decline in financial performance and a weakening of the financial result of operations. Measures from the domain of restructuring can help businesses to financially stabilise and in certain conditions contribute to the growth. Proper implementation of the enterprise restructuring strategy needs an adequate definition of right problems. Interpretation of the obtained results should serve as the basis for professional and scholarly discussion on the role of restructuring in the function of improving business operations. In this chapter, the authors attempt to give a comprehensive answer to the following question "What is the significance of certain sources of financing for the enterprise restructuring...?" by using a number of countries from the EU and the Western Balkans.

Chapter 6 From the analysis of the results, the authors in this chapter have identified measured indicators of the motives of entrepreneurial behaviour which are apparently a direct consequence of achieved level of economic development. It is expected that the indicators of opportunity motives and necessity motives do not deviate from the logical to the now established tendency. Transition of society generates specific conditions and has some typical features, but there is no direct link with motive of entrepreneurial behaviour.

Chapter 7 The main purpose of this chapter is to compare female entrepreneurial activities in transition economies. A comparison of female entrepreneurship in Central Europe and the Baltic States is interesting because, although they are transition countries and the members of the European Union, their development paths in the late twentieth century were quite different. This has affected the economic, technological and social development of these countries. This chapter aims to draw conclusion from the way in which macro-level factors explain the differences of female entrepreneurship in Central Europe and the Baltic States. The basic hypotheses used as the starting point of this research are as follows: female entrepreneurial activity in transition countries depends on macro-level factors, and cultural factors have a dominant influence on the female entrepreneurial activity.

Chapter 8 It is widely known that universities or other similar entities have an impact on the national and regional economies. A growing demand generates more precise studies regarding the quantification of the economic impact of these entities. The topic of the examination of economic impact is especially interesting and exciting when we can compare regions with different levels of development, yet both with the presence of an internationally successful university (e.g. here the University of Lorraine in France and the University of Szeged in Hungary). The main goal of this chapter is to compare the local economic impact of universities in two university towns, one in a relatively rich and the other in a relatively poor region of Europe. To avoid bias, the same methodology based on the available data was applied.

Chapter 9 The globalisation of the economy and the growth of competition brought forward tremendous challenges for small and medium enterprises. SMEs play a key role in transition countries by generating employment, innovation and competition and creating economic wealth. The size of the firm is a focal factor for the business performance. This chapter is focused on the intangible factors such as distinctive competencies, the abilities to evaluate and use culture, skills, work experience and capabilities to create qualitative products and services, to manage human resources, to use technologies, to generate business plans and to make clear how ideas can be turned into reality, as well as on the tangible assets like land, buildings, machinery, inventory, etc. The author attempts to articulate the complications faced by SMEs, by focusing on the Albanian case. In this country, a large number of firms are family-owned businesses. This study assesses small and medium enterprises and particularly intangible and tangible assets and their involvement in the success of a business.

Chapter 10 In strategic documents, like the Strategy for Development of Entrepreneurship in the Republic of Croatia 2013–2020, Croatian government has recognised their importance and outlined it as one of the top priorities. This strategic document is focused on strengthening entrepreneurial potential and improving entrepreneurial culture, and its programmes and projects are implemented through a wide infrastructure network of business support institutions. However, despite these initiatives and multiple efforts, recent evidence suggests that these firms in Croatia struggle to sustain their business activates thus losing competitive advantage with those from the EU. This research has identified a number of barriers that small and medium-sized companies face in Croatia. This chapter is particularly concerned with business networks, an important part of the small business management.

Chapter 11 The size of public procurement markets worldwide is impressive. For developed economies, the ratio of government procurement markets to GDP is about 15–20% of GDP (OECD 2012). The government procurement markets in post-transition countries make a significant share of national economy, and seemingly, its importance rises in the times of economic crisis. Most of the previous research is focused on the government procurers, i.e. the demand side of public procurement markets and its (in)efficiencies. The shift to the supply side makes the new stream of research in developed countries, yet comprehensive assessment of this process in transition economies is missing. Thus, this chapter aims to fulfil the gap in the literature by investigating the accession policy impact on the role of SMEs in post-transition countries. Based on the experience of companies in two post-transition countries, Croatia and Bosnia and Herzegovina (B&H), it analyses the role of the EU in public procurement generally and specifically the effect of EU membership on public procurement for SMEs.

Chapter 12 Market liquidity, as an important factor of making investment decisions at the capital market, provides security for the investors and reduces the risk of not being able to close their positions without significant loss of financial assets. Considering the complexity of the liquidity term, there is more than one definition of liquidity. Generally, liquid market can be described as one where participants can quickly accomplish large transactions with no significant impact on the price. How can the liquidity on the capital market be measured is the ultimate question of this research. The chapter focuses on the hypothesis that market liquidity has a positive impact on the performance and operating profitability of the companies and thereby on the value of the companies. In order to confirm this hypothesis, the measures of market liquidity have been analysed, and the overview of previous research and studies of this subject has been given. The authors used data from the Banja Luka Stock Exchange and Institute of Statistics of Republic of Srpska, as well as data from New York Stock Exchange, International Monetary Fund, World Bank and studies of other relevant institutions and authors.

Chapter 13 In order to construct effective context for entrepreneurial learning, this chapter aims to identify students' potentials for the entrepreneurial and innovative activities. This will be achieved by summarising answers given to a custom-made survey by student sample from the Western Balkans region. In the next step, this chapter will try to propose a model that describes teaching-and-working space within a university that could help students improve their knowledge and skills relative to business thinking and enterprise.

Chapter 14 There is no doubt that managers are facing a number of ethical challenges in their everyday activities, trying to respond better to all demands of all stakeholders they are directly and indirectly linked to. Today, in emerging economies in particular, the ethical behaviour of managers is a strategic important term when it comes to decision-making and successful business. This chapter contributes to the knowledge of this important area of management focusing on both negative and positive effects of the ethical behaviour of managers, but also all relevant frameworks are presented when it comes to ethics in decision-making that affects employee satisfaction. Croatia is used as the empirical context, in which country many businesses still straggle to get full recognition by the EU business community.

References

International Monetary Fund. (2000, April 12, Corrected January 2002). *Globalization: Threat or opportunity?* (Issue Briefs 00/01).
International Monetary Fund. (2008). *Globalization: A brief overview* (Issue Briefs 00/08).
OECD. (2012). *Recommendation of the council of fighting bid rigging in public procurement*. Paris: OECD Publishing. Accessed August 4, 2015, from http://acts.oecd.org/Instruments/ShowInstrumentView.aspx?InstrumentID=284&InstrumentPID=299&Lang=en&Book=False

Part I
Entrepreneurship in Post-Transition Context

The Influence of the Motives of Entrepreneurial Activity on Economic Growth of Developing Countries in Southeast Europe

Suzana Stefanović, Maja Ivanović-Đukić, Vinko Lepojević, and Jovo Ateljević

1 Introduction

Economic growth is one of the most extensively studied macroeconomic phenomena in the economic literature. How to stir economic growth and what are the drivers of growth are the issues that a number of economists are trying to answer. In the early twentieth century, it was believed that the key drivers of economic growth are large enterprises, because they took advantage of the effects of economies of scale and scope, so they were very efficient, generating huge profits and employing large numbers of people (Burns 2011, p. 516). Therefore, most developed economies paid great attention to the development of large enterprises, while small and medium-sized enterprises and entrepreneurs were considered remnants of the past which cannot extensively contribute to economic growth.

However, in the 1970s, a number of big companies were affected by serious economic difficulties. With intensified global competition, increasing market fragmentation, technological advances, and other changes that increased market dynamism and uncertainty, large companies faced a number of problems. It turned out that large enterprises were inflexible, slowly adapting to new market conditions. In contrast, small and medium enterprises and entrepreneurs (SMEEs) were much more successful in coping with the new reality (Toma et al. 2014). As a result, an increasing number of scholarly papers appeared, pointing to the importance of SMEEs, and politicians, such as Ronald Reagan in the USA and Margaret Thatcher

---

S. Stefanović (✉) · M. Ivanović-Đukić · V. Lepojević
Faculty of Economics, University of Niš, Niš, Serbia
e-mail: suzana.stefanovic@eknfak.ni.ac.rs

J. Ateljević
Faculty of Economics, University of Banja Luka, Banja Luka, Bosnia and Herzegovina

© Springer International Publishing AG, part of Springer Nature 2018
J. Ateljević, J. Budak (eds.), *Entrepreneurship in Post-Communist Countries*,
https://doi.org/10.1007/978-3-319-75907-4_2

in Great Britain, focused on a policy which strongly encouraged the advancement of small business and entrepreneurship. Consequently, the rapid development of this sector ensued, which stirred the economy and gained increasing share in economic activities (Cornelius et al. 2006).

The increasing contribution of SMEEs to employment and gross domestic product in most developed countries of the world has led to a change of economists' perception regarding the drivers of economic growth. They started devoting considerable attention to analyzing the phenomenon of entrepreneurship and its links with economic growth. What is more, there are a number of empirical studies demonstrating the positive impact of entrepreneurship on economic growth (Valliere and Peterson 2009; Van Stel et al. 2005, 2010).

Unlike developed countries where there is strong empirical evidence that the development of entrepreneurial activity has a significant impact on economic growth, in developing countries there are a number of dilemmas regarding the relationship between entrepreneurship and economic growth. Although theorists emphasize that the contribution of entrepreneurship to economic growth in developing countries is also large, there is no empirical evidence to confirm these theoretical assumptions. In other words, Schumpeter's view that entrepreneurship is the main driver of economic growth has not been empirically proven in developing countries. Koster and Kumar Rai (2008, p. 132), therefore, question whether entrepreneurship has such a significant and positive role in developing countries as it does in developed countries. Empirically, the impact of entrepreneurship on the development of low-income countries still remains to be determined (Sautet 2013).

A number of scholars explain different impact of entrepreneurship on economic growth in developed and developing countries by the characteristics of the macroeconomic environment in less developed countries (compared with developed countries), the presence of the gray economy and informal entrepreneurship, etc. (Sabella et al. 2014). Furthermore, some studies suggest that different impact of entrepreneurship on economic growth in developing countries may, to some extent, be caused by the different types of entrepreneurial activity that is present in the above groups of countries (Valliere and Peterson 2009; Wong et al. 2005).

Given these and other unresolved dilemmas, the impact of SMEE sector on economic growth in developing countries is still not completely clear, and it is the subject of a large number of empirical studies. The subject of this chapter will also be an empirical study of the relationship between the total entrepreneurial activity and economic growth in Southeast Europe, as well as a comparative analysis of the impact of different types of entrepreneurship on economic growth in the abovementioned group of countries (developed and underdeveloped countries). The aim of our study is to identify the types of entrepreneurial activities based on the motives of entrepreneurial activity as well as some elements of the macroeconomic environment and to consider their impact on economic growth in selected developed EU countries and also in underdeveloped countries of Southeast Europe. We perceive economic growth over the gross domestic product rate (GDPR), but also through the unemployment rate (UR), which, we believe, can have a significant impact on the achievement of the objectives of economic growth and development in developing countries of the SEE region. The SEE region is interesting for the authors of the chapter because it involves the authors' native country Serbia and comprises (with the exception of Slovenia and Greece) underdeveloped countries. It is also the region where most of the countries have passed or are passing through a period of transition from state-planned to market economy.

In addition to the assumption that entrepreneurial activity affects economic growth and development, in both developed and developing countries, our second starting hypothesis is that the motives of entrepreneurship affect economic growth and development (measured by GDPR and UR) in both developed and underdeveloped countries. This starting hypothesis can be divided into two subhypotheses, which aims to demonstrate that (a) the effect of opportunity-driven early-stage entrepreneurship activity (OEA) on GDPR is greater than the impact of the necessity-driven early-stage entrepreneurship activity (NEA), both in developed and in developing countries, and (b) the impact of the NEA on UR is greater than the impact of OEA, especially in developing countries. Also, our third assumption was that larger financial incentives from the state aimed at development of the SMEEs sector lead to economic growth.

The chapter first gives an overview of literature that links entrepreneurship with economic growth. The second part of the chapter presents the starting hypotheses and describes models and methodology. The third part shows the results obtained and discusses them. The final part of the chapter presents conclusions and recommendations to macroeconomic policy makers.

2 Overview of Literature

Entrepreneurship is considered one of the key drivers of economic growth. It contributes to increasing economic stability and sustainable economic development, by creating new jobs (Belka 1995; Richter and Schaffer 1996; Sexton and Landstrom 2000; Audretsch and Thurik 2000), by contributing to the rise in GDP, i.e., economic growth, poverty reduction, and ensuring the welfare of the whole society in the long term (Wennekers and Thurik 1999; Berkowitz and DeJong 2011; Petković and Tešić 2013; Toma et al. 2014; Smith and Chimucheka 2014; Kritikos 2014; Ateljevic et al. 2016).

In developed countries, a number of studies have been conducted on the relationship between entrepreneurship and economic growth. There are a number of empirical studies demonstrating the positive impact of entrepreneurship on economic growth (Valliere and Peterson 2009; Carree and Thurik 1998). Acs and Varga (2005) find that entrepreneurship has a positive and statistically significant impact on economic growth, due to the effect of knowledge spillover, which is generated during growth. Wong et al. (2005) point to similar conclusions, claiming that business creativity and innovation, characteristics of SMEEs, have great significance for economic growth in developed countries. Naude (2013) proves that entrepreneurship has a positive impact on the economy, because it contributes to increasing employment and intensifying competition.

Although theorists emphasize that the contribution of entrepreneurship to economic growth in developing countries is also large, there is no empirical evidence to confirm these theoretical assumptions. Empirically, the impact of entrepreneurship on the development of low-income countries still remains to be determined (Sautet 2013). The regression analysis by Sabella et al. (2014), conducted in Palestine, confirms that entrepreneurship (measured in their study by the rate of business start-ups), among other things, has a positive effect on the GDP growth rate. However, this correlation is not statistically significant. Furthermore, research conducted by Valliere and Peterson (2009), based on a sample of 20 developing countries, does not confirm that entrepreneurship significantly affects economic growth, and they conclude that developing countries need to reach a certain development threshold so that entrepreneurship could make its full contribution to economic growth. Also, a lot of scholars explain different impact of entrepreneurship on economic growth in developed and developing countries by the characteristics of the macroeconomic environment in less developed countries (compared with developed countries), the presence of the gray economy and informal entrepreneurship, etc. (Sabella et al. 2014).

In addition to the macroeconomic environment, the differences in the contribution of entrepreneurship to economic growth may be affected by different structures of entrepreneurial activity, i.e., different types of entrepreneurship prevailing in some countries. Commonly cited classification of the types of entrepreneurship is the one based on the motives that drive people to start a business. There are mainly two dominant reasons or motives that drive individuals into start-ups, namely: use of the opportunities and necessity. This classification has also been accepted in the GEM research. In this regard, there are two different types of entrepreneurship. Opportunity-driven early-stage entrepreneurship activity (OEA) includes all start-ups and newly established businesses (younger than 42 months), which emerge as a result of perceived business market opportunities. Necessity-driven early-stage entrepreneurship activity (NEA) occurs in a situation where individuals perceive entrepreneurship as a last resort and start a business because they either do not have other employment options or such options are unsatisfactory (Singer et al. 2014).

This distinction between two types of early-stage entrepreneurship activity has been made to explain the paradoxically high levels of entrepreneurship in developing countries, defined under the GEM project. It has been shown that the greater the poverty, the greater the level of necessity-based entrepreneurship. The higher number of entrepreneurs entering into business out of necessity results in high rates of entrepreneurial activity. As the level of development of a country increases, the share of necessity entrepreneurship decreases and opportunity entrepreneurship increases.

"The theory of necessity" can explain the high levels of entrepreneurship in developing countries. The basic idea is that people from the poorest developing countries, driven by poverty, survival, and lack of business choices, are forced to start their businesses. In contrast, in developed countries, individuals have much more alternatives to provide a source of income, so that they are not forced to start a business at any cost and enter entrepreneurial ventures only if they recognize market opportunities or have new original ideas and concepts (Serwanga and Rooks 2013).

If one starts from the assumption that entrepreneurship contributes to economic development (as is the case in developed countries) and bears in mind a large number of new businesses in developing countries, it is logical to conclude that entrepreneurial activity has a significant impact on the GDP growth rate. However, this has not been proven yet. This can be explained by the fact that necessity entrepreneurship has a much lower contribution to economic growth, compared to other forms of entrepreneurship, as proven by numerous studies (Poschke 2013; Acs and Varga 2005; Fritsch 2007). First of all, necessity entrepreneurship is largely present among self-employed people (defined as those who work for themselves), which increases the probability that the firm has no employees. Even if the self-employed have other employees, their number is, in case of necessity entrepreneurship, by about 3.2 times lower than the average number of employees in entrepreneurial organizations (9.6 employees). It is economically very important, because it affects the employment rate and value added (Poschke 2013). Furthermore, one research shows that necessity entrepreneurship does not create knowledge that leads to the development of the business, so that it has a much lower contribution to economic growth, compared to other types of entrepreneurship (Acs and Varga 2005). Moreover, Acs et al. (2008) conclude that higher levels of necessity entrepreneurship may have a negative effect on economic growth of the country, while opportunity entrepreneurship has a significant, positive effect on economic performance.

The relationship between the total early-stage entrepreneurial activity (TEA) rate in certain countries and their national per capita income usually appears as a curve in the shape of the letter U. The countries with low income per capita have high total early-stage entrepreneurial activity rate, as well as countries with high income per capita, whereas countries between them have lower total early-stage entrepreneurial activity rate (Carree et al. 2007). What is more, in less developed countries, the contribution of entrepreneurship to economic growth significantly differs, compared to the contribution of entrepreneurship to economic growth in countries with higher levels of development (Valliere and Peterson 2009). Developing countries are characterized by the dominance of entrepreneurship in low-productive activities, so that it does not produce adequate returns, commensurate with those achieved in developed countries (Acs et al. 2008). This, on the one hand, results in lower contribution to economic growth, while at the same time discourages potential entrepreneurs to start their own business. In addition, Acs (2006, p. 102) stressed that if entrepreneurship is identified with self-employment, it will not lead to economic development. He pointed out that the data in his study showed that the ratio of opportunity-to-necessity entrepreneurship is a key indicator of economic development. As more and more people leave necessity entrepreneurship (i.e., self-employment), and get more involved in opportunity-driven entrepreneurship, the level of economic development of a country is going to rise in prospect of time.

Despite the fact that a number of papers and empirical studies point to this conclusion, it faces a certain amount of criticism. First of all, one of the limitations of GEM research is that it does not take into account other ways of entering into a entrepreneurial career. In addition to start-ups, there are other ways to get into the business world, like buying a firm, inheriting family business, or becoming a franchisee (Stefanović and Ivanović-Djukić 2015). Van Teeffelen (2012) distinguishes two types of entrepreneurs, namely, starters who are starting their own business and acquirers who are taking over existing firms, and the latter comprise of family successors, management buy-ins, and management buy-outs. These two types of entrepreneurs differ by factors of human capital and motives to enter into a business, as well as by personality traits and competences and, also, by prediction of turnover as a business performance. When it comes to differences in motives to enter into a business, there is a significantly large difference between starters and acquirers in one of them: dissatisfaction with their job (Van Teeffelen 2012, p. 34). So, Van Teeffelen concludes that some of the entrepreneurs who start up their own business opt for entrepreneurship out of necessity. On the other hand, the study did not show a large difference between starters and acquirers where market opportunities as a motive are concerned. Although the study showed that there are differences between start-ups and acquirers in turnovers, these differences seem to be "not always significant enough to predict business results" (ibid., p. 37). But, other authors consider the difference in performance of new entrants in relation to the existing ones. In developed countries, as GDP per capita increases, established firms can satisfy increasing demand of growing market, due to the exploitation of economies of scale and new technologies' implementation, and have a relatively greater impact on economic development (Acs 2006, p. 104). Further increases in GDP per capita may contribute to the increased strength of new businesses, as more and more individuals have the resources to start up their own businesses in order to exploit the opportunities in the growing market.

Thus, Kritikos (2014, p. 4) states that even though overall employment may decline, because existing firms fail to compete on market and lay off their staff or go out of business, newly established businesses can foster productivity in the medium term. Although there is an evidence that failure rates are high within the first 5 years of starting a business (around 40–50%), with the highest failure rate in the first year (Kritikos 2014, p. 6), Audretsch and Thurik (2000, p. 28) cite some research, based on longitudinal data sets, that wages and productivity of new firms increase as the firm ages. They highlight the evidence that there is a positive relationship between firm age and the likelihood of survival, and also between firm size and the likelihood of survival. Many start-up firms enter upon a business to "experiment with new ideas," and although many of these new firms fail, "some succeed, resulting in low survival rates but high growth rates of the successful new start-ups" (ibid.).

Some authors suggest that the view presented above is too simplistic (Rosa et al. 2006), because there are a variety of motives that drive individuals to start a business, i.e., necessity and opportunities are only part of a broader debate about what motivates business start-ups. Furthermore, GEM notes some other classifications of entrepreneurial activity as well. Thus, for example, there is the classification of entrepreneurial activity on the basis of growth expectations, and all entrepreneurs are divided into three groups: entrepreneurs with low, medium, and high growth expectations (Singer et al. 2014). Previous research suggests that fast-growing companies (established by entrepreneurs with high growth expectations) make the greatest contribution to economic growth in developed countries (Autio 2005).

However, consideration of entrepreneurial motives in terms of the level of economic development is twofold. There is a reasonable assumption that different motives of entrepreneurial activities have different effects on the economic development of individual countries. The causal connection is bidirectional, so there is an assumption that the higher stages of economic development create the appropriate environment for development of opportunity-driven entrepreneurship (Leković 2015). In addition, Leković cited Deli (2011), who has in her research analyzed the impact of the unemployment rate on necessity/opportunity-driven entrepreneurs' inclination and transition to self-employment. The results of conducted study have shown a high positive correlation between the observed phenomena, unemployment rates, and the transition to self-employment for necessity-driven entrepreneurs. Leković found that a positive correlation between a high level of economic development and opportunity-driven entrepreneurship, with a higher degree of achieved economic development, presented in the nominal amount of GDP per capita, leads to a higher percentage of opportunity-driven entrepreneurial ventures within the total early-stage entrepreneurial activity. On the other hand, he has calculated that a strong negative correlation between the level of achieved economic development and entrepreneurship out of necessity, with a higher degree of achieved economic development, which is presented in nominal amount of GDP per capita, means a lower percentage of necessity-motivated entrepreneurial ventures within the total early-stage entrepreneurial activity.

However, the aim of the chapter is to prove the opposite effect, i.e., the impact of necessity/opportunity-driven early-stage entrepreneurial activity, within total early-stage entrepreneurial activity, on economic growth and development in both developed and developing countries. At the same time, we analyze economic growth by looking at the gross domestic product rate (GDPR), but also through the unemployment rate (UR), which we believe can have a significant impact on the achievement of the objectives of economic growth and development in developing countries.

3 Model, Hypotheses, and Methodology of Research

Previous research suggests that entrepreneurial activity can have different effects on economic growth in developed and developing countries. The reason for this lies in the fact that economic growth can be driven by varying factors in developing and developed countries and that it may be affected by the conditions that impact the development of entrepreneurial activity at the national and regional level. In addition, the number and economic role of different types of entrepreneurs may vary in different countries and have different effects on economic growth in both developed and developing countries. For example, necessity entrepreneurship in developing countries can be primarily manifested in self-employment as the form of basic subsistence activities (nonmarket agriculture, individual job replacement, "mom and pop" firms, etc.), while in developed countries, entrepreneurship activity can predominantly occur in the form of individual self-actualization, i.e., self-employment in order to achieve personal noneconomic objectives (Valliere and Peterson 2009). In the countries of Southeast Europe (as well as in developing countries in general), entrepreneurs largely depend on the financial incentives from the government, as well as from the development-oriented international financial institutions, which provide them with legitimacy in the international market and risk-sharing, although this dependence carries the risk of excessive bureaucracy and political interference (Bartlett and Bukvic 2001).

However, despite all the problems that the small and medium enterprises and entrepreneurship sector in Southeast Europe faces, a significant share of SMEEs in total economic activity points to the fact that this sector positively affects economic growth in this group of countries as well as in developed countries. Our second starting hypothesis is that the motives of entrepreneurship affect economic growth and development (measured by GDPR and UR) in both developed and underdeveloped countries. Also, our third assumption was that larger financial incentives aimed at development of new entrepreneurial ventures lead to economic growth.

So, hypotheses, i.e., basic assumptions, in the chapter are:

H1 The development of SMEEs sector has a positive effect on economic growth and development (measured by GDPR and UR) in both developed and underdeveloped countries.

H2 Motives for entrepreneurship activity affect the economic growth and development (measured by GDPR and UR) in both developed and underdeveloped countries.

In order to operationalize the proof of the hypothesis H2, it has been decomposed into the following subhypotheses (H2a and H2b):

H2a Opportunity-driven entrepreneurship (OEA) has a greater impact on economic growth, as measured by GDPR, but entrepreneurship out of necessity (NEA), both in developed and in underdeveloped countries.

H2b Entrepreneurship out of necessity (NEA) has a greater impact on reducing unemployment rates than opportunity-driven entrepreneurship (OEA) in developed but especially in underdeveloped countries.

H3 State measures in the form of financial incentives for the development of SMEE sector have a significant impact on the growth of entrepreneurial activity, and consequently on economic growth, where the influence is greater in underdeveloped countries.

So, in the chapter dependent variables are GDP rate (GDPR) and unemployment rate (UR), and independent variables are total early-stage entrepreneurial activity (TEA), opportunity-driven early-stage entrepreneurial activity (OEA), and necessity-driven early-stage entrepreneurial activity (NEA). However, aware of the great influence of other primarily macroeconomic variables to economic growth, as well as the significant role of the state, which with primarily financial incentives affect the development of SMEEs and economic activity in a country, we also introduce a control variable, namely, financial incentives of the state for small and medium enterprises and entrepreneurship sector development (F for E). The values of key macroeconomic indicators that were used in the analysis—GDPR and UR—are downloaded from the World Bank website, while the values for the NEA, OEA, and TEA were downloaded from the GEM (Global Entrepreneurship Monitor) database. The analysis covered 21 countries over a period of 9 years, of which 15 countries are categorized as developed countries, while 6 countries of Southeast Europe belong to the group of developing countries. Missing values for some of the indicators were assessed based on the value of these indicators in recent years or have been estimated based on the value of a given indicator for similar countries in the region.

The GEM data is observed especially in respect of developing countries, belonging to the region of Southeast Europe (a total of six countries with a GDP per capita of less than US$20,000, making all the countries in the SEE region, with the exception of Greece and Slovenia, as their GDP is greater than US$20,000, which puts them in the group of developed countries). Out of the group of SEE countries, the research does not take into consideration Montenegro, Albania, and Bulgaria, since GEM does not contain data on these countries). At the same time, 15 developed EU countries are observed as well (with GDP per capita greater than US$20,000). Data for all countries is analyzed for the period 2007–2015. Countries involved in the research are presented in Table 1.

In the research we used correlation analysis and multiply regression. The methods of correlation analysis are used to examine whether there is a statistically significant correlation between entrepreneurial activity and economic growth and unemployment rate in those two groups of countries. Also, hierarchical regression models are developed, in trying to predict the GDP growth rate and the unemployment rate. List of indicators included in the study is presented in Table 2.

4 Results and Discussion of Obtained Results

The correlation between independent variables and UR as well as GDPR (considered with a 2-year lag effect) in developed as well as in underdeveloped countries of SEE is presented in tables that follow (Tables 3 and 4):

By analyzing the interdependence of selected variables, we found that between GDPR and other independent variables, in developed countries, correlation is not expressed with respect to the fact that the value of the Pearson correlation coefficient is less than 0.30 (as defined by Cohen 1988).

In underdeveloped countries of SEE, there is a moderate correlation between a dependent variable GDPR and independent variables F for E and TEA (Pearson correlation coefficient larger than 0.30), but not between GDPR and opportunity-driven entrepreneurship (OEA), and entrepreneurship out of necessity (NEA) as a

Table 1 Countries included in the study

Category	Country
Underdeveloped countries of Southeast Europe	Bosnia and Herzegovina
	Croatia
	Macedonia
	Romania
	Serbia
	Turkey
Developed countries	Belgium
	Denmark
	Finland
	France
	Germany
	Greece
	Iceland
	Ireland
	Italy
	Netherlands
	Norway
	Portugal
	Slovenia
	Spain
	Sweden

Source: Authors

Table 2 List of used variables

Variable	Variable type	Model
Lagged 2-year GDPR	Dependent	M1, M3
UR	Dependent	M2, M4
F for E	Control	All
Total early-stage entrepreneurial activity (TEA)	Predictor	All
Opportunity-driven entrepreneurship activity (OEA)	Predictor	All
Necessity-driven entrepreneurship activity (NEA)	Predictor	All

Source: Authors

part of the total early-stage entrepreneurial activity (TEA), which means that the motives of entrepreneurship are not correlated with economic growth, measured by GDPR.

There is a statistically significant correlation, measured by Pearson's coefficients, between the unemployment rate and independent variables in developed EU countries. This connection is in the case of OEA and F for E the inverse, meaning that an increase in entrepreneurship activity in order to use the opportunities and also an increase in the financial allocation of resources for the development of SMEE sector by the state lead to a decrease in the unemployment rate, which is logical.

Table 3 Correlation for UR

<table>
<tr><th></th><th colspan="6">Developed countries</th><th colspan="6">Underdeveloped countries of Southeast Europe</th></tr>
<tr><th></th><th>UR</th><th>F for E</th><th>TEA</th><th>OEA</th><th>NEA</th><th>UR</th><th>F for E</th><th>TEA</th><th>OEA</th><th>NEA</th></tr>
<tr><td>UR</td><td>1.000</td><td></td><td></td><td></td><td></td><td>1.000</td><td></td><td></td><td></td><td></td></tr>
<tr><td>F for E</td><td>−0.447 (0.000)</td><td>1.000</td><td></td><td></td><td></td><td>−0.425 (0.001)</td><td>1.000</td><td></td><td></td><td></td></tr>
<tr><td>TEA</td><td>0.284 (0.000)</td><td>−0.142 (0.051)</td><td>1.000</td><td></td><td></td><td>0.155 (0.132)</td><td>0.042 (0.381)</td><td>1.000</td><td></td><td></td></tr>
<tr><td>OEA</td><td>−0.477 (0.000)</td><td>0.338 (0.000)</td><td>−0.116 (0.091)</td><td>1.000</td><td></td><td>−0.689 (0.000)</td><td>0.174 (0.104)</td><td>−0.153 (0.134)</td><td>1.000</td><td></td></tr>
<tr><td>NEA</td><td>0.444 (0.000)</td><td>−0.313 (0.000)</td><td>0.044 (0.307)</td><td>−0.685 (0.000)</td><td>1.000</td><td>0.832 (0.000)</td><td>−0.380 (0.000)</td><td>0.018 (0.448)</td><td>−0.663 (0.000)</td><td>1.000</td></tr>
</table>

Source: Authors

Table 4 Correlation for GDPR

<table>
<tr><th></th><th colspan="5">Developed countries</th><th colspan="5">Underdeveloped countries of Southeast Europe</th></tr>
<tr><th></th><th>GDPR</th><th>F for E</th><th>TEA</th><th>OEA</th><th>NEA</th><th>GDPR</th><th>F for E</th><th>TEA</th><th>OEA</th><th>NEA</th></tr>
<tr><td>GDPR</td><td>1.000</td><td></td><td></td><td></td><td></td><td>1.000</td><td></td><td></td><td></td><td></td></tr>
<tr><td>F for E</td><td>−0.114 (0.144)</td><td>1.000</td><td></td><td></td><td></td><td>0.326 (0.018)</td><td>1.000</td><td></td><td></td><td></td></tr>
<tr><td>TEA</td><td>0.089 (0.125)</td><td>−0.215 (0.014)</td><td>1.000</td><td></td><td></td><td>0.345 (0.013)</td><td>0.004 (0.090)</td><td>1.000</td><td></td><td></td></tr>
<tr><td>OEA</td><td>0.157 (0.081)</td><td>0.391 (0.000)</td><td>−0.035 (0.363)</td><td>1.000</td><td></td><td>0.035 (0.013)</td><td>0.179 (0.029)</td><td>−0.299 (0.027)</td><td>1.000</td><td></td></tr>
<tr><td>NEA</td><td>−0.122 (0.896)</td><td>−0.391 (0.000)</td><td>0.027 (0.393)</td><td>−0.673 (0.000)</td><td>1.000</td><td>0.199 (0.093)</td><td>0.386 (0.006)</td><td>0.191 (0.013)</td><td>−0.639 (0.000)</td><td>1.000</td></tr>
</table>

Source: Authors

However, entrepreneurship out of necessity and total early entrepreneurial activity, on the one hand, and the unemployment rate, on the other hand, just stand in proportion, which is an illogical result. It turns out that the higher the entrepreneurial activity out of necessity and the total entrepreneurial activity, the higher the unemployment rate in developed countries, and vice versa. A possible explanation is that the total early-stage entrepreneurial activity, especially those motivated by necessity, in developed countries does not lead to reduction in the unemployment rate, because it is determined by other factors, such as employment in large companies, as well as a number of other variables, i.e., macroeconomic factors.

There is a statistically significant correlation (except for TEA) between independent variables and the unemployment rate in selected countries of Southeast Europe. This connection is in the case of F for E and OEA inverse, meaning that an increase in the financial allocation of resources for entrepreneurship as well as an increase in opportunity-driven entrepreneurship leads to a decrease in the unemployment rate in the countries of Southeast Europe, and vice versa. However, this correlation in the case of TEA and NEA stands in proportion, which means that growth of total early entrepreneurial activity and increase of entrepreneurship out of necessity lead to an increase in the unemployment rate, and vice versa, which are illogical results. Possible explanation is that both entrepreneurship out of necessity and total early entrepreneurial activity barely affect the general reduction of unemployment because they lead to self-employment, i.e., they contribute to resolution of the problem of layoff in big companies, but not to employing new workers to reduce unemployment in the country. Just entrepreneurship motivated by using the opportunities at the market leads to further economic growth and development and generate new employment.

The results of the regression models are presented in Table 5.

Determined regression model, which describes the correlation between GDPR and other variables (2-year lag effect), in the case of selected developed countries explains only 14.5% of the total variability. We were unable to prove a simple statistical significant contribution of any independent variable on the variability of GDPR in selected developed countries of EU.

In the case of the underdeveloped countries of Southeast Europe by selected regression model, we were able to explain 25.5% of the variability in GDPR (2-year lag effect) by the changes in the independent variable, during the time period we have analyzed. The largest effect is due to the TEA and indicates that with the increase of TEA of 1%, there is an increase in GDPR of 0.49%. The OEA variable has small but a statistically significant contribution to explaining the total variability of dependent variable. The increase of the OEA variable by 1% leads to an increase of GDPR of 0.068%. Also, a great impact on GDPR (significant at the level of 0.1) has a control variable F for E, but these variables stand in inverse proportion. The increase in variable F for E of 1% leads to a decrease of 3.6% in GDPR. Entrepreneurship out of necessity (NEA) has no statistically significant contribution to changes in GDPR.

By observing the relationship of given variables and UR, we can conclude that in the case of developed countries observed selected regression model explains 37.8%

Table 5 Estimation results of models over period 2007–2015[a]

	Developed countries		Underdeveloped countries of Southeast Europe	
	Lagged 2-year GDPR	UR	Lagged 2-year GDPR	UR
	(Model 1)	(Model 2)	(Model 3)	Model (4)
Constant	0.520	21.426**	0.936	12.063
	(0.152)	(5.746)	(0.136)	(1.185)
F for E	−0.348	−3.552**	−3.613*	−5.611**
	(−0.427)	(−3.775)	(−1.968)	(−2.031)
TEA	0.017	0.014**	0.494**	0.428
	(0.109)	(2.994)	(2.576)	(1.582)
OEA	0.010	−0.094**	0.068**	−0.189**
	(0.293)	(−2.324)	(2.239)	(−2.486)
NEA	−0.022	0.128**	0.052	0.548**
	(−0.391)	(2.012)	(2.805)	(6.064)
R^2	0.145	0.378	0.255	0.758
Adjusted R^2	0.139	0.359	0.174	0.738

Source: Authors
[a]t-values are between brackets
* Significant at 0.10 level
** Significant at 0.05 level

of the total variability in UR. The largest contribution to the change in the unemployment rate in the given developed countries is given by F for E, while the influence of other variables is slightly smaller and relatively uniform. The influence of these variables on the UR is statistically significant at the 0.05 level. Changes in F for E and OEA, in terms of their increase, lead to reduction of UR and vice versa, meaning that the growth of financial incentives as well as entrepreneurship based on the opportunities leads to the reduction of unemployment in developed countries, and vice versa. On the other hand, the increase in TEA and NEA leads to an increase in UR, and vice versa, so regardless of their statistical significance we cannot conclude that the hypothesis H1 and H2b has been proven.

In the case of the selected countries of Southeast Europe regression model we developed, 75.8% of variability in UR is explained by changes in selected independent variables. In underdeveloped countries of Southeast Europe, the largest contribution to the change of UR, in addition to financial incentives of the state, is given by the NEA. If the NEA increased by 1%, the UR will increase to 0.548, and vice versa. Since the impact of the change of NEA on UR change is statistically significant, but variables stand in proportion, we cannot say that we have proved our hypothesis H2b. The impact of changes in the OEA is statistically significant, but inverse, meaning that a 1% increase in the OEA impacts the reduction of the unemployment rate for 0.189. In this model, only the TEA is not a statistically significant variable, and therefore, the hypothesis H1 cannot be proved in the case of underdeveloped countries of Southeast Europe.

In conclusion, if we consider the hypotheses H1 and H2 (as well as subhypotheses H2a and H2b), we could not prove these hypotheses by presented regression model in the case of selected developed countries. As for the developing countries of Southeast Europe, we were able to prove that total early entrepreneurial activity (TEA) affects growth of GDPR (with a lag of 2 years), so we confirmed the hypothesis H1, but also we confirmed that opportunity-driven entrepreneurship has a positive effect on increase of GDPR, although this impact is not large. Bearing in mind that the NEA's impact on the unemployment rate is higher than the OEA, but stands in proportion, we cannot conclude that the hypothesis H2b has been proved in the case of underdeveloped countries of Southeast Europe. Also, in the case of underdeveloped countries of Southeast Europe, hypothesis H3 was indirectly proved, i.e., that larger financial incentives aimed at development of SMEEs sector lead (by increasing of total entrepreneurial activity—TEA) to economic growth measured by the decrease in unemployment rate.

5 Conclusion

It can be concluded that entrepreneurship is very important for economic development, but its contribution to economic development is significantly different in the countries at different levels of economic development. Also, the contribution of certain types of entrepreneurship to economic development is significantly different. Previous research has shown that opportunity-driven entrepreneurship activity has had greater contribution to economic growth in developed countries, while the contribution of necessity-driven entrepreneurship activity is much smaller.

Our research has showed that the relationship between the total early-stage entrepreneurship activity and economic growth measured by GDP growth rate is not very strong in developing countries of Southeast Europe. This may be explained by the fact that in these countries a large share in total early-stage entrepreneurship activity goes to necessity-driven early-stage entrepreneurship activity, the contribution of which to the GDP growth rate is significantly lower than the contribution of opportunity-driven early-stage entrepreneurship activity. This points to the fact that these countries should work on encouraging opportunity-driven early-stage entrepreneurship activity. This is supported by the fact that correlation between unemployment rate and opportunity-driven early-stage entrepreneurship activity is very strong in the developing countries of Southeast Europe. Also, contribution of this type of entrepreneurship has significant contributions to increasing employment.

Increase in entrepreneurial activity generally should not be regarded as a universal solution to solve the problem of economic development in the developing countries of Southeast Europe. Instead, these countries should primarily focus their policies of economic development on the increase of the share of OEA in the formal economy. At the same time, it is necessary to substantially improve macroeconomic environment in these countries as it largely affects the development of the most productive types of entrepreneurship. As we noticed above, one of the limitations of GEM research is that it does not take into account other ways of entering into business. In addition to start-ups, there are other ways to enter into a business, like buying a firm, inheriting family business, or becoming a franchisee. It is important because often businesses that were transferred to another entrepreneur outperform start-ups in survival rate, growth in terms of wages and productivity (due to exploiting economies of scale), and new job creation (because of more intensive investment). But new start-ups, although characterized by low survival rates, often achieve high growth rates. This is especially true for innovative start-ups, established to exploit the new ideas and opportunities in the market. As more and more people leave necessity entrepreneurship (i.e., self-employment) and get more involved in opportunity driven entrepreneurship, the country prospers in economic development. So, one of the goals of policy creators should be to reduce the number of self-employed and strengthen the existing small and medium enterprises and entrepreneurs. Financial incentives from the state should be assigned not only for new start-ups but also for growing established businesses. Also, measures aimed to attract foreign direct investment may contribute to employment of people leaving self-employment businesses as well as people who were laid off in large companies. In addition, it is necessary to provide more financial incentives from the state to start new innovative businesses because our research has shown that this factor is noticeably important for entrepreneurial activity and economic development in developing as well as in developed countries.

Theoretical knowledge and the best entrepreneurial practice should be, to a greater extent, included in general education programs of schools and universities in the abovementioned countries, and greater transfer of ideas and knowledge obtained by scientific research should be also transferred to SMEEs, because this can contribute to easier identification of market opportunities and their exploitation in order to start up new innovative businesses. This is important because it has been shown that those with less education, management, and entrepreneurship knowledge in developing countries usually end up in necessity entrepreneurship that contributes much less to economic development in developing countries as well as in developed countries.

References

Acs, Z. J. (2006, Winter). How is entrepreneurship good for economic growth? *Innovations*, 97–107.
Acs, Z. J., & Varga, A. (2005). Entrepreneurship, agglomeration and technological change. *Small Business Economics, 24*(3), 323–334.
Acs, Z. J., Desai, S., & Klapper, L. F. (2008). What does "entrepreneurship" data really shows? A comparison of the global entrepreneurship monitor and World Bank group datasets. *Small Business Economics, 31*, 265–281.
Ateljevic, J., Stefanovic, S., Ivanovic-Djukic, M., & Jankovic-Milic, V. (2016). Researching the entrepreneurial sector in Serbia. In J. Ateljevic & J. Trivic (Eds.), *Economic development and*

entrepreneurship in transition economies: Issues, obstacles and perspectives (pp. 129–146). Cham: Springer International Publishing Switzerland.

Audretsch, B. D., & Thurik, A. R. (2000). Capitalism and democracy in the 21st century: From the managed to the entrepreneurial economy. *Journal of Evolutionary Economics, 10*(1–2), 17–34.

Autio, E. (2005). Global Entrepreneurship Monitor (GEM) – 2005 Report on High-Expectation Entrepreneurship. Accessed July 20, 2015, from http://papers.ssrn.com/sol3/papers.cfm

Bartlett, W., & Bukvic, V. (2001). Barriers to SME growth in Slovenia. *MOST: Economic Policy in Transitional Economies, 11*(2), 177–195.

Belka, M. (1995). Enterprise adjustment in Poland: Evidence from a survey of 200 private, privatized, and state-owned firms. Centre for Economic Performance London School of Economics and Political Science. Accessed July 20, 2015, from http://eprints.lse.ac.uk/20765/1/Enterprise_Adjustment_in_Poland_Evidence_from_a_Survey_of_200_Private.pdf

Berkowitz, D., & DeJong, D. (2011). Growth in post-Soviet Russia: A tale of two transitions. *Journal of Economic Behavior & Organization, 79*(1–2), 133–143.

Burns, P. (2011). *Entrepreneurship and small business*. New York: Palgrave Macmillan.

Carree, M., & Thurik, A. R. (1998). Small firms and economic growth in Europe. *Atlantic Economic Journal, 26*(2), 137–146.

Carree, M. A., Stel, R., Thurik, A. R., & Wennekers, S. (2007). The relationship between economic development and business ownership revisited. *Entrepreneurship & Regional Development, 19*, 281–291.

Cohen, J. W. (1988). *Statistical power analysis for the behavioural sciences* (2nd ed.). Hillsdale: Lawrence Erlbaum Associates.

Cornelius, B., Landström, H., & Persson, O. (2006). Entrepreneurial studies: The dynamic research front of a developing social science. *Entrepreneurship Theory and Practice, 30*(3), 375–398.

Deli, F. (2011). Opportunity and necessity entrepreneurship: Local unemployment and the small firm effect. *Journal of Management Policy and Practice, 12*(4), 38–57.

Fritsch, M. (2007). How does new business formation affect regional development? *Small Business Economics, 30*, 1–14.

Global Entrepreneurship Monitor Data. Accessed December 10, 2016, from http://www.gemconsortium.org/data/sets?id=aps

Koster, S., & Kumar Rai, S. (2008). Entrepreneurship and economic development in a developing country: A case study of India. *Journal of Entrepreneurship, 17*(2), 117–137.

Kritikos, A. S. (2014). Entrepreneurs and their impact on jobs and economic growth. *IZA World of Labor, 8*, 1–10.

Leković, B. (2015). *Kauzalitet preduzetničkog ponašanja, faktora uspešnosti preduzetničkog poduhvata i ambijentalnih uslova*, dok.dis., Ekonomski fakultet Subotica.

Naude, W. (2013). *Entrepreneurship in economic development* (IZA Discussion Paper No. 7507). http://ftp.iza.org/dp7507.pdf

Petković, S., & Tešić, J. (2013). SMEs and entrepreneurship development and institutional support in Republic of Srpska (Bosnia and Herzegovina). In V. Ramadani & R. C. Schneider (Eds.), *Entrepreneurship in the Balkans: Diversity, support and prospects* (pp. 293–315). New York: Springer.

Poschke, M. (2013). Entrepreneurs out of necessity: A snapshot. *Applied Economics Letters, 20*, 658–663.

Richter, A., & Schaffer, M. (1996). The performance of de novo private firms in Russian manufacturing. In S. Commander, Q. Fan, & M. E. Schaffer (Eds.), *Enterprise restructuring and economic policy in Russia* (pp. 253–274). Washington, DC: World Bank.

Rosa, P., Kodithuwakku, S., & Balunywa, W. (2006). *Reassessing necessity entrepreneurship in developing countries* (pp. 1–13). Institute for Small Business & Entrepreneurship.

Sabella, R. A., Farraj, A. W., Burbar, M., & Qaimary, D. (2014). Entrepreneurship and economic growth in West Bank, Palestine. *Journal of Developmental Entrepreneurship, 19*(1), 1450003-1–1450003-15.

Sautet, F. (2013). Local and systemic entrepreneurship: Solving the puzzle of entrepreneurship and economic development. *Entrepreneurship Theory and Practice, 3*, 387–402.

Serwanga, A., & Rooks, G. (2013). Identifying high potential entrepreneurs in developing country: A cluster analysis of Ugandan entrepreneurs. *Journal of Developmental Entrepreneurship, 18* (2), 1350010–1350025.

Sexton, D. L., & Landstrom, H. (2000). *Handbook of entrepreneurship*. Oxford: Blackwell Publishers, Ltd.

Singer, S., Amoros, J., & Moska, D. (2014). Global Entrepreneurship Monitor 2014 Global Report. Accessed June 12, 2015, from http://www.gemconsortium.org/report

Smith, W., & Chimucheka, T. (2014). Entrepreneurship, economic growth and entrepreneurship theories. *Mediterranean Journal of Social Sciences, 5*(14), 160–168.

Stefanović, S., & Ivanović-Djukić, M. (2015). *Upravljanje malim i srednjim preduzećima: strateški i operativni aspekt*. Niš: Ekonomski fakultet.

The World Bank Data. Accessed December 15, 2016, from https://data.worldbank.org/indicator

Toma, S.-G., Grigore, A.-M., & Marinescu, P. (2014). Economic development and entrepreneurship. *Procedia Economics and Finance 8 from the 1st International Conference*: '*Economic Scientific Research – Theoretical, Empirical and Practical Approaches', ESPERA 2013* (pp. 436–443). Elsevier.

Valliere, D., & Peterson, R. (2009). Entrepreneurship and economic growth: Evidence from emerging and developed countries. *Entrepreneurship & Regional Development, 21*, 459–480.

Van Stel, A., Carree, M., & Thurik, R. (2005). The effect of entrepreneurial activity on national economic growth. *Small Business Economics, 24*, 311–321.

Van Stel, A., Thurik, R., Wennekers, S., & Carree, M. (2010). The relationship between entrepreneurship and economic development: Is it U-shaped? *Scales Research Reports*, H200824, EIM Business and Policy Research.

Van Teeffelen, L. (2012). *Avenues to improve success in SME business transfers: Reflections on theories, research and policies*. Utrecht: Hogeschool Utrecht.

Wennekers, S., & Thurik, R. (1999). Linking entrepreneurship and economic growth. *Small Business Economics, 13*(1), 27–56.

Wong, P. K., Ho, Y. P., & Autio, E. (2005). Entrepreneurship, innovation and economic growth: Evidence from GEM data. *Small Business Economics, 24*(3), 335–350.

Financial Instruments for Boosting Entrepreneurship in Selected Post-Communist EU Countries

Mihaela Grubišić Šeba

1 Introduction

Several studies have emphasised the importance of venture capital and private equity funds for boosting SME competitiveness and growth (IKED 2007; EVCA 2014). The data show that the EU lags behind the USA in terms of venture capital investments. It is particularly true in the aftermath of the financial crisis (Invest Europe 2016). However, the EU regulation strives to smooth the huge differences in development of entrepreneurship by allowing convergence regions to use a portion of the EU funds with other financial instruments to spur the competitiveness and economic growth. It does it via three mechanisms: grants from the ESI funds within the Cohesion policy that are accessed via national calls for application; local financial intermediaries that offer lower interest rates for certain programmes by help of the European Investment Bank and/or European Investment Fund; and by applying directly for the programmes managed by the European Commission.

Besides the specific types of the available EU funds and the main aim of their usage, the operational programmes' contribution to boosting the competitiveness of the new EU member states have not been widely researched. It is mostly due to the late evaluation results of certain programme achievements that spread years ahead of the programmes' closure.

There are many of the EU thematic goals, and it is up to the member states to fine-tune the available funds with the EU thematic and national goals. Boosting entrepreneurship, i.e. SME competitiveness, is just one of the twelve thematic goals the countries are requested to follow. However, other thematic goals such as research and innovation, information and communication technologies, low-carbon economy, or education and training may indirectly be related to encouraging entrepreneurship.

M. G. Šeba (✉)
Consultant, Zagreb, Croatia

The role of this chapter is to research the contribution of the EU funds to boosting the entrepreneurship in the new EU member states of the CEE and SEE region. Even though there are some less developed areas, i.e. below the 75% of EU average GDP per citizen in the old member states (Portugal, Malta, southern Italy, and east Great Britain), this research focuses on the continental EU member countries.

The research strives to answer to what extent the available EU funds make up for the difference in venture capital retreat in the last decade. For this purpose, the chapter firstly explores the statistical data on venture capital and private equity presence in the chosen EU countries. Then it analyses the operational programmes of the EU member states targeted to boosting the entrepreneurship and the amount of ESI funds contribution for investing in SMEs competitiveness. The data used in the analysis shall be obtained from the publicly available Invest Europe and the EC Directorate-General for Regional and Urban policy databases. Subject to data availability, the research goes further to analyse the blending mechanics of ESI funds with other available financial instruments.

1.1 SME Financing in Selected Post-Communist EU Countries

There is a multiannual debate on access to finance, affordability of external finance for SMEs and finance-growth nexus of SMEs (Beck 2007; Udell 2015). There seem to be many credit and guarantee programmes tailored to SMEs, but the bottom line is that young and small SMEs can't borrow funds until they have sufficient long-term assets to pledge as collateral, good reputation on the market, a strong guarantee from a related business, wealthy natural people or state institutions, or promissory notes issued as a guarantee for generating sufficient market turnover during the loan repayment period. If SMEs cannot fulfil such conditions, a loan is either not approved to them at all, or a very small amount of the required loan is available to them. The latter makes the loan prohibitively expensive in terms of benefit–cost ratio due to various fees charged for loan approval. Although there are few alternatives to bank borrowing in bank-based systems, Barth et al. (2011) found that SMEs in more concentrated bank-based markets of Central and Eastern Europe have better access to loans and lower interest rates. The more transparent firms are, the easier they get access to external finance. However, it takes time to achieve transparency and gain confidence (reputation) in the market. Bonin et al. (2014) reported that the transition process of banking systems of post-communist countries of Europe ended successfully as these countries today have mature banking systems in which privately owned banks replaced once state-owned banks, banks are well capitalised and operate in modern regulatory framework, and they are closely monitored by the national central banks.

Current territory of the EU encompasses many former communist countries which have undergone or have been still passing through transition process from social to the market economy. These countries include: former Soviet republics of Estonia, Latvia and Lithuania, Poland, Czech Republic, Hungary, Slovakia, countries of former Yugoslavia (Slovenia, Croatia), Bulgaria, and Romania, as well as the accession countries of the Western Balkans and Western Asia. Although some economies are more advanced, all post-communist European countries more or less share some common features embedded to countries moving from centrally planned to market economies. As partly elaborated by Smallbone and Welter (2001) these are: privatisations of once social enterprises and the need for restructuring entire business sectors related to government enterprises, bureaucracy, inadequate and changing legal frameworks, high tax burden, corruption, increasing competition, inadequate and investment finance lacking financial infrastructure, informal networks, government institutions unaware of the market economy functioning, dominant relationship-based lending, etc.

Most European SMEs are financed internally, especially SMEs in Eastern European countries. Bank loans take more than 90% stake in debt capital of European SMEs as opposed to the US, where almost 90% of debt capital is related to debt securities issued (Demary et al. 2016). The European Union tries to attract private capital to SME financing by means of various programmes that are run centrally (through European Commission or European agencies and banks) and via intermediaries (either national public authorities or commercial banks). Some EU initiatives for SME financing are listed in Ciani et al. (2015). The main difference between financing SMEs in Western and Central and Eastern European countries, i.e. post-communist countries, is that the latter are eligible for a greater portion of the EU grants. There are various forms of government interventions aimed to fostering access to finance by broadening the palette of available financial instruments, reforming laws and institutions' role (Beck 2007). The regulatory framework adaptation in transitory post-communist economies, which is conditional on accepting the EU acquis, has the largest achievement in terms of broadening the supply of other financial institutions, except for credit institutions, and other financial instruments. Recently, the European Bank for Reconstruction and Development has had a broad initiative to develop factoring and capital market for SMEs. The International Finance Corporation gave its contribution in developing corporate governance manuals in post-communist countries, while the European Investment Bank group unlocked the funds of commercial banks by providing guarantees for loans approved to certain types of SMEs and/or entrepreneurs.

According to the EU definition, all the enterprises fulfilling at least two of three criteria of having less than 250 employees, less than 50 million euros turnover, or less than 43 million euros assets belong to the SME population (2003/361/EC). Purely by the criterion of employment, the SMEs account for 57% of the share of the total value added generated by non-financial business sector in the EU, while large enterprises account for the remaining 40% of the value added (Muller et al. 2016).

Table 1 Contributions of SMEs to the economic development in selected countries in 2015

Country	Number of inhabitants (est 2017)	Number of SMEs per 1000 inhabitants	Value added (%)	Employment (%)	Enterprises (%)
Czech Republic	10,555,130	**0.94**	55	68	**99.9**
Slovakia	5,432,157	0.75	57	71	**99.9**
Slovenia	2,071,252	0.64	63	72	99.8
Hungary	9,787,905	0.53	52	70	99.8
Bulgaria	7,045,259	0.44	**66**	**76**	99.8
Austria	8,592,400	0.38	61	68	99.7
Croatia	4,209,815	0.35	56	67	99.7
EU-28 average	*510.1 million*	*0.45*	*57*	*67*	*99.8*
Poland	38,563,573	0.41	52	69	99.8
UK	65,511,098	0.29	52	54	99.7
Ireland	4,749,153	0.35	47	71	99.7
Germany	80,636,124	0.27	53	63	99.5
Romania	19,237,513	0.22	50	67	99.7

Source: Eurostat, National Statistical Offices

The Small Business Act, though legally not mandatory, encourages growth of the SME sector throughout the EU, by pronouncing importance of ten core principles, i.e. skills and innovation, single market presence, internationalisation, environment protection, creating entrepreneurship-supportive environment with responsive administration, facilitating access to finance to SMEs, facilitating SMEs' participation in public procurement, ensuring better access to state aid for SMEs, designing the rules tailored to the "Think small principle", and ensuring the honest bankrupted entrepreneurs a second opportunity to succeed (Commission of the European Communities 2008, COM(2008) 394). The results of three consecutive SAFE surveys conducted in 2016 reveal that access to finance is the sixth most important problem SMEs are faced with, after finding customers, availability of skilled staff and managers, competition, regulation, costs of production and labour, which is unchanged order in the last couple of years.

The data in Table 1 reveal not much difference in relative contribution of SMEs to total non-financial business sector enterprises in EU-28. SMEs in new EU member states outpace the SMEs in old member states in terms of employment and some of them in terms of relative contribution to value added (Bulgaria, Slovenia).[1] The SME

---

[1] EU-15 are considered old member states, other countries that joined the EU later are regarded as new member states. Czech Republic, Hungary, Poland, Slovakia, Slovenia, Estonia, Latvia, Lithuania, Cyprus, and Malta joined the EU in 2004; Bulgaria and Romania in 2007; and Croatia in 2013.

sector developed strongly in the new EU member states, particularly in the Czech Republic and Slovakia, which have a significant number of SMEs per 1000 inhabitants. Why?

Available external funds are one of preconditions for SME expansion. Grants or subsidised bank loans in EU-28 take the fifth place in importance of sources of financing (32%), after credit line or overdraft (55%), bank loans (50%), leasing (47%), and trade credit (35%), exceeding internal funds which were reported at 27% (SAFE survey analytical report, 2016). Overall, debt financing contributes 85% to total financing gap of the SMEs (ibid., 2016). A breakdown of the debt financing shows that only 15% of all EU-28 SMEs have made use of internal funds, 9% used other types of loans, 7% grants or subsidised bank loans, and another 6% factoring. Equity (2%), other sources (1%), and debt securities (1%) were the least popular types of financing (SAFE survey analytical report, 2016). Confidence in ability to take a loan is the highest (67%), while the confidence in negotiating with equity investors and venture capital funds is three times lower (22%) in EU-28.

Even though several studies have emphasised the importance of venture capital and private equity funds for boosting SME competitiveness and growth (Andersson and Nopier 2007), the data show that the EU lags behind the USA in terms of venture capital investments. It is particularly true in the aftermath of the financial crisis (Invest Europe 2016). Even SMEs in the countries with more market-based financial systems such as the UK and Ireland favour bank borrowing. Private investors and venture capital funds are prone to financing SMEs in stable economies, while relationship lending is dominant in any economy. A comparison between venture capital financing in USA and Europe is illustrated in Graph 1.

European venture capital market, though recovering, has not reached the levels seen in 2000. Europe was lagging behind the US market 2.65 times in terms of deals and over 5.5 times in terms of raised funds in 2016 (WilmerHale 2017). The statistical numbers, however, quite vary depending on the applied methodology. Private equity market, that among other private sources of capital encompass venture capital funds, reached 551 billion of raised capital globally in 2015 (Prequin Global Private Equity and Venture Capital Report 2016). Business angels in Europe typically provide first round of financing of 500,000 €, while the second round of financing for growth, estimated at about 2 million euros, is not approved without difficulties (AFME 2017). One reason is the fact that an average venture capital backed company in EU receives 1.3 million euros capital compared to the average US company which receives 6.4 million euros (AFME 2017). Compared to the GDP levels, private equity investments are very low, only 0.13% on average in the CEE countries (Invest Europe CEE Private Equity Statistics 2016).

Table 2 reveals strong loans preference for financing SME growth throughout the EU as approximately 64% of enterprises apply for loans. Loans from other sources follow, so that overall sum of loan financing reaches 80% on average. Financial instrument(s) popularity is highlighted in bold in Table 2. Other sources of finance, which are primarily grants, significantly exceed equity investments in some new EU

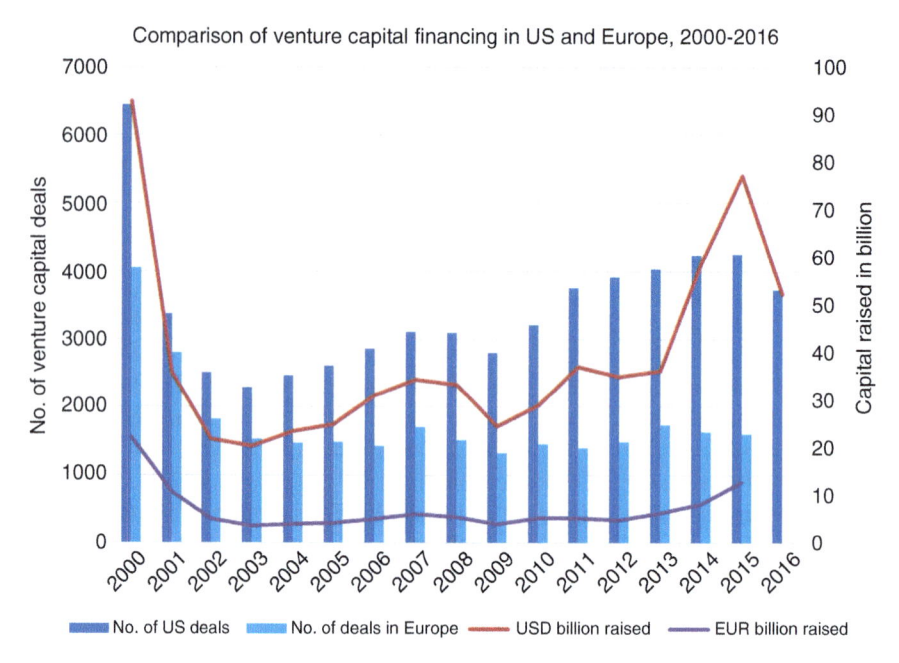

Graph 1 Venture capital financing in US and Europe, 2000–2016. Source: WilmerHale (2017) Venture Capital Report

member states, such as Slovakia, the Czech Republic, Hungary, and Romania, with Slovenia and Croatia as exceptions. Austria has been put among post-communist countries for several reasons: size of the country measured by the number of inhabitants, its historic cultural influence on Slovenia, Croatia, Hungary, and partly to the Czech Republic, and for the reason of comparing the advancement of post-communist countries to the developed countries of continental Europe. It is very interesting that grants have equal importance as equity investments in the UK, a country with developed capital market for SMEs. As far as the EU-28 average is concerned, equity investments have a negligible 1% advantage over other sources of financing, whereby debt financing makes up for the difference of 80% in supporting the growth of SMEs.

According to Udell (2015), venture capital and crowdfunding are two most interesting alternatives to bank financing. However, they may work in market-based economies with developed capital markets that allow exit to investors. In countries with illiquid capital markets, there is little chance that such financing forms may support the growth of businesses that the banks are not willing to finance. Hence, venture capitalists in Europe mostly go out through M&A transactions (Felix et al. 2013).

The statistics shows less than 0.05% venture capital investments as a percentage of GDP in most European countries, except in Denmark which had 0.109% and

Table 2 Preferred financial instruments and confidence levels in obtaining debt and external equity financing by SMEs in selected countries

Country	Bank loans (%)	Loans from other sources (%)	Equity investment (%)	Other (%)	Obtaining a loan (%)	Negotiating with venture capital funds and private investors (%)
Czech Republic	66	17	0	9	69	9
Slovakia	61	22	2	10	69	23
Slovenia	64	18	11	4	62	12
Hungary	48	29	1	9	59	18
Bulgaria	67	17	2	3	75	22
Austria	62	19	7	4	72	26
Croatia	55	19	9	6	62	16
EU-28 avg	*64*	*16*	*6*	*5*	*67*	*22*
Poland	61	21	4	5	67	25
United Kingdom	56	14	9	9	71	30
Ireland	66	13	8	5	63	25
Germany	67	17	6	4	73	28
Romania	45	19	5	14	51	14

Source: SAFE survey analytical report 2016

Luxembourg with 0.079% venture capital investment share in GDP (AFME 2017). Just for comparison, Cohesion policy for supporting growth and jobs in 2006–2013 engaged 6.5% of the EU average GDP in the EU member states, with an estimate of additional GDP creation of 2.74 € by 2023 (European Commission Ex post evaluation of ERDF and Cohesion Fund 2007–2013). Financing alternatives to SMEs such as crowdfunding, although existing, do not have notable market share in selected CEE countries, except in Austria where over seven million investors invested through three crowdfunding platforms (AFME 2017).

2 The Role of Grants in Financing SME Development

There are 12 thematic goals the member countries are expected to follow in 2014–2020 period. It is up to the member states to fine-tune the available funds with the EU thematic and national goals. Despite the EU attempts, the financing schemes are not evenly distributed across the EU area. Both supply and demand factors influence financial instruments use; hence, the EU policy should step in and try to correct market imbalance.

According to EU 1407/2013 rules, the total amount of de minimis aid granted per member state to a single undertaking shall not exceed 200,000 € over any period of three fiscal years. This rule applies to most business sectors, except for freight transport which has 50% lower threshold, SMEs from fishery and aquaculture sector, SMEs with primary production of agricultural products, SMEs with export activities to third countries, and where the amount of aid is fixed to price or quantity of the products purchased from primary producers and where the aid is conditional on being partly or entirely passed on to primary producers.

Apart from de minimis grants, whenever possible, the EU favours a horizontal approach under which the benefits of the grants are widespread to a vast number of beneficiaries. However, direct state aid can be approved to certain SMEs if they fulfil one or more goals of the common EU policy and submit project proposals to open public calls of national authorities, whereby their project proposals have to be in line with the rules of the national operational programmes of the EU member countries. The common EU goals are defined for each 7-year financing framework, they address overall harmonious development of the EU member countries and regions, and they strengthen economic and social cohesion by reducing development disparities between the regions. While European Social Fund is targeted to employment measures and better access to labour market, the other regional development issues are, depending on the purpose of co-funding, mostly supported by either European Regional Development Fund or Cohesion Fund, or from both funds. Since all three funds back the Cohesion policy, they are often jointly called Cohesion Funds.

Cohesion policy and Cohesion Fund apply to member states with a gross national income of less than 90% of the EU-28 average, i.e. to member states that joined the EU community in and after 2004, and to Greece, Portugal, and southern Italy. The Cohesion Funds are distinguished according to their priorities for financing. European Regional Development Fund supports programmes related to regional development, economic change, enhanced competitiveness, and territorial cooperation throughout the EU. It typically finances research, innovation, environmental protection and risk prevention, and investments in infrastructure. Cohesion Fund is mostly targeted to investments in environment protection and transport infrastructure. Cohesion Funds, together with the European Agricultural Fund for Rural Development and European Maritime and Fisheries Fund, belong to European structural investment funds which are run decentralised by the member states.

The evaluation of financial instruments provided to SMEs through financial institutions mentions 17 billion euros support in the financial perspective 2007–2013 until the end of 2014, of which 14 billion euros has been approved from the European Regional Development Fund (EC ex-post evaluation financial instruments for enterprise support 2016). The EU policy goal of enhancing the competitiveness through SME development is much clearer if this number is compared to the financial support of 1.3 billion euros offered to SMEs in 2000–2006 period. Europe supports smart, sustainable, and inclusive growth in 2014–2020 period, whereby SMEs are directly co-funded under the thematic objective of enhancing the competitiveness of SMEs under smart growth target. The amount of the EU contribution is determined according to the average GDP. Hence, the countries/regions are distinguished as being less developed regions (GDP per capita is less than 75% of EU average), transition regions (GDP per capita is between 75 and 90% of the EU average), and more developed regions with GDP per capita above 90% of the EU average.

The national priorities that are not specified in countries' operational programmes cannot be co-funded. Each member state sets one or more operational programme with priority axes that conform to the EU overall 7-year strategy. Some operational programmes are independent of each other, while some overlap in co-funding the sectors of specific interest of the member country. Employment programmes are mostly funded through European Social fund; hence the operational programmes available through Cohesion Fund are investigated as they concern direct injection of funds to the SME sector.

The share of public support to SME growth, both from the EU funds and by national authorities, typically ranged from 9.31% (in Slovakia) to 18.25% (in Hungary) of the total allocated public funds for all operational programmes in selected countries in the period 2007–2013, whereas Austria had minimum 25.96%. Slovenia is not accounted in the average as it had only one operational programme for all priorities in both 2007–2013 and 2014–2020 period. Bulgaria decreased the participatory part of SMEs in 2014–2020 compared to the previous financing period unlike Hungary that almost doubled the share of SMEs' co-funding. Austria, although entitled to much smaller financial envelope from the EU, split the total available EU funds from 2007–2013 into nine regional operational programmes, whereby more than 72% went to financing SMEs.

The number of operational programmes varies, and countries allocate the funds in operational programmes based on their own preferences in line with the EU targets as the European Commission approves the operational programmes. The highest number of operational programmes in the period 2014–2020, seven, is noted in Czech Republic, Bulgaria, and Hungary, whereas Slovakia has determined six operational programmes. Slovenia is the only country that has had one main operational programme in the two consecutive 7-year financing periods. In the financial perspective from 2014 to 2020, Croatia and Austria followed this path too as it gives much flexibility in allocating multiannual budget according to the given priorities.

The percentage of co-funding from the EU funds compared to the national contribution also varies from country to country. Croatia, Bulgaria, and Hungary have the highest share of EU funding in total public contribution in 2014–2020 period. The share of EU funds in total public contribution reached 85% in almost all countries in the years from 2007 to 2013. The contribution of EU funds to SME development is shown in Table 3.

SMEs are primarily financed from the European Regional Development Fund. Not only SMEs have to compete with other SMEs at a national level when requesting the EU grant, but SME financing has to be balanced with financing other EU priorities. In 2007–2013 financial perspective, most EU grants have been allotted to transport (from 29% of the total budget and above), environment and energy (26+% of the total budget), SMEs, research and innovation infrastructure,

Table 3 Funds available as a direct support for SME development from the EU funds and national budgets in selected EU countries, 2007–2020

Country name	Operational programme name	EU contribution	OP budget	Share of EU contribution in OP budget (%)	EU contribution for all OPs	Percentage of total EU funds allocated for direct SME support (%)	Public budget for all OPs
In 2014–2020 time frame							
Slovakia	Research and Innovation	2,266,776,537.00	3,707,210,258.00	61.15	13,489,867,864.00	16.80	17,622,818,217.00
Czech Republic	Enterprise and Innovation for Competitiveness	4,331,062,617.00	7,942,151,282.00	54.53	19,497,481,083.00	22.21	26,104,606,192.00
Hungary	Economic Development and Innovation OP	7,733,969,530.00	8,813,195,514.00	87.75	21,544,112,983.00	35.90	25,420,858,577.00
Croatia	OP Competitiveness and Cohesion 2014–2020	6,881,045,559.00	8,095,347,794.00	85.00	6,881,045,559.00	N/A	8,095,347,794.00
Slovenia	OP for the Implementation of the EU Cohesion policy in the Period 2014–2020	3,011,899,768.00	3,756,236,661.00	80.18	3,011,899,768.00	N/A	3,756,236,661.00
Austria	Investments in Growth and Employment Austria 2014–2020—OP for the use of the ERDF funds	536,262,079.00	2,065,579,275.00	25.96	536,262,079.00	N/A	2,065,579,275.00
Bulgaria	Operational Programme "Innovations and Competitiveness"	1,079,615,516.00	1,270,135,903.00	85.00	7,408,299,092.00	14.57	8,817,646,008.00

In 2007–2013 time frame						
Slovakia	Operational Programme 'Competitiveness and Economic Growth'	777,000,000.00	914,117,648.00	85.00	8,349,016,794.00	9.31	9,895,263,758.00
Czech Republic	Operational Programme 'Enterprises and Innovations'	3,041,312,546.00	3,578,014,760.00	85.00	17,634,115,065.00	17.25	20,746,017,733.00
Hungary	Operational Programme 'Economic Development'	2,839,044,884.00	3,340,052,807.00	85.00	15,555,590,016.00	18.25	18,305,012,157.00
Croatia	Operational Programme 'Regional Competitiveness' for Croatia	187,779,594.00	199,865,510.00	93.95	805,460,086.00	23.31	930,866,486.00
Slovenia	Operational Programme 'Strengthening Regional Development Potentials'	1,709,749,522.00	2,011,470,033.00	85.00	1,709,749,522.00	N/A	2,011,470,033.00
Austria	Nine regional operational programmes "Innovation and knowledge base economy"	491,266,958.00	940,507,681.00	52.23	680,066,021.00	72.24	1,276,780,733.00
Bulgaria	Operational Programme 'Development of the Competitiveness of the Bulgarian Economy'	987,883,219.00	1,162,285,551.00	84.99	5,505,168,381.00	17.94	6,641,608,988.00

Source: DG Regio, own calculations

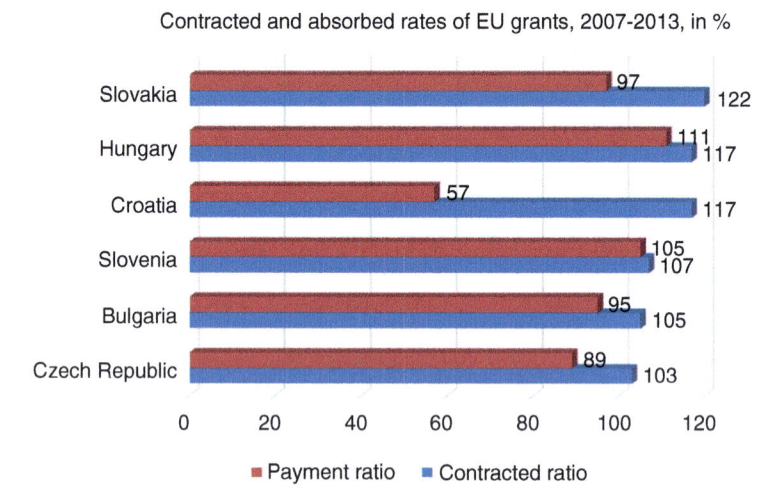

Contracted and absorbed rates of EU grants, 2007-2013, in %

Country	Payment ratio	Contracted ratio
Slovakia	97	122
Hungary	111	117
Croatia	57	117
Slovenia	105	107
Bulgaria	95	105
Czech Republic	89	103

Graph 2 Absorption of EU funds per member countries, 2007–2013. Source: KPMG (2016) (At the EU level there are daily refreshed data on the absorption of EU funds per member countries and per Cohesion Funds. The data are available at: https://cohesiondata.ec.europa.eu/dataset/2007-2013-Funds-Absoption-Rate/kk86-ceun)

social infrastructure, strengthening public administration and e-services, and technical assistance (1–2% of the total budget).

Getting funds from the EU is bound to certain achievements through the funding period and at least 2 years after the funding seizure. It is subject to initial promise of a company to achieve a certain increase in revenues, exports, net gain, the number of employees, and hopefully in intellectual property protection filings. All types of intellectual property creation and filings are strongly encouraged by the European Commission as they directly add to the smart growth goal. There is usually the difference between the available, contracted, and paid grants. A study by KPMG (2016) shows that contracted grants exceed the available budget, while paid grants to beneficiaries are, sometimes substantially, below the budget (Graph 2).

A popular alternative to de minimis grants are targeted loans up to 100,000 or 200,000 € to certain target groups of enterprises and/or entrepreneurs, typically young entrepreneurs, start-ups, women-led enterprises, exporters, or innovators. A variant of loans are public guarantee schemes developed by development agencies which often pool national funds with regional and/or funds of local authorities to boost entrepreneurship in certain area. The public guarantee schemes are typically used for small investment needs, instead of collateral. According to Gozzi and Schmukler (2015), public guarantee schemes have been used worldwide from 1950s. The statistics has shown that 476,000 SMEs throughout the EU can't get the loans due to the lack of collateral only.[2]

---

[2]https://ec.europa.eu/digital-single-market/en/financial-guarantee-facility-culture-creative

The availability of EU grants creates expectations among SMEs and, hence, SMEs that are capable of investing their own funds rather sustain investments and wait for the public call for submission of project proposals for a grant. Regardless of the size of the grant, any grant is better than either debt or equity as only administrative costs emerge when requesting the grant. Due to administrative costs, many SMEs give up from requesting the grant up front, while those that managed to get the funds for growth attempt to use grants again and again. Even financial institutions issue letters of intent promising financing conditional on grant receipt, which in a way ruins the relationship-based lending as credit scoring is targeted to risk estimate conducted by public authorities instead of a credit institution. On the other hand, public authorities often give up financing projects submitted for ESI co-funding, unless a credit institution issues a binding letter of intent to finance the project for the portion of the entrepreneur's funds that are missing. Hence, lots of projects end up waiting which institutions would give in first—a credit institution or a public authority. If none of the institutions, i.e. the credit institution that should close an entrepreneur's financial gap, or the public institution that runs a call for ESI co-funding does not make a decision, a project will never be financed no matter what its quality is as it is perceived too risky.

3 Public Financial Engineering for SME Financial Support

European institutions have recognised the shortage of risk capital for small companies and have been intensively working on making more use of the EU funds by creation of guarantee and loan schemes as well as risk capital funds for SMEs for more than a decade. JEREMIE fund, abbreviated from Joint European Initiative for Micro to Medium Enterprises, was developed by the European Commission and the European Investment Fund that operatively manages the programme in 2005. EU countries can use a part of their EU budget allocation which is then used as guarantees, loans, and/or equity for supporting: creation and expansion of businesses, access to investment capital, business-oriented research and development, technology transfer, investments aimed to safeguard sustainable jobs, and technological modernisation. Returns from investments are retained in the companies; hence, the invested capital is used constantly for development purposes of SMEs. However, only twelve countries have had benefits from this initiative, including Slovakia and Bulgaria. The current financial perspective has been the richest in various programmes available for financing. Yet, the selected countries almost do not benefit from the broadened choice of financing programmes.

A joint effort of European Commission, European Investment Bank, and the European Bank for Reconstruction and Development has created a palette of various financing programmes for SMEs. EBRD supports certain target groups of entrepreneurs such as women, young entrepreneurs, social entrepreneurship, as well as advisory services and capital market initiatives for SMEs.

European Investment Fund typically does not enter into transactions directly with final beneficiaries. However, it has contracts with most major financial intermediaries in the EU member countries that enter into contracts with final beneficiaries. Still, almost 90% of financing schemes available to the SMEs in the member countries are either loans or guarantees.[3] The list of EU-supported financing programmes is shown in Table 4, but it is not ultimate.

Of the selected CEE countries, Austria benefited most from the EU financial engineering instruments. After most innovative Iceland, it shares the second place with Denmark and Ireland in using Horizon's 2020 SME instrument for innovative companies from 2014 to 2017 (European Commission 2017).

Brander et al. (2015) found that mixed funding of publicly and privately backed venture capital funds is more efficient for supporting corporate growth than either public or private investment only. In case of mixed funding, the investment is higher and exit opportunities are greater. Pan-European initiatives for SMEs, such as Start-up and Scale-up initiative, were launched in November 2016. Startup Europe aims to strengthen the business environment for web and ICT entrepreneurs. Startup Europe Partnership has been launched by the European Commission in the beginning of 2014. It is led by Mind the Bridge Foundation present in Europe and the USA with institutional support of UK's innovation foundation—NESTA, European Investment Bank group, London Stock Exchange group, EBAN, Cambridge University, IE Business School, and Alexander von Humboldt Institute for Internet and Society, and corporate partners. It is estimated that Europe hosts about 4200 fast growing ICT companies with the EU average of 0.9 such companies per 100,000 citizens.[4] Based on the Startup Europe database which covers 12 countries, 3444 such companies collectively raised USD 50.8 billion in funding from either venture capital or via IPO or USD 14.75 million per company on average (SEP Monitor 2017). However, only 2% of the European fast-growing, high-tech companies go public and raise 15% of the total funds available globally through equity issuance. More than one-third of fast growing companies come from the UK, and they collected about 40% of total available funds, i.e. USD 20.2 billion or USD 14.3 million per company. For comparison, 1441 companies from Germany, France, Sweden, and Spain jointly collected USD 24.8 billion and slightly higher funds, USD 17.2 million, per company.

The creation of Capital Market Union is envisaged by 2019 to enable SMEs, large enterprises, and infrastructure projects easier access to capital. It should gather the excess of funds and demand for funds at one central place to complement bank financing with a pan-European capital market. Financial engineering and engagement of private sector funds is expected to continue as investments in SME projects

---

[3]The data on financial intermediaries, types of financing scheme available, the maximum amount of financing, and the total available funds can be obtained from: http://europa.eu/youreurope/business/funding-grants/access-to-finance/

[4]Nordic countries and UK exceed the EU average with 2.4 and 2.3 fast growers per 100,000 citizens, respectively.

Table 4 Financial instruments created by EU institutions for SME support, 2014–2020

Programme name	Purpose	Financial instruments supported	Execution of support	Total budget 2014–2020 in billion euro
COSME	Provides easier access to finance for SMEs in all phases of their lifecycle, including business transfer	Guarantees to loans up to 150,000 €, equity	Through local financial intermediaries that respond to EASME	2.3
InnovFin (Horizon 2020)	Provides financial support to research and innovation SMEs regardless of their size, including advisory help	Loans and guarantees which can be tailored to innovators' needs	Financing is either provided directly or via a financial intermediary that contract with EIB	N/A
SME instrument (Horizon 2020)	Financing close-to-market, export-oriented, high growth, disruptive, and scalable SMEs, preferably with a prototype; concept and feasibility study is financed by up to 50,000 €, while demonstration, market replication, R&D, and product development are financed from 0.5 to 2.5 million euros, i.e. up to 70% of project cost	Equity	Directly	3 (7000 companies)
Creative Europe	To cover financial intermediaries' potential losses when they engage with cultural and creative sector projects up to 70% of individual loans' losses and up to 25% for portfolios losses	Guarantee facility to the cultural and creative sector only	Through local financial intermediaries	0.121
Programme for Employment and Social Innovation (EaSI)	Supports microloans of up to 25,000 € for vulnerable groups and microenterprises and investments of social enterprises of up to 500,000 €	Guarantee and capacity building of financial intermediaries	Through interested microcredit providers and social enterprise that contract with European Investment Fund	0.112

(continued)

Table 4 (continued)

Programme name	Purpose	Financial instruments supported	Execution of support	Total budget 2014–2020 in billion euro
ESI funds	Multi-annual EU financing programmes	Loans, guarantees, equity financing, and business grants	Through national authorities	Determined separately for each country
European investment bank/European investment fund	Depends on detailed specification of each financing instrument	Business loans, microfinance, guarantees, and venture capital	Through local financial intermediaries	Negotiated with local financial intermediaries

Source: http://europa.eu/youreurope/business/funding-grants/access-to-finance/

bring faster rates of return and faster impact on GDP levels than investments in infrastructure. Though it seems that such investments target directly limited number of enterprises, the indirect spillover effects on overall economy are beneficial. Hence, the financing schemes available to SMEs are expected to develop further as well as their evaluation programmes with the ultimate message that Europe has sufficient funds for financing projects that help achievement of their common goals of smart and sustainable growth.

4 Conclusion

SME development is held crucial for overall EU economy competitiveness, employment, and growth and as such, it is heavily supported by the EU institutions, either directly or in a decentralised manner according to the EC pre-approved member countries' operational programmes. European Commission manages competitive programmes for SMEs or coordinates design and usage of financial engineering instruments with other European institutions such as European investment bank (fund) or and/or the EBRD. The purpose of the financial engineering instruments is to engage additional funds by the private sector or to enable capital multiplication. The most frequently used are loan guarantees provided to the financial intermediaries whereby case-by-case financing is solved by local financial intermediaries under commercial terms. There is a long way ahead to encourage more active participation of equity investors.

There are numerous programmes that enable access to market to all types of entrepreneurs. However, no unified statistics exists on the variety of programmes available to SMEs and the value-added effect they achieve. The sole evaluations are done for all programmes, but running a joint statistical database on the financing programmes impact remains a long-term challenge.

While it can't be expected that the EU contribution will solve all the problems until the end of the funding period, the catch is in spill-over effect on employment, value added, and competitiveness that can be provoked by joint investment of the EU and national funds. Such investments demonstrate the long-term goals of the EU member countries that will be visible and quantifiable many years ahead. Eventually, investing in determined priorities may change the competitiveness picture in the European continent.

References

AFME – The Association for Financial Markets in Europe. (2017). *The shortage of risk capital for Europe's high growth businesses*. https://www.afme.eu/en/reports/publications/the-shortage-of-risk-capital-for-europes-high-growth-businesses/

Andersson, T., & Nopier, G. (2007). *The role of venture capital global trends and issues from a Nordic perspective*. IKED. http://www.iked.org/pdf/THE%20ROLE%20OF%20VENTURE%20CAPITAL,GLOBAL%20TRENDS%20AND%20ISSUES.pdf

Barth, J. R., Lin, D., & Yost, K. (2011). Small and medium enterprise financing in transition. *Atlantic Economic Journal, 39*, 19–38.

Beck, T. H. L. (2007). *Financing constraints of SMEs in developing countries*. Tilburg University. https://pure.uvt.nl/portal/files/1107677/Financing_Constraints_of_SMEs.pdf

Bonin, J., Hasan, I., & Wachtel, P. (2014). Banking in transition countries. Bank of Finland. Institute for Economies in Transition (BOFIT) Discussion Paper No. 8.

Brander, J. A., Qianqian, D., & Hellman, T. (2015). The effects of government-sponsored venture capital: International evidence. *Review of Finance, 19*, 571–618.

Ciani, D., Russo, P. F., & Vacca, V. (2015). *Financing SMEs in Europe: Stylised facts, policies, challenges*. Instituto Afferi Internazionali (IAI) Working Paper 15/46, November.

Commission of the European Communities. (2008). "Think Small First" A "Small Business Act" for Europe, Brussels, 25.6.2008 COM(2008) 394 final, Brussels, 25.6.2008 COM(2008) 394 final.

Commission Recommendation of 6 May 2003 concerning the definition of micro, small, and medium-sized enterprises. (2003). 2003/361/EC, Official Journal of the European Union, L 124/36, 20 May 2003.

Demary, M., Hornik, J., & Watfe, G. (2016). *SME financing in the EU: Moving beyond one-size-fits-all*. Institut der Deutschen Wirtschaft Köln, IW-Report 11/2016.

European Commission. (2017). *Accelerating innovation in Europe*. https://ec.europa.eu/easme/sites/easme-site/files/2016_smei_report_updated.pdf

EVCA – European Private Equity and Venture Capital Association. (2014). *2014 European private equity activity – Statistics on fundraising, investments and divestments*. https://www.investeurope.eu/media/385581/2014-european-private-equity-activity-final-v2.pdf

Felix, E. G. S., Pires, C. P., & Gulamhussen, M. A. (2013). The determinants of venture capital in Europe-evidence across countries. *Journal of Financial Services Research, 44*, 259–279.

Global Private Equity and Venture Capital Report. (2016). Prequin.

Gozzi, J. C., & Schmukler, S. (2015). Public credit guarantees and access to finance. *European Economy: Banks, Regulation and the Real Sector, 2*, 101–117.

IKED – International Organisation for Knowledge Economy and Enterprise Development. (2007). *The role of venture capital, global trends, and issues from a nordic perspective*. http://www.iked.org/pdf/THE%20ROLE%20OF%20VENTURE%20CAPITAL,GLOBAL%20TRENDS%20AND%20ISSUES.pdf

Invest Europe. (2016). *Central and Eastern Europe statistics 2015*. https://www.investeurope.eu/media/504370/invest-europe-cee-statistics-2015.pdf

KPMG. (2016). EU funds in Central and Eastern Europe. Progress Report 2007–2015. https://assets.kpmg.com/content/dam/kpmg/pdf/2016/06/EU-Funds-in-Central-and-Eastern-Europe.pdf

Muller, P., Devnani, S., Julius, J., Gagliardi D., & Marzocchi, C. (2016). Annual report on European SMEs – 2015/2016 – SME performance review. https://ec.europa.eu/jrc/sites/jrcsh/files/annual_report_-_eu_smes_2015-16.pdf

Smallbone, D., & Welter, F. (2001). The role of government in SME development in transition countries. *International Small Business Journal, 19*(4), 63–77.

Startup Europe Partnership (SEP) Monitor, Scaleup Europe. (2017). Mind the bridge. http://startupeuropepartnership.eu/

Udell, G. F. (2015). Issues in SMEs access to finance. *European Economy: Banks, Regulation and the Real Sector, 2*, 61–72.

Venture Capital Report. (2017). WilmerHale. https://www.wilmerhale.com/uploadedFiles/Shared_Content/Editorial/Publications/Documents/2017-WilmerHale-VC-Report.pdf

FDI Flows and Regional Development: Lessons for Transition Countries

Kurt A. Hafner and Jörn Kleinert

1 Introduction

Multinational enterprises (MNEs) are important players on many goods and factor markets worldwide, while their foreign affiliates and FDI flows play an increasing role in spurring economic development. Firms set up by multinational firms are more productive and integrated in the international division of labor than the average domestic firm. Due to size and potential to substitute among intermediate goods and input factors, their impact on regional supplier and customers is also larger. Moreover, export activities of foreign affiliates allow domestic firms to (indirectly) compete in international market as local trade relationships increase and spillover effects arise. However, FDI flows do not necessarily increase the welfare of regions or push regional economic development if there is no match between the profile (and therefore the needs) of the region and the activities of MNEs. While the EU and its member states pursue FDI policy in several sectors and on different regional levels, the European territorial development policy and its Agenda 2020 focuses on the regional components of economic development for attracting MNEs. Research in international economics suggests that heterogeneous MNEs can pursue welfare-enhancing activities in some but not every foreign location. Obviously, a one-size-fits-all FDI policy does not work, as finding the best match between MNEs and host locations is not a simple task.

K. A. Hafner (✉)
Faculty of International Business, Heilbronn University, Max-Planck-Straße 39, 74081 Heilbronn, Germany
e-mail: kurt.hafner@hs-heilbronn

J. Kleinert
Institut für Volkswirtschaftslehre, Universität Graz, Universitätsstraße 15/F4, 8010 Graz, Austria
e-mail: joern.kleinert@uni-graz.at

© Springer International Publishing AG, part of Springer Nature 2018
J. Ateljević, J. Budak (eds.), *Entrepreneurship in Post-Communist Countries*,
https://doi.org/10.1007/978-3-319-75907-4_4

The appropriate match between the profiles of potential regions and the activities of MNEs seems to be the key factor for a positive effect of FDI on regional welfare and economic development. Not surprisingly, the heterogeneity of foreign affiliates of MNEs and regions for firm locations is huge. Firms differ, for example, with respect to their home country, sector category, motives of internationalization, size, activities, use of resources, and technological knowledge. Regions are very different too and compete according to their comparative advantage such as rural versus urban regions, capital cities versus second-tier cities, regions with a well-connected versus remote infrastructure, abundance of resources, labor skills, and sector expertise. While both lists are far from being complete, the challenge is to find the best firm-location match between the particular need (and strength) of the region and firm.

There are many empirical studies regarding FDI flows, location choices of MNEs, and their economic impact on both home and host countries. In the advance of our research project, we will add to the literature a fundamentally microeconomic view of an optimal location choice of a firm among heterogeneous regions. We take into account macroeconomic and regional characteristics and combine firm-specific characteristics with regional data to model the match between firms and locations. However, we refrain from delivering a precise micro-level analysis in this contribution as the data basis is still to be developed. Instead, we show the relationship between FDI flows and regional economic development across European countries on a Nuts-2 level. We back up the empirical analysis by a theoretical approach of a two-sided matching problem and address the following points: (1) the patterns of inward FDI flows to EU regions, (2) the impact of MNE activity on regional economic development in Europe, and (3) regional factors for attracting FDI. Specifically, we start from the empirical observation that regions conduct different policies to attract FDI and foreign affiliates of MNEs. We model the firm-location decision as a two-sided matching of firms and locations, where firms choose among different locations and regional administrations try to "guide" the decision by conducting different policies and offering specific incentives. While rankings of regions usually address vertical differentiation, our firm-location approach focuses on the horizontal component of regional differentiation. We address this in our empirical part and use regional data from the Eurostat Structural Business Survey (SBS) and the Eurostat Regional Competitiveness Index (RCI). Combining both data types at the NUTS-2 level, we expect insights between the matching of heterogeneous firms and regions.

The chapter is organized as follows. In Sect. 2, we review the literature on location choice of FDI and the impact of multinational firms' activities on regional development. The model of a two-sided matching of firms and locations is described in Sect. 3. We present descriptive empirical results for regional FDI flows and regional economic development across European countries in Sect. 4. Finally, we conclude in Sect. 5.

2 Literature Review

Theoretical advances in the field of international trade lead to a renewed interest in the empirical analysis of the location choice of MNEs. Summarized by Markusen (2002), the theoretical literature suggests that the location choice of foreign affiliates is driven by demand factors (i.e., market size and market potential), supply factors (i.e., labor costs, human capital, knowledge base, and costs of doing business such as corporate tax rates), firm heterogeneity, and agglomeration economies (i.e., spillover effects). Most of the empirical studies find that *market access* and *market size* are positively linked to a regions' probability being selected as a host (Head et al. 1999; Disdier and Mayer 2004; Head and Mayer 2004; Basile et al. 2008), while the evidence on the role of *labor costs* and *taxation* is somehow mixed (Devereux and Griffith 1998). Eaton and Kortum (2002) and Melitz (2003) introduced *firm heterogeneity* in general equilibrium models to study firm-specific location decisions, where firms differ systematically even within the same industry. Chen and Moore (2010) test the effect of firm heterogeneity on location-specific investment decisions using a sample of French multinational corporations. They find that MNEs' productivity affects their investment decisions and high productive MNEs are likely to invest in economies with a smaller market potential, higher fixed costs of investment, and lower import tariffs. At the regional level, Siedschlag et al. (2013) modeled 446 location decisions of R&D firms across EU regions over the period 1999–2006 and link the location choice to a range of region- and country-specific covariates. They find that the probability to choose a particular region is positively affected by the regions' FDI stock and endowments and therefore driven by comparative advantage. *Agglomeration economies* are found to play an important role in attracting foreign-owned firms (Basile et al. 2008; Head et al. 1995; Feldman and Audretsch 1999). Basile et al. (2008), for example, use data on 5509 foreign subsidiaries across 50 European regions in eight European countries over the period 1991–1999 to test the determinants of multinational firms' location choices. Using a mixed logit approach model, they find that agglomeration economies play a key role in determining location choices and that MNEs are more likely to set up new plants in locations, where firms from the same country of origin or the same business group are located. Head et al. (1995) provide evidence that Japanese firms tend to locate in regions with other firms from the same industry, whereas Feldman and Audretsch (1999) find that industries relying on the same technology tend to cluster geographically.

Turning to the impact of FDI on regional economic development, theoretical advances in endogenous growth theory renewed the interest on micro- and macroeconomic effects of FDI on host country's economic development. From the *microeconomic perspective*, FDI is a source of technology and knowledge transfer, which occur directly from parent firms to foreign affiliates, and indirectly from foreign affiliates to domestic firms (Hirschmann 1958; Markusen and Venables 1999; Rodriguez-Clare 1996). Moreover, FDI leads to positive technological spillover effects through competition, imitation, and training (Blomstrom and Kokko 1997; Smarzynska Javorcik 2004) and depends on the technological and social capabilities of the foreign affiliates and their host countries (Dunning 1994, 1996;

Verspagen 1991). Such spillover effects to arise require a minimum level of absorptive capacity by the local firms and are more likely if there is a (good) match between the firm and region. From the *macroeconomic perspective*, FDIs are thought to have an immediate impact on the host country in terms of higher physical capital stock and therefore higher GDP. Like physical capital investments, FDI flows are less volatile than other financial sources (e.g., portfolio investments) and foreign investors usually make long-term commitments. However, growth theories have not completely confirmed the role played by MNEs. Neoclassical growth theories suggest that an (exogenous) increase in the FDI stock (such as an increase in the physical capital stock) has a temporary effect on the growth rate of the host economy shifting their economy to higher GDP levels. However, there is an increase in the long-run growth rate only if FDI spurs technological change or increases the effective labor force. This leads us to the endogenous growth theories, where technological change, learning-by-doing, and technology diffusion are the important determinants for economic growth (Temple 1999). Accordingly, FDI flows are investments in fixed assets, knowledge (tacit and codified), and technology and therefore create economic growth endogenously through direct (and indirect) transfer of technology. Surprisingly, only few endogenous growth models explicitly model FDI as a main driver for long-run growth (De Mello 1997; Grossman and Helpman 1991; Baldwin et al. 1999), whereas empirical studies find mixed evidence for MNEs' activities in fostering long-run growth in host countries (Hafner 2008, 2014). Evidence for positive spillover effects from foreign firms varies by the level of human capital in the host country (Borensztein et al. 1998), the degree of openness of the host economies (Balasubramanyam et al. 1996), and the development of local financial markets (Alfaro et al. 2004).

Firm level studies of particular countries show that enhanced growth and positive spillovers from foreign to domestic firms are not the rule but rather the exception (Aitken and Harrison 1999; Haddad and Harrison 1993; Konings 2000; Altomonte and Resmini 2002). Interestingly, most of these studies do not pay serious attention to a bidirectional relationship between FDI and growth, although a bidirectional causality is very likely as GDP and its growth rate as well as the availability of infrastructure facilities and well-functioning institutions may influence the choice of the location and level of FDI. The few existing studies such as Ericsson and Irandoust (2001) and Zhang (2001) that explicitly address this issue provide evidence of both unidirectional and bidirectional causality.

3 Theory: Two-Sided Matching Model

We see the location choice for a foreign affiliate of an MNE as a two-sided matching problem as the firms decide about the engagement in a particular location and public authorities try to influence the firm-location decision. There is a wide range of regional targeted-policy actions both directly such as the permission to construct establishments and facilities and indirectly such as a well-disposed attitude toward foreign engagement and rich cultural life. Each of the regional characteristics affects firms and their investment decisions differently. The availability of wood, for instance, is of particular interest for the paper industry but not for business services. Thus, Krugman's (1993) first nature (e.g., wood) and second nature (e.g., wood mill or furniture plant) characteristics of a location shape the investment decision of a firm.

Taking into account that firms choose their most preferred location among heterogeneous regions, we are unable to assess the mutual influence of each characteristic on realized and non-realized (but possible) firm-location matches. We rely instead on sample averages of characteristics that might affect firms' decision. Hence, we see matches as the rational choices of firms for their (most) preferred location and model the profit π_{ik} of firm k generated by the decision to invest in location i as:

$$\pi_{ik} = \underbrace{\sum_{j=1}^{m} \delta_j \omega_{ikj}}_{\omega_{ik}} + \varepsilon_{ik}, \qquad (1)$$

where the vector ω reflects the known characteristics of the firm, location, or firm-location relationship; δ is the weight of the characteristic in the profit function; and ε is the firm-location specific component of the decision. The latter is unknown to us but possibly known by the body deciding on behalf of the firm.

Firm k compares profits among different locations l and decides to invest in one location i. The probability P_{ik} of firm k to choose location i is thus given by:

$$P_{ik} = Pr\left[\omega_{ik} + \varepsilon_{ik} = \max_{l=1...n}(\omega_{lk} + \varepsilon_{lk})\right], \qquad (2)$$

where we do not know the firm-specific characteristics ω, but sector or region averages $\overline{\omega}_h$. We rewrite the firm-specific characteristic as: $\omega = \overline{\omega}_h + \vartheta$, where $h = i, k, ik$, and ϑ is the deviation from the characteristics' average. The unobserved component is thus the sum of $u = \sum_{j=1...m} \vartheta_j + \varepsilon$. If the unobserved component u is normally distributed, the probability that firm k chooses location i is according to Anderson et al. (1992):

$$P_{ik} = \frac{e^{(\omega_{ik}-\mu)/\beta}}{\sum_{l=1}^{n} e^{(\omega_{lk}-\mu)/\beta}}, \qquad (3)$$

where μ is the mean and β is a scale parameter (proportional to the standard deviation) of a logistic distribution. Hence, the probability that firm k chooses location i is affected by the characteristics of location i relative to the characteristics of all other locations. We will estimate the (average) weights δ of the different characteristics on the location decision using discrete choice logit or probit models. Since many of the location variables do not have the same effect on all firms, it is essential to aggregate over meaningful, not too heterogeneous, groups of firms or locations in order to reduce the deviation ϑ from the average realization of a specific characteristic.

In addition, we are able to analyze comparative advantages of locations in attracting FDI and MNEs. This extends the two-sided matching model if the location characteristics can be adjusted and targeted toward groups of firms or individual firms (i.e., in terms of subsidies, land offers, specific infrastructure investments). Hence, locations compete for firms and their investments trying to increase their attractiveness and thus the probability by Eq. (3). Since characteristics of regions appeal differently to firms, a relative change leads not only to a change in the absolute number of firms but also in the firm mix. For example, a new school established abroad, where the teaching language is French, increases the (relative) attractiveness of the foreign region for MNEs headquartered in France. Locations can, thus, create comparative advantages rather than just to exploit them. As these advantages might accrue in a rather small area, regional data has to be analyzed. The region might, for instance, establish a new business or engage in a large investment in already established business areas. This can cause follow-up investment from suppliers and customers as well as competitors seeking proximity for enjoying spillover effects. The overall economic gain might be much larger than the gain from the new establishment as the probability of attracting other firms increases. A good measure of a region's success with respect to attracting investments is the number of newly attracted firms. For a large number of firms looking independently for their best match, the number of new establishments equals the product of the probability and the total number of firms investing in a (new) location. Hence, multiplied with the total number of FDI establishment N^{FDI}, we write the gravity equation explaining FDI activities by relative characteristics of locations and the total number of investment projects as:

$$N_i = \frac{e^{(\omega_{ik}-\mu)/\beta}}{\sum_{l=1}^{n} e^{(\omega_{lk}-\mu)/\beta}} N^{FDI}. \qquad (4)$$

Equation (4) is usually estimated by a Poisson regression, which addresses the problem of heterogeneity according to Santos Silva and Tenreyro (2006) and handles zero outcome of FDI in some locations.

4 Results: Empirical Evidence of FDI Flows

The empirical analysis focuses on the relationship between inward FDI flows, activities of foreign affiliates of MNEs, and their firm-location choice. Hence, a firm-level dataset that constructs the explanatory variables at the regional level by firm aggregation combined with a detailed regional dataset (preferably at a NUTS-2 level or more disaggregated) allows us to model the match between firms and locations. However, such a dataset is not available yet, but can be constructed using AMADEUS firm-level data and Eurostat data on regional development. While such an empirical analysis is beyond the scope of this contribution, it will be the goal of our research project to match the theory with a firm-location dataset on a regional level.

FDI Flows and Regional Development: Lessons for Transition Countries   53

For the purpose of this contribution, we rely on the Eurostat Regional Competitiveness Index (RCI) (Annoni and Dijkstra 2013; Annoni et al. 2017) and its three subindexes available at a NUTS-2 level. The three subindexes are (1) the *basis* subindex reflecting the regional quality of institutions, macroeconomic stability, infrastructure, health, and basic education; (2) the *efficiency* subindex taking into account higher education and lifelong learning, labor market efficiency, and market size; and (3) the *innovation* subindex related to the level of technological readiness of enterprises and households, business sophistication, and innovation.[1] In addition, we make use of the regional data from the Eurostat Structural Business Survey (SBS) database to analyze the link between FDI flows and economic development across European regions.[2] The total RCI and its ranking show the strong component of horizontal differentiation among regions. In principle, higher ranked regions perform better, but the ranking reflects not the location choice of firms. The Northwest region of Romania, for example, is ranked 241 out of 275 NUTS-2 regions in 2016 but had been chosen by Nokia as the location for its mobile phone production in 2008. At that time, the regions' RCI position would have been comparable if the Eurostat had calculated such rankings. Although many locations (i.e., 240 out of 275 regions according to the RCI of 2016) are better ranked than Romania Northwest, Nokia decided to produce there and calculated the expected return by the use of Eq. (2), which exceeded the expected return in all other regions. Consequently, Nokia moved out of the German region Dusseldorf (i.e., ranked 32 out of 275 according to the RCI of 2016). Thus, there must be an important component of horizontal differentiation between regions in order to attract activities.

We use the discrete choice model by Eq. (2) to analyze vertical and horizontal differentiation within and across regions. In the case of perfect vertical differentiation, the market shares by the use of Eq. (3) of all locations except one location would be zero. In the case of perfect horizontal differentiation, the market shares for all locations would be the same. However, the total RCI pattern shown in the data is different. Figure 1 shows the regional distribution of the total RCI of 2016 with respect to the national average for 28 EU countries arranged by an increasing order. The vertical element is shown by the dominance of the capital region in almost all countries, whereas the horizontal element becomes apparent by the within-country variances of the regions in Fig. 1. Specifically, there is no capital region that is below the country average, and it outperforms the average in all countries with the exception of Germany. In many countries, the capital region is the only region

---

[1] See http://ec.europa.eu/eurostat/statistics-explained/index.php/Regional_competitiveness_statistics

[2] There is a wide range of data on FDI flows and activities of MNEs from different sources and aggregation levels. Regional data can be found in the Eurostat Structural Business Survey (SBS). At a country level, MNE data is provided by OECD databases, whereas the United Nations Conference on Trade and Development, World Bank, International Monetary Fund, and International Trade Center provide FDI data. Moreover, the AMADEUS database of the Bureau van Dijk offers regional FDI stocks, number of foreign-owned firms, sales, value added, and employment of MNEs and their affiliates. However, access and use of the AMADEUS database is restricted to subscriptions.

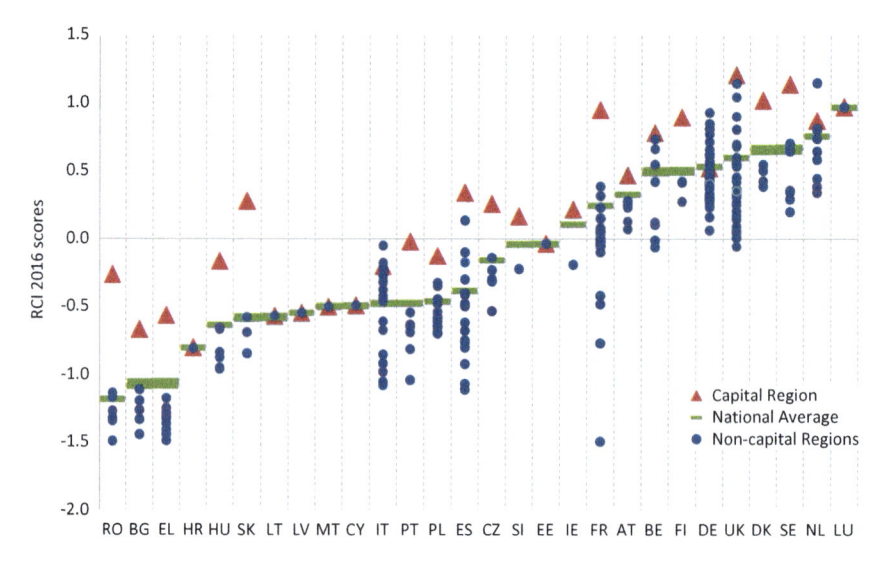

Fig. 1 Distribution of RCI scores between and within countries, 2016. Source: Annoni et al. (2017, p. 6)

above the average. The within-country variance is smallest for Austria, Germany, Finland, and Denmark and largest for Romania and Greece, which is likely to be the results of very heterogeneous regions compared to their capital region within countries of the European periphery.

Unfortunately, regional FDI flows are not available from Eurostat, which leads us to the RCI subindex "innovation" as a (regional) proxy for FDI flows. It reflects most likely the regional impact of FDI activity, as technological readiness and innovation competence are key characteristics of MNEs. For the economic development in 272 European regions, we use the indexed GDP per capita of 2011 (i.e., with value of 100 for the 2011-regional average of the EU-28 countries) and, as an alternative indicator, the RCI of 2013 as it reflects the readiness and capabilities of regions to compete at different dimensions. Since NUTS-2 regions are very heterogeneous, various patterns across regions and countries emerge. We therefore group the EU-28 countries and their regions into four country aggregates (i.e., nine "EU-core countries," three "Mediterranean countries," three "post-cold war countries," and thirteen "Eastern-enlargement countries") according to the year of EU accession.[3]

Figure 2 shows the scatterplot of the subindex "innovation" across regions and country aggregates, respectively, both GDP per capita in the left panel and RCI in the right panel, while the last two columns of Table 2 in the appendix show the correlation coefficients. Looking at country aggregates, there is a common pattern of FDI flows across countries and regions irrespective of whether we use GDP per capita or total RCI as an indicator for economic development. On average, regions

---

[3]Tables 1 and 2 in the appendix provide specific information and descriptive statistics for the regions of the EU-28 countries and their country aggregates.

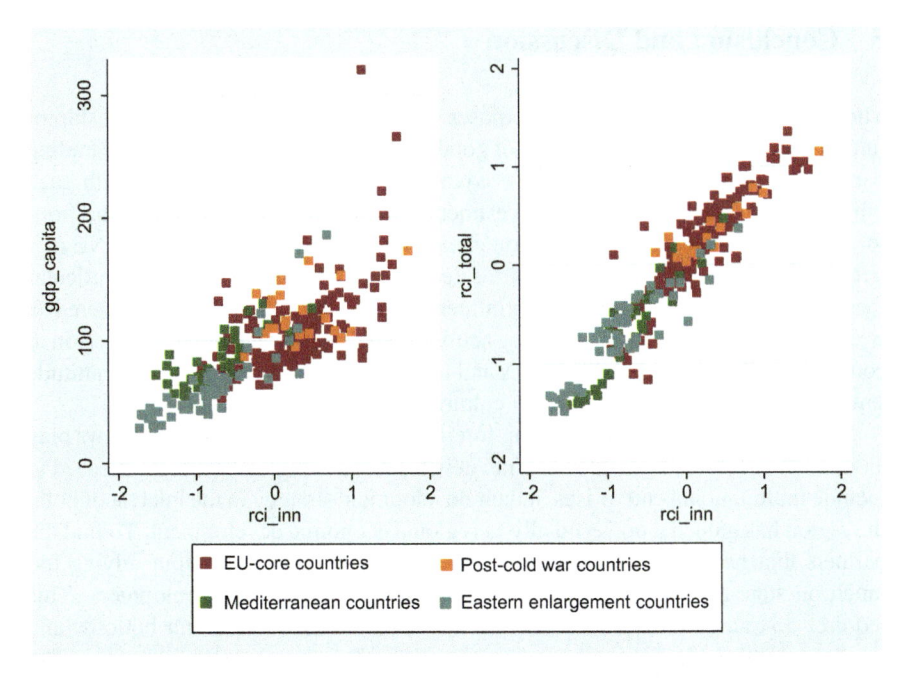

Fig. 2 Regional competitiveness subindex "innovation," 2013. Source: Annoni and Dijkstra (2013), own calculation

belonging to "EU-core countries" or "post-cold war countries" score higher in terms of both economic development and FDI flows compared to those belonging to "Mediterranean countries" or "Eastern enlargement countries." Not surprisingly, there is a high correlation (i.e., 90% or higher according to Table 2 in the appendix) between total RCI and its subindex "innovation" irrespective of whether regions belonging to a certain country aggregate or not. In contrast, no such correlation is shown in the case of GDP per capita especially within regions of "EU-core countries" or "post-cold war countries." Hence, FDI flows seem to be an important key factor for Europe's economic development of its periphery regions as the correlation coefficient is much higher in regions of "Mediterranean countries" and "Eastern enlargement countries."

To sum up, there are regions with particularly large or low innovation capacities given their GDP per capita and total RCI, but to elaborate further we have to rely on disaggregated firm data. It will be interesting to relate firm data to FDI inflows at a regional level in order to analyze if the RCI index reflects investment decisions of individual firms. Moreover, size distributions, home-country and sector concentration measures, heterogeneity, and specialization measures at a regional level allow us to make inference regarding a regions' capacity (and success) to attract new firms.

5 Conclusion and Discussion

The European integration process exposes its regions to a particular relationship of intensive competition and exchange of goods and services. While looking for trading partners to exploit their comparative advantages, regions also compete with each other for resources and (foreign) investment. Public authorities can affect the firm-location decision. We see the location choice for a foreign affiliate of an MNE as a two-sided matching problem as the firms decide about the engagement in a particular location and public authorities try to influence the firm-location decision. There is a wide range of regional targeted-policy actions both directly such as the permission to construct establishments and facilities and indirectly such as a well-disposed attitude toward foreign engagement and rich cultural life.

With further economic integration, foreign affiliates of MNEs and FDI flows play an increasing role in regional economic development. If regional policies succeed to include multinational enterprises in their development strategy in the interest of both, the region has gained a powerful ally in regional economic development. To find the partners that help to boost economic activities in the regions without relying too much on state-allocated resources is the challenge of regional development. This requires a strategy for a future development path based on the contributions (and support) of firms guided by incentives rather than directed by influence. The encouraging result of this contribution is that there is a suitable strategy for every region building on its strengths and visions as regional heterogeneity is large and regions are likely to find a niche and thereby the suitable partners.

Appendix

Table 1 Country aggregation (Annual data for 28 EU countries of 2011 and 2013)

EU-28 countries	Country aggregates
EU-core countries: six founding members in 1967 (i.e., Belgium, France, Germany, Italy, Luxembourg, the Netherlands) and 1973-enlargement countries (i.e., Denmark, Ireland, United Kingdom)	"EU-core countries"
Mediterranean countries: Greece (1981), Portugal (1986), and Spain (1986)	"Mediterranean countries"
Post-cold war countries (1995): Austria, Finland, and Sweden	"Post-cold war countries"
Eastern enlargement countries (2004, 2007): Bulgaria, Croatia, Cyprus, Czech Republic, Estonia, Hungary, Latvia, Lithuania, Malta, Poland, Romania, Slovakia, Slovenia	"Eastern enlargement countries"

Notes: Country aggregates according to EU accession

Table 2 Descriptive and correlation analysis (Annual data for 28 EU countries of 2011 and 2013)

	Obs.	Mean	Std. Dev.	Min	Max	GDP per capita	RCI Total
EU Nuts-2 regions							
GDP per capita	272	95.83456	36.78067	29.00	321.00	1	
RCI total	272	−0.05526	0.68121	−1.48	1.36	0.7077	1
RCI innovation	272	−0.09313	0.75427	−1.74	1.73	0.7395	0.9474
EU-core countries							
GDP per capita	153	107.33990	35.25194	53.00	321.00	1	
RCI total	153	0.29013	0.52710	−1.16	1.36	0.5482	1
RCI innovation	153	0.28549	0.57569	−0.95	1.58	0.5953	0.8982
Mediterranean countries							
GDP per capita	39	83.64103	20.47269	55.00	130.00	1	
RCI total	39	−0.70897	0.49431	−1.42	0.48	0.7849	1
RCI innovation	39	−0.74872	0.44957	−1.52	0.50	0.7758	0.9435
Post-cold war countries							
GDP per capita	22	122.04550	22.71034	87.00	173.00	1	
RCI total	22	0.35500	0.29479	0.04	1.15	0.3182	1
RCI innovation	22	0.34227	0.48958	−0.38	1.73	0.3528	0.9265
Eastern enlargement countries							
GDP per capita	58	63.74138	29.63554	29.00	186.00	1	
RCI total	58	−0.68241	0.43892	−1.48	0.38	0.7931	1
RCI innovation	58	−0.81621	0.56036	−1.74	0.68	0.8396	0.9101

Notes: Country aggregates according to EU accession

References

Aitken, B. J., & Harrison, E. (1999). Do domestic firms benefit from direct foreign investment? Evidence from Venezuela. *American Economic Review, 3*, 605–618.

Alfaro, L., Chanda, A., Kalemli-Ozcan, S., & Sayek, S. (2004). FDI and economic growth: The role of local financial markets. *Journal of International Economics, 64*, 89–112.

Altomonte, C., & Resmini, L. (2002). Multinational corporations as a catalyst for local industrial development. The case of Poland. *Scienze Regionali. The Italian Journal of Regional Science, 2*, 29–58.

Anderson, S., De Palma, A., & Thisse, J. (1992). *Discrete choice theory of product differentiation.* Cambridge, MA: MIT Press.

Annoni, P., & Dijkstra, L. (2013). *The EU regional competitiveness index 2013*. http://ec.europa.eu/regional_policy/sources/docgener/studies/pdf/6th_report/rci_2013_report_final.pdf

Annoni, P., Dijkstra, L., & Gargano, N. (2017). *The EU regional competitiveness index 2016* (Working Papers 02/2017). http://ec.europa.eu/regional_policy/sources/docgener/work/201701_regional_competitiveness2016.pdf

Balasubramanyam, V. N., Salisu, M., & Sapsford, D. (1996). Foreign direct investment and growth in EP and IS countries. *Economic Journal, 106*, 92–105.

Baldwin, R., Braconier, H., & Forslid, R. (1999). *Multinationals, endogenous growth and technological spillovers: Theory and evidence*. CEPR discussion paper 2155, London.

Basile, R., Castellani, D., & Zanfei, A. (2008). Location choices of multinational firms in Europe: The role of EU cohesion policy. *Journal of International Economics, 74*(2), 328–340.

Blomstrom, M., & Kokko, A. (1997). *How foreign investment affects host countries* (The World Bank Policy Research Working Paper n. 1745). Washington, DC: The World Bank.

Borensztein, E., De Gregorio, J., & Lee, J.-W. (1998). How does foreign direct investment affect economic growth? *Journal of International Economics, 45*, 115–135.

Chen, M., & Moore, M. O. (2010). Location decision of heterogeneous multinational firms. *Journal of International Economics, 80*(2), 188–199.

De Mello, L. (1997). Foreign direct investment in developing countries and growth: A selective survey. *The Journal of Development Studies, 34*(1), 1–34.

Devereux, M. P., & Griffith, R. (1998). Taxes and the location of production: Evidence from a panel of US multinationals. *Journal of Public Economics, 68*(3), 335–367.

Disdier, A.-C., & Mayer, T. (2004). How different is Eastern Europe? Structure and determinants of location choices by French firms in Eastern and Western Europe. *Journal of Comparative Economics, 32*(2), 280–296.

Dunning, J. (1994). Re-evaluating the benefit of foreign direct investment. *Transnational Corporation, 3*(1), 23–51.

Dunning, J. (1996). The Geographical sources of the competitiveness of firms. *Transnational Corporations, 5*(3), 1–30.

Eaton, J., & Kortum, S. (2002). Technology, geography, and trade. *Econometrica, 70*(5), 1741–1779.

Ericsson, J., & Irandoust, M. (2001). On the casualty of foreign direct investment and output: A comparative study. *International Trade Journal, 15*(1), 122–132.

Feldman, M., & Audretsch, D. (1999). Innovation in cities: Science-based diversity, specialization and localized competition. *European Economic Review, 43*(2), 409–429.

Grossman, G., & Helpman, H. (1991). *Innovation and growth in the global economy*. Cambridge, MA: MIT Press.

Haddad, M., & Harrison, H. (1993). Are there positive spillovers from direct foreign investment? Evidence from panel data from Morocco. *Journal of Development Economics, 42*(1), 51–74.

Hafner, K. A. (2008). The pattern of international patenting and technology diffusion. *Applied Economics, 40*(21), 2819–2837.

Hafner, K. A. (2014). Technology spillover effects and economic integration – Evidence from integrating EU countries. *Applied Economics, 46*(25), 3021–3036.

Head, K., & Mayer, T. (2004). Market potential and the location of Japanese investment in the European Union. *The Review of Economics and Statistics, 86*(4), 959–972.

Head, K., Ries, J., & Swenson, D. (1995). Agglomeration benefits and location choice: Evidence from Japanese manufacturing investments in the United States. *Journal of International Economics, 38*(3–4), 223–247.

Head, K., Ries, J., & Swenson, D. (1999). Attracting foreign manufacturing: Investment promotion and agglomeration. *Regional Science and Urban Economics, 29*(2), 197–218.

Hirschmann, A. O. (1958). *The strategy of economic development*. New Haven: Yale University Press.

Konings, J. (2000). *The effects of direct foreign investment on domestic Firms: Evidence from firm level panel data in emerging economies*. CEPR Discussion paper 2586.

Krugman, P. (1993). First nature, second nature, and metropolitan location. *Journal of Regional Science, 33*(2), 129–144.

Markusen, J. (2002). *Multinational firms and the theory of international trade*. Cambridge, MA: MIT Press.

Markusen, J., & Venables, A. (1999). Foreign direct investment as a catalyst for industrial development. *European Economic Review, 43*, 335–356.

Melitz, M. (2003). The impact of trade on aggregate industry productivity and intra-industry reallocations. *Econometrica, 71*(6), 1695–1725.

Rodriguez-Clare, R. (1996). Multinationals, linkages, and economic development. *American Economic Review, 86*(4), 852–873.

Santos Silva, J. M. C., & Tenreyro, S. (2006). The log of gravity. *The Review of Economics and Statistics, 88*(4), 641–658.

Siedschlag, I., Zhang, X., Smith, D., & Turcu, C. (2013). What determines the location choice of R&D activities by multinational firms? *Research Policy, 42*, 1420–1430.

Smarzynska Javorcik, B. (2004). Does foreign direct investment increase the productivity of domestic firms? In search of spillovers through backward linkages. *American Economic Review, 94*(3), 605–627.

Temple, J. (1999). The new growth evidence. *Journal of Economic Literature, 37*(1), 112–156.

Verspagen, B. (1991). A new empirical approach to catching up or falling behind. *Structural Change and Economic Dynamics, 2*, 359–380.

Zhang, K. (2001). How does FDI affect economic growth in China? *Economics of Transition, 9*(3), 679–693.

Sources of Financing in the Process of Enterprise Restructuring Focusing on Transitional Countries

Dragan Milovanović, Saša Vučenović, and Igor Mišić

1 Introduction

The need to restructure the company during the last economic and financial crisis is gaining in importance. Under such conditions, a large number of companies faced a crisis of business, a decline in financial performance, and a weakening of the financial result of operations. Measures from the domain of restructuring can help rehabilitate, financially stabilize, and in certain conditions contribute to the growth of the company through improving the financial performance of the business. In this regard, the sources of funding directly influence the creation and implementation of the enterprise restructuring strategies. One thing is certain: the existence of several symptoms definitely leads to the conclusion that something is wrong with the company. Proper implementation of the enterprise restructuring strategy needs an adequate and timely diagnosis of the situation in the company and adequate definition of right problems. Based on this, the company managers will create an adequate strategy for enterprise restructuring in a crisis. It rarely happens that only one cause affects the crisis and that it is isolated. A more common case is that several of them simultaneously exert pressure on the management and the company, which significantly blurs the situation and makes it difficult to diagnose correctly the right problems. The basic research questions that are reflected in the problem of this chapter, which we will try to answer, are: "What is the significance of certain sources of financing for the enterprise restructuring in the Republic of Srpska, Serbia, and other EU countries?" In this regard, the main problem of the research is: "What are the differences in the evaluation of the significance of certain sources of financing for

D. Milovanović (✉) · S. Vučenović · I. Mišić
University of Banja Luka, Banja Luka, Bosnia and Herzegovina
e-mail: dragan.milovanovic@ef.unibl.org; sasa.vucenovic@ef.unibl.org; igor.misic@auraosiguranje.com

the enterprise restructuring in the Republic of Srpska, Serbia, and the countries of Western, Central, and Eastern Europe?"

Interpretation of the obtained results should serve as the basis for professional and scientific discussion on the role of restructuring in the function of improving business operations, as well as the basis for improving the existing analytical framework. After the introductory part, in the first part of the paper, the research problems are analyzed from the perspective of the previous research through scientific literature. The second part is called "Research methodology and analysis of the sample", where the basic methodological concept of research is developed, sampling is done, and scientific research methods are applied. The third part of the chapter presents the results of the research and the discussion of the results. Final conclusions are elaborated in the final part of the chapter.

2 Overview of Literature and Previous Research

Financing is an important factor that determines the survival and growth of a company. Establishment of a company, expansion of business activities, new product development, and investment in plant, equipment, and human resources are directly conditioned by the ability of companies to meet capital needs. The choice of adequate sources of financing for every economic organization is one of the most sensitive issues. The decision on how and from which sources to finance the daily business, investment, growth, and development has a strategic importance for every owner, entrepreneur, or manager. In the initial stages of growth, most small businesses rely on their own sources of financing. In later stages of the life cycle, the need for capital outperforms the internal capacities of the owner, and they must then consider the use of external sources of financing to provide the resources for necessary investment and business development. The concept of financial restructuring has attracted the attention of experts over the past twenty years, emphasizing the importance of this concept of enterprise restructuring (Roland Berger Strategy Consultants 2014). Hence, restructuring as a method and a strategy of radical changes in the companies should not be seen only as a one-time event. It is a continuous activity that organizations undertake from time to time, when they feel the need for change, that is, when they are dissatisfied with the existing situation, structures, or strategies that affect the overall level of performance. The approach to the concept of financial restructuring is increasingly being considered as a part of the overall process of enterprise restructuring, which is confirmed for the reason, taking into account the connections of business functions in the company's operation, especially in times of economic crisis (Damodaran 2010). The concept of restructuring will be systematized through a couple of approaches. One group of approaches sees restructuring as a set of activities that an organization implements when facing a crisis and the need for healing. These approaches are based on the assumption that organizations have already started to crash and that healing measures need to be undertaken (Slatter et al. 2006). They see restructuring as a reduction in the number of hierarchical levels in the organization and the number of employees (Hill and Jones 2008). Then, there is a group of approaches that look at restructuring only from the financial point of view with respect to changes in the financial structure. Financial restructuring refers to the changes that occur in the capital structure of the company (Todorović 2010). Gilson, in his work called "Creating Value Through Corporate Restructuring": Case Studies in Bankruptcies, Bayouts in 2010, under the financial restructuring subsumes (Gilson 2010):

– Changes in the structure and relationship between debt, preferential, and ordinary shares
– Changes in maturities of loans and/or debt instruments
– Changes in the amount of the interest rate or the method of its calculation (fixed/variable)
– The use of exotic financial instruments
– Changes in the owners of securities

Restructuring of debt implies a freeze in repayment of liabilities, temporary delays in the execution of obligations, write-off of receivables, restriction or reduction of interest rates, conversion of debt into equity, and Leverage Buy Out (LBO) (Erić and Stošić 2013). On the other hand, the conversion of debt into equity can be carried out in three ways: Debit to Equity Swap (a part of the old debt is written off and a new capital structure is created and adapted to existing assets), Debit to Equity conversion with recapitalization, and a combination of Debit to Equity conversion and investment of new funds. In addition to debt restructuring, the restructuring of equity capital implies recapitalization through changes in share capital. Recapitalization can be realized through the emission of a new series of shares through a public offer, private offer, offer of rights, or combined (Erić and Stošić 2013). New funds can be invested in the company in the form of loans or equity, a conversion through the sale of the company (one part of the assets is sold for cash and the other part of the debt is written off) (Gilson 2010). LBO transactions are related to an increase in the level of indebtedness on the basis of new loans or issuance of securities as instruments of debt. Certainly, one of the most important groups of financial restructuring activities is related to debt restructuring (Gaughan 2007).

Financing through debt (by borrowing or issuing securities of debt instruments) is treated as one of the alternatives to external financing. It brings a number of advantages, primarily through lower capital costs and the effect of a financial leverage, i.e., tax protection that debt brings. More recently, banks have been more actively engaged in resolving the issue of debt restructuring (Lazonick 2004). Such a practice began in the UK called the London Approach. According to the International Turnaround Management Standard, the crisis implies limited resources and limited time for decisions and actions to be taken (Lymbersky 2013). Also, the crisis refers to a situation where there is a danger for the business of high intensity enterprises (Smart et al. 1978). We can say that there are almost no companies that have not faced or are faced with business difficulties and problems in their business and existence. In order to formulate and implement successfully a company restructuring strategy, it is necessary to analyze the factors that lead the company to business difficulties and failures (Walker 2010). Also, it is necessary to identify

Table 1 Top 10 enterprise restructuring in Europe per year in the period (2004–2014)

Years	Company	Created new jobs	Location of business	Sector	Type of restructuring
2004	Legnica SEZ	5200	Poland	Information Technology	Internal restructuring
2005	PSA Peugeot-Citroën	3500	Slovakia	Car industry	Business growth
2006	IPS Alpha	12,000	Czech Republic	Post and Telecommunications	Business growth
2007	GDF-Suez	60,000	France	Electricity, gas, vapor, etc.	Mergers/acquisitions
2008	Edeka	25,000	Germany	Retail	Business growth
2009	Hyundai Motor	18,000	Czech Republic	Manufacture of motor vehicles	Business growth
2010	ASDA	6000	United Kingdom	Retail	Business growth
2011	McDonald's France	9000	France	Hotels–Restaurants	Business growth
2012	Sainsbury's	6000	United Kingdom	Wholesale and retail trade	Business growth
2013	Amazon	4000	Czech Republic	Transport and Storage	Business growth
2014	Barratt Developments[a]	3000	United Kingdom	Construction	Mergers/acquisitions

Source: European Commission, European Parliament: The European Monitoring Centre on Change (EMCC), European Restructuring Monitor (ERM), 2004, 2005, 2006, 2007, 2008, 2009, 2010, 2011, 2012, 2013, 2014
Based on the criteria of most new jobs created
[a]As of the second quarter of 2014

and on the basis of business forecasts predict on time "early" signals and symptoms of problems that lead to business difficulties, as well as to properly define the causes of business difficulties. If entrepreneurial managers respond quickly to the first signs of the crisis and predict business difficulties on the basis of business forecasts, they can prevent profound consequences and enable growth of the company (Kotter 1995). It is important to point out that the success of financial restructuring is almost impossible without effective and efficient cost management. Savings must be achieved in different types of costs, both direct and indirect.

The remainder of this chapter provides an overview of types of restructuring in Europe and their effects. In Table 1 gives an overview of types of restructuring of enterprises in each year, according to the criteria most new jobs are being created.

Based on the above table, we can see that the French company GDF-Suez, through the process of business restructuring, has created majority of new jobs (60,000) in Europe in the past decade. Peer research group consisted of 36 transition countries, classified according to the classification of the European Bank for

Reconstruction and Development. In continuation, Table 2 gives an overview assessment of the degree of restructuring of companies around the country.

Worryingly operate fact that there are no positive developments in the field of restructuring in Bosnia and Herzegovina since 2003. Also, based on the data in the table above, we can see that the odds score for Bosnia and Herzegovina at the level 2 from 2003 until 2014. In comparison with the transition of the most highly marks, Bosnia and Herzegovina is lagging significantly behind (Table 3).

Statistically, based on the above analysis, we can conclude that the average value of the assessments in the area of enterprise restructuring in transition economies in the period 2003–2014 ranged from 2.32963 to 2.49655. In the decision-making process, each management activity, including business restructuring, includes planning activities and a restructuring program. Restructuring programs represent a detailed elaboration and concretization of specific measures and activities that need to be undertaken in order to change the established structures, strategies, and positions which are the basic pillars of restructuring. In economic theory and practice, a number of business restructuring programs have been developed that have many similarities, but also differences, both in terms of the content, mode, intensity, and timing of the realization of the envisaged changes. When creating a restructuring program, a high quality diagnosis of the company's operating status is of great importance, which is the starting point of the restructuring program (Pomerleano and Shaw 2005). There are programs tailored for business enterprise restructuring in transitional economies, as well as the concepts of restructuring programs which favor the goal of enterprise restructuring.

3 Model, Hypotheses, and Methodology of Research

A detailed analysis showed a small number of papers in our area that dealt with the issues. The basic research was realized in the second half of 2014 and the first half of 2015 in the Republic of Srpska on a sample of 81 companies which implemented some form of restructuring of the structure, strategy, and/or position of the company. On the basis of the given survey, data, which are the basis for confirmation or rejection of the research hypothesis, were collected. Research issue is very up to date in scientific-research circles abroad, and as such it is a field suitable for the realization of new scientific truths based on research. To examine the foreign practice and the situation from the given area, the obtained results of the survey were compared with the results of the research in Europe, respecting the methodological concept of Roland Berger Strategy Consultants. Therefore, we have tested the basic research hypotheses:

H1 In the Republic of Srpska, in the processes of enterprise restructuring, loans are most used source of financing.

H2 Companies in the Republic of Srpska restructure mostly (>50%) due to the identification of certain business difficulties.

Table 2 The values of the coefficient EBRD assessment on progress in the area of enterprise restructuring in the period from 2003 to 2014

Country	2014	2013	2012	2011	2010	2009	2008	2007	2006	2005	2004	2003
Albania	2.3[a]	2.3	2.3	2.3	2.3	2.3	2.3	2.3	2.3	2	2	2
Armenia	2.3	2.3	2.3	2.3	2.3	2.3	2.3	2.3	2.3	2.3	2.3	2.3
Azerbaijan	2	2	2	2	2	2	2	2	2	2.3	2.3	2.3
Byelorussia	1.7	1.7	1.7	1.7	1.7	1.7	1.7	1	1	1	1	1
Bosnia and Herzegovina	2	2	2	2	2	2	2	2	2	2	2	2
Bulgaria	2.7	2.7	2.7	2.7	2.7	2.7	2.7	2.7	2.7	2.7	2.7	2.7
Croatia	3.3	3.3	3.3	3.3	3	3	3	3	3	3	3	2.7
Estonia	3.7	3.7	3.7	3.7	3.7	3.7	3.7	3.7	3.7	3.7	3.3	3.3
Macedonia	2.7	2.7	2.7	2.7	2.7	2.7	2.7	2.7	2.7	2.3	2.3	2.3
Georgia	2.3	2.3	2.3	2.3	2.3	2.3	2.3	2.3	2.3	2.3	2	2
Hungary	3.7	3.7	3.7	3.7	3.7	3.7	3.7	3.7	3.7	3.7	3.3	3.3
Kazakhstan	2	2	2	2	2	2	2	2	2	2	2	2
Kyrgyzstan	2	2	2	2	2	2	2	2	2	2	2	2
Latvia	3.3	3.3	3.3	3	3	3	3	3	3	3	3	3
Lithuania	3	3	3	3	3	3	3	3	3	3	3	3
Moldova	2	2	2	2	2	2	2	2	2	2	1.7	1.7
Mongolia	2	2	2	2	2	2	2	2	2	–	–	–
Montenegro	2.3	2.3	2.3	2.3	2	2	2	2	2	–	–	–
Poland	3.7	3.7	3.7	3.7	3.7	3.7	3.7	3.7	3.7	3.7	3.3	3.3
Romania	2.7	2.7	2.7	2.7	2.7	2.7	2.7	2.7	2.7	2.3	2	2
Russia	2.3	2.3	2.3	2.3	2.3	2.3	2.3	2.3	2.3	2.3	2.3	2.3
Serbia	2.3	2.3	2.3	2.3	2.3	2.3	2.3	2.3	2.3	2.3	2	2
Slovakia	3.7	3.7	3.7	3.7	3.7	3.7	3.7	3.7	3.7	3.7	3	3
Slovenia	3	3	3	3	3	3	3	3	3	3	3	3
Tajikistan	2	2	2	2	2	2.3	1.7	1.7	1.7	1.7	1.7	1.7
Turkey	2.7	2.7	2.7	2.7	2.7	2.7	–	–	–	–	–	–

Turkmenistan	1	1	1	1	1	1	1	1	1	1	1	1
Ukraine	2.3	2.3	2.3	2.3	2.3	2.3	2.3	2	2	2	2	2
Uzbekistan	1.7	1.7	1.7	1.7	1.7	1.7	1.7	1.7	1.7	1.7	1.7	1.7
Egypt	2	2	2	–	–	–	–	–	–	–	–	–
Jordan	2.3	2.3	2.3	–	–	–	–	–	–	–	–	–
Morocco	2.3	2.3	2.3	–	–	–	–	–	–	–	–	–
Tunis	2	2	1.7	–	–	–	–	–	–	–	–	–
Kosova	2	2	–	–	–	–	–	–	–	–	–	–
Cyprus	3	–	–	–	–	–	–	–	–	–	–	–
Czech Republic	–	–	–	–	–	–	3.3	3.3	3.3	3.3	3.3	3.3

Source: (EBRD—European Bank for Reconstruction and Development) (*Transition Report* 2003–2014)

[a]The ratings range from 1, representing little or no progress, and 4.3, which represents the maximum value for companies in transition economies. In this regard, the coefficient assessment of the degree of restructuring of companies of developed market economies of the EU, moving through 5. Empty fields relating to the classification of countries into the category of transition

Table 3 Calculation of statistical parameters' evaluation of enterprise restructuring in transition countries in the period (from 2003 to 2014, years)

Observations	2014	2013	2012	2011	2010	2009	2008	2007	2006	2005	2004	2003
Mean	2.46571	2.45000	2.45455	2.49655	2.47586	2.48621	2.44643	2.45172	2.45172	2.45556	2.34074	2.32963
Min	1.00	1.00	1.00	1.00	1.00	1.00	1.00	1.00	1.00	1.00	1.00	1.00
Max	3.70	3.70	3.70	3.70	3.70	3.70	3.70	3.70	3.70	3.70	3.30	3.30
Standard deviation	0.63917	0.64180	0.65509	0.66617	0.66106	0.65586	0.68582	0.72949	0.72949	0.74403	0.65955	0.65082
Variance	0.40854	0.41191	0.42915	0.44378	0.43700	0.43015	0.47034	0.53215	0.53215	0.55358	0.43501	0.42357
Coefficient of variation	0.25922	0.26196	0.26689	0.26684	0.26700	0.26380	0.28033	0.29754	0.29754	0.30300	0.28177	0.27937
Median	2.30	2.30	2.30	2.30	2.30	2.30	2.30	2.30	2.30	2.30	2.30	2.30

Source: Research and authors' calculations based on (EBRD—European Bank for Reconstruction and Development) (*Transition Report 2003–2014*)

H3 Successfully restructured enterprises in the Republic of Srpska realize growth with a probability of more than 0.5.

H4 Businesses in the Republic of Srpska that applied the restructuring strategy in the function of corporate growth, realized the growth.

The purpose of the research was to highlight the level, trends, and a role of managers in the process of enterprise restructuring in the Republic of Srpska in relation to the Republic of Serbia and the countries of Western, Central, and Eastern Europe. The results were collected on the basis of the questionnaire, where opinions of managers and owners of companies in the Republic of Srpska were given. Observing the legal form of company organization, the structure of the research sample consisted of limited liability companies (Ltd.) in the amount of 65.43% and joint stock companies (JSC) in the amount of 34.57%. In the structure of the sample by activity, the trade activity has the largest share of 20.99%. In addition, the wood industry and the metal industry have a significant share of 18.52% and 16.05%, respectively. Also, 16.05% of the research sample were the companies from the category of other activities. The survey was conducted by submitting a questionnaire on the basis of e-mail, in person (in writing), and by telephone through the contact of managers/owners of the company. According to the obtained values, a statistically based estimate of the proportion based on the relation (Žižić et al. 2000) $p - Z\alpha/2$ p sp $\leq \pi \leq Z\alpha+/2$ sp is $0.47314457 \leq \pi \leq 0.62889625$. Based on the obtained interval evaluation, we prove that our research sample is large and statistically representative for the given scientific research. Also, on the basis of the Pearson Chi-Square test, we tested the significance of the difference in the obtained research results in the Republic of Srpska in relation to the results of the Roland Berger Strategy Consultants.

On the basis of the second part of the research, the opinions of experts in the field of enterprise restructuring were collected. Research stratum consisted of 67 randomly selected experts in the field of enterprise restructuring. The study used three strata, one for professors, one for associates (assistants), and one for consultants from consulting houses. Experts from the category of professors and associates are employed at the faculties of economics: Faculty of Economics in Ljubljana, Faculty of Economics in Zagreb, Faculty of Economics in Niš, Faculty of Economics in Kragujevac, Faculty of Economics in Belgrade, Faculty of Economics in Novi Sad, Faculty of Economics in Banja Luka, Polytechnic in Knin, Faculty of Economics in Split, Faculty of Business Economics in Bijeljina, Faculty of Economics in Zenica, Faculty of Economics in Priština, Indiana University Department of Economics, Erasmus School of Economics, LSE (London School of Economics and Political Science), Harvard Business School, Gea College in Ljubljana, and consultants are employed at the consulting houses: Roland Berger, McKinsey, KPMG, PWC (PricewaterhouseCoopers) and Deloitte company and Hypo Alpe-Adria-Bank a.d. Banja Luka (now Addiko Bank). On the basis of the research, 17 expert opinions were collected. The results of the research are presented below.

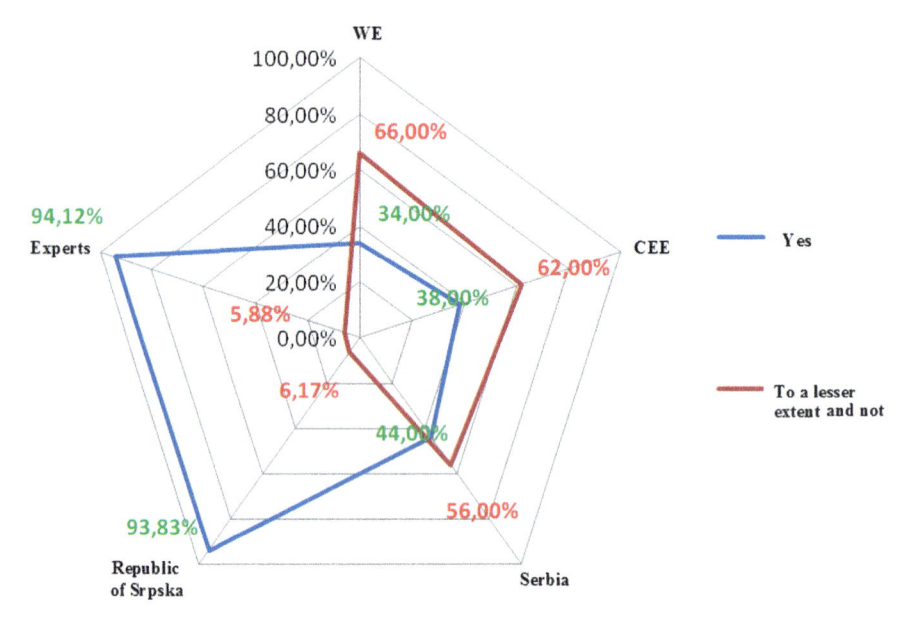

Fig. 1 The adequacy of funding as a barrier to the growth of enterprises through restructuring. Source: Research authors and Roland Berger Strategy Consultants. *WE* Western Europe, *CEE* Central and Eastern Europe

4 Results and Discussion of Obtained Results

In this section of the chapter, a comparison of the obtained research results with similar research carried out in the neighboring countries and countries around the world is made. Regarding the assessment of the enterprise restructuring practice in the Republic of Srpska, the results we obtained will be compared with the results of research conducted by Roland Berger Strategy Consultants. The results of the survey published in February 2012 in an international study titled "Restructuring as a Precondition for Competitiveness" comprised of the basic set of 6000 companies. The results are systematized in three contingents: Western Europe (WE), Central and Eastern Europe (CEE), and Serbia. In the next part of the chapter, a comparison of the results of the basic research we obtained and the results of the given international study is presented (Fig. 1).

Positive response yielded 93.83% of the companies that make the Republic of Srpska Peer research group. It is more for the 49.83% respect of Serbia (44.00%) 55.83% compared to the countries of Central and Eastern Europe (38%), 59.83% in relation to the countries of Western Europe (34%). It is important to point out that research experts of peer group are of an even greater importance given the positive response to 94.12% (Table 4).

According to the survey, 55.56% of the company date research Peer group assessed is that the loans were the major source of funding during their restructuring

Sources of Financing in the Process of Enterprise Restructuring... 71

Table 4 Distribution of answers to the question: "Rank the sources of financing of the restructuring of enterprises according to their importance in the Republic of Srpska?"

Answers	Number answer	The frequency response of the (%)
(a) Internal sources	28	34.57
(b) Credits	45	55.56
(v) The issue of shares	4	4.94
(g) The bond issue	0	0.00
(d) EU Funds	0	0.00
(d) A grant (subsidies and incentives)	4	4.94
(e) Other	0	0.00
Total	81	100.00

Source: Authors

upgrades the company. What we confirm the first research hypothesis H1, i.e., that the Republic of Srpska companies in restructuring processes, mostly use loans as a source of funding. As the second most important source of financing during the restructuring of state enterprises are internal sources of funding with a percentage of 34.57%. Financing issue of shares and on the basis of grant (stimulus) companies are equally assessed each with 4.94%. Other sources of financing enterprises in their restructuring process are not used.

The remainder of this chapter will conduct testing hypotheses concerning the proportion of the basic set based on large samples. Data statistical testing requires the application of the normal schedule and statistics Z-test. In the remainder of this paper we provide calculation of the parameters of the hypothesis test on the proportion of basic group on the basis of large samples with a reliability coefficient of $(1 - \alpha) = 95\%$, i.e., the risk of error of $\alpha = 0.05$ based on the computer. We will test the hypothesis H2 that enterprises in the Republic of Srpska mostly do (>50%) restructuring exercise, to identify specific business problems. In this connection the null and alternative hypothesis is:

Ho $\pi \leq \pi 0 \ (=0.50)$

H1 $\pi > \pi 0 \ (=0.50)$

The remainder of this paper will carry out testing of the sample size. Criterion of large sample volumes is related to the fulfillment of requirements that $n\pi 0 \geq 5$ and $n(1 - \pi 0) \geq 5$.

Statistical testing 1. Testing hypotheses about the proportion of the basic set based on large samples

	Value
n	81
$n1$	68
$(1-\alpha)$	0.95
α	0.05
$\pi 0$	0.50
p value	0.839506
$n\pi 0 \geq 5$	40.500000
$n(1-\pi 0) \geq 5$	40.500000
sp	0.055556
$Z\alpha$	1.64
Z value	6.111111

Source: Authors

Since $Z > Z\alpha$ reject Ho: $\pi \leq \pi 0$ (=0.50) hypothesis, we accept the alternative hypothesis H1: $\pi > \pi 0$ (=0.50), and we conclude that the enterprises in the Republic of Srpska majority (>50%) perform restructuring, to identify specific business problems, which is confirmed by another research work hypothesis H2.

The remainder of this paper will conduct testing hypotheses concerning the proportion of the basic set based on large samples. Statistical testing requires the application of the normal schedule and statistics Z-test. In the remainder of this chapter, we provide calculation of the parameters of the hypothesis test on the proportion of basic group on the basis of large samples with a reliability coefficient of $(1-\alpha) = 95\%$, i.e., the risk of error of $\alpha = 0.05$ based on the computer. We will test the hypothesis that successfully restructured company in the Republic of Srpska achieves growth with the degree of probability of greater than 0.5. In this connection, the null and alternative hypothesis is:

Ho $\pi \leq \pi 0$ (−0.50)

H1 $\pi > \pi 0$ (=0.50)

The remainder of this chapter will carry out testing of the sample size. Criterion of large sample volumes is related to the fulfillment of requirements that $n\pi 0 \geq 5$ and $n(1-\pi 0) \geq 5$.

Statistical testing 2. Testing hypotheses about the proportion of the basic set based on large samples

	Value
n	81
n1	55
(1 − α)	0.95
α	0.05
π0	0.50
p value	0.679012
nπ0 ≥ 5	40.500000
n(1 − π0) ≥ 5	40.500000
sp	0.055556
Zα	1.64
Z value	3.222222

Source: Authors

Since $Z > Z\alpha$ reject Ho: $\pi \leq \pi 0$ (=0.50) hypothesis, we accept the alternative hypothesis H1: $\pi > \pi 0$ (=0.50), and we conclude that successfully restructured company in the Republic of Srpska achieve growth with a degree of probability greater than 50%, which have confirmed the third research hypothesis H3.

The remainder of this chapter will analyze whether and to what extent companies that had business difficulties, after applying the strategy of business restructuring in the function of the company growth realized growth and thus overcome business problems associated with it. In this regard, the continuation of interdependence of analysis of the response of companies that have applied the strategy of business restructuring in the function of the growth of company and the answer to the question: "Are you on the basis of restructuring the business realized a growth of the company?" (Table 5)

Based on the previous analysis, we have identified 42 companies which had business difficulties, applied the business restructuring strategy in the function of company growth, and achieved growth in the company, thus overcoming the business difficulties associated with it. The growth rate was (42/61 × 100 = 68.85%) 68.85%. Also, it is important to note that out of 26 companies, i.e., 32.10% of research peer group of companies that did not realize growth, 7 companies, i.e., 8.64% of companies that were restructured, applied the business restructuring strategy in the function of contraction of business activities of the company. Based on the previous analysis, we can confirm the fourth auxiliary hypothesis H4 which says that the companies that applied the restructuring strategy in the function of the growth of the company in the Republic of Srpska realized the growth.

Table 5 Interdependence (impact factor) responses of companies that have applied the strategy of restructuring as a function of growth enterprises (*R*1) and the answer to question (*R*2) "Are you on the basis of restructuring achieved a growth company?"

Analysis		*R*1 variable	Total
		Business restructuring strategy as a function of the growth companies	
*R*2 variable	Yes	42	42
	No	19	19
	Total	61	

Source: Authors

5 Conclusion

In the context of contemporary economic science, the problems of enterprise restructuring have been of particular importance in recent years. We have paid special attention to our current reality, trying to analyze some key issues, attitudes, and problems in the field of restructuring and to point out the possible directions of their overcoming. Directions of restructuring depend to a large extent on the nature and severity of the problems that companies face in their business. In this chapter, enterprise restructuring is analyzed from the perspective of business forecasts and their impact on the process and the effects of enterprise restructuring.

Also, the enterprise restructuring program must be created on the basis of a high-quality diagnosis of the situation, respecting the life cycle phase of the company. In addition, to implement the phases of the enterprise restructuring process, it is necessary to provide adequate sources of financing enterprise restructuring, which is in many cases extremely difficult. For this reason, it is necessary to make a quality selection of sources of financing enterprise restructuring and to use the cheapest sources of financing which favor the given phases of the enterprise restructuring process. According to the results of the survey, 55.56% of the companies surveyed by the peer group estimated that loans were the most important source of financing during the enterprise restructuring. This confirms the first research hypothesis H1. Considering that $Z > Z\alpha$, we reject Ho: $\pi \leq \pi 0$ (=0.50) hypothesis, and we accept the alternative hypothesis H1: $\pi > \pi 0$ (=0.50) and conclude that the majority of enterprises in the Republic of Srpska (>50%) perform restructuring to identify certain business difficulties, thus confirming the second research hypothesis H2.

Considering that $Z > Z\alpha$, we reject Ho: $\pi \leq \pi 0$ (=0.50) hypothesis, and we accept the alternative hypothesis H1: $\pi > \pi 0$ (=0.50), and we conclude that successfully restructured companies in the Republic of Srpska achieve growth with probability greater than 50%, which confirmed the third research hypothesis H3. Based on the analysis, we have identified 42 companies which had business difficulties, applied the business restructuring strategy in the function of company growth, and achieved growth in the company, thus overcoming business difficulties associated with it. The growth rate was (42/61 × 100 = 68.85%) 68.85%. Based on the previous analysis, we can confirm the fourth auxiliary hypothesis H4 which says that the companies that applied the restructuring strategy in the function of the growth of the company in the Republic of Srpska realized the growth. What can be said with certainty is that it is necessary to respect the contingent approach in the process of enterprise restructuring. Also, there is a need for strategic thinking in decision-making processes of restructuring domestic enterprises. There are several possible directions for further research, which could complement the scientific and pragmatic aspect of enterprise restructuring in our country. First of all, it is necessary to highlight the lagging of enterprise restructuring practice of transitional countries behind the enterprises of the countries of the European Union. On the other hand, research papers indicate the practice of lagging of the enterprise restructuring practices of the European Union behind the enterprises in the USA and Japan.

References

Damodaran, A. (2010). *The dark side of valuation-valuing young, distressed, and complex businesses* (2nd ed.). Upper Saddle River: Pearson Education/FT Press.
EBRD – European Bank for Reconstruction and Development) (Transition Report 2003–2014). Accessed May 20, 2015., from http://www.ebrd.com/downloads/research/transition/TR03-14.pdf
Erić, D. D., & Stošić, I. S. (2013). *Korporativno restrukturiranje*. Belgrade: Čigoja Print.
European Commission. (2013). ERM Annual Report 2013 Monitoring and managing restructuring in the 21st century (p. 25). Brisel.
Gaughan, P. A. (2007). *Mergers, acquisitions, and corporate restructurings*. Hoboken: John Wiley and Sons.
Gilson, S. C. (2010). *Creating value through corporate restructuring – Case studies in bankruptcies, bayouts and breakups*. Hoboken: John Wiley and Sons.
Hill, C. W. L., & Jones, G. R. (2008). *Strategic management – An integrated approach* (8th ed.). Boston: Houghton Mifflin Company.
Kotter, P.J. (1995). *Leading change: Why transformation efforts fail*. Boston: Harvard Business Review.
Lazonick, W. (2004). Corporate restructuring. In S. Ackroyd, R. Batt, P. Thompson, & P. Tolbert (Eds.), *The Oxford handbook of work and organization* (pp. 577–601). Oxford: Oxford University Press.
Lymbersky, C. (2013). *International turnaround management standard version 1.1* (p. 47). Hamburg: MLP Management Laboratory Press UG.
Pomerleano, M., & Shaw, W. (2005). *Corporate restructuring – Lessons from experience* (p. 92). Washington: The World Bank, The International Bank for Reconstruction and Development.
Roland Berger Strategy Consultants. (2014). *Entrepreneurial restructuring, crafting tailor-made business models for sustainable success*. Munich: Roland Berger.
Slatter, S., Lovett, D., & Barlow, L. (2006). *Leading corporate turnaround: How leaders fix troubled companies*. New York: John Wiley and Sons.
Smart, C. F., Thompson, W. A., & Vertinsky, I. (1978). A cross-impact simulation of corporate susceptibility to crisis: The case for organizational reform. *Journal of Business Administration, 9*(2), 585–592.
Todorović, M. (2010). *Poslovno i finansijsko restrukturiranje preduzeća*. Beograd: CID Ekonomski fakultet.
Walker, L. W. (2010). Strategic restructuring: A critical requirement in the search for corporate potential. In M. L. Rock & R. H. Rock (Eds.), *Corporate restructuring*. New York: McGraw-Hill.
Žižić, M., Lovrić, M., & Pavličić, D. (2000). *Metodi statističke analize*. Beograd: Ekonomski fakultet Beograd.

Dominant Motives of Entrepreneurial Behaviour in Transitional Countries

Božidar Leković and Slobodan Marić

> *Clearly, in order to abolish classes completely, it is not enough to overthrow the exploiters, the landowners and capitalists... it means overthrowing small commodity producers (entrepreneurs), but they cannot be banished; they cannot be destroyed; we can and must coexist with them and reform them. (This quotation testifies to the strength of entrepreneurial will!)*
>
> V. I. Lenin

1 Introduction

With the processes of concentration and centralisation of capital, and massification of production, which characterised the period of the nineteenth century, the role and position of independent entrepreneurial enterprises becomes marginal. In such an environment, independent entrepreneurial ventures (small enterprises) fill in the gaps in the mosaic of economic structure, opting for individual production with high participation of live labour, where large-scale industry had no interest. The above-mentioned orientation of small enterprises, which was relevant in the historical period of development, still features as an area with great opportunities for the development of entrepreneurship. The first cases of separating ownership from management and the first forms of money lending are stated as key moments in the emergence and development of independent entrepreneurship and small enterprises. Separation of ownership from management emerged as a consequence of increase in the volume and complexity of operation. The owners detach themselves from the working process and employ experts and professionals whose knowledge and skills meet the requirements of tasks and operations for which they are employed.

B. Leković · S. Marić (✉)
Department for Management, The Faculty of Economics Subotica, University of Novi Sad, Subotica, Republic of Serbia
e-mail: bolesu@ef.uns.ac.rs; marics@ef.uns.ac.rs

© Springer International Publishing AG, part of Springer Nature 2018
J. Ateljević, J. Budak (eds.), *Entrepreneurship in Post-Communist Countries*,
https://doi.org/10.1007/978-3-319-75907-4_6

This process of separating of ownership from property occurred gradually, in the following iterations:

- The owner stops managing the property, but retains the right of ownership, manifested through possessing shares in a joint-stock company.
- The owner is temporarily separated from property, but is reunited with it at the end of a certain period, while receiving rent for the given period.
- The owner is permanently separated from property, receiving preferred shares in return (Jojić 1973).

The development of entrepreneurship is influenced not only by the separation of ownership from management, but by investment process itself, which started developing with the first forms of money lending. What we can identify as making a significant impact on the development of entrepreneurship is the stability of the value of money, which was mostly provided through long-term loan agreements, guaranteeing the payment of the fixed amount. These processes were intensely developed in the eighteenth, nineteenth, and twentieth century—the period which saw the crystallisation of two groups of people, referred to as investors and business people. Investors and business people have opposing interests, which still remain in force in joint-stock companies, and are related to the conflict of interest between managers and shareholders.

A very important role in this process is played by the value of money, which, if stable, does not harm investors with long-term loan agreements and fixed remuneration. "In the period of change, when prices grow, entrepreneurs receive a favourable opportunity to increase profit, because purchases occur at more favourable prices.... The decline in the value of money results in the discouragement of investment and decline in entrepreneurial activities. It affects them in such a way that they are reluctant to undertake a long-term production process which demands investment of money long before the possibility of return. Rather than only 'profiteers', the burning issue is unemployment" (Kejns 1937). The above cited Keynes' opinion speaks about another essential condition for the development of entrepreneurship, that is, stability of the value of money, which, if absent, makes a negative impact.

Socialism collapsed in the East because three most important human rights were not respected: religion, freedom, and property (Zlatković 1994). "...people do not work, do not produce, do not buy and do not sell for the benefit of others, nor to enhance society as such, but for their own interest, and thus, at the same time, not intending and not knowing, they advance the interest of society and enlarge social wealth...; only the individuals' absolute freedom to do as they think is best for them and their competition with other, likewise free individuals to pursue their own interest in the struggle for scarce goods result in the natural order of freedom which inevitably leads to the advancement and benefit of humanity" (Smith). Smith firmly believed that all one has to do on the path to progress is remove obstacles and hindrances used by the state and its regulation to limit the natural order, the best for all; "as a specific feature of nature and product of society, man accepts this society only if it does not prevent him from using his work, skill and knowledge, to be venturesome, and that thwarting his acquisition of wealth based on work and ability represents an obvious violation of a natural human right and hindering the liberation of his existence" (Jojić 1973).

The above claims feature as parallel representation of the basic economic (entrepreneurial) motives stimulating in an individual the interest to initiate individual entrepreneurial venture and essential environmental preconditions for initiating and developing entrepreneurship. Thus, we can conclude that the basic preconditions and motives of development of entrepreneurship have no temporal limitations, which implicates the basic research question within this topic: how does the passage of time influence the development of entrepreneurship, especially the transformation of social, economic, and political system?

2 Theoretic Foundation of the Paper: Transition and Entrepreneurial Motives

Holistic definition of transition including next events, alongside the liberalization of prices and the creation of market institutions, the transformation of centrally planned into market economies involves the development of a privately owned business sector, through a combination of the privatization of former state-owned companies and the creation of completely new enterprises (Smallbone and Welter 2006). Transition from one economic system to another has created unique opportunities for entrepreneurs to create new businesses that fill voids in the structure of industry and services (Estrin et al. 2006). Entrepreneurs in transition economies build their businesses in view of high uncertainty and a not very supportive institutional environment. As McMillan and Woodruff (2002) argue, entrepreneurs in transition economies "succeeded by self-help: they built for themselves substitutes for the missing institutions". Despite the significant role that the business environment plays for the development of entrepreneurship in terms of volume and structure, it is also necessary to include the human aspect of entrepreneurship in the form of the motive of entrepreneurial personality for initiating the entrepreneurial process.

2.1 Transition as a Social Process, Business Environment, and Condition for Development of Entrepreneurship

Transition in most former socialist countries, especially in our country, did not represent a commitment, but rather an escape from the past, and a search for a solution for a deep social, political, economic, and social crisis. Such an approach to the reform of social and economic system contributed to the emergence of "transitional recession", which was reflected in the decline in the population's living standards, rise in inflation, instability of foreign exchange rates, rise in foreign trade deficit, rise in unemployment, and other macroeconomic indicators, which showed only negative trend. The burning issue in transition countries is, by all means, growing unemployment caused by the demise of huge enterprises in state and public ownership (Drnovsek 2002).

The main cause of the economic collapse at the beginning of the transition period that befell all the countries of Central and Eastern Europe and former Soviet republics, including our country, is the huge pressure of simultaneous impact of the following factors:

- Inflation, which was characteristic of almost all countries, caused by strict programmes of stabilisation and adjustment aimed at ending inflation in the shortest possible period, balancing the budget, closing gaps in balances of payments, price liberalisation aimed at removing disparities, combined with deflationary policies, resulted in a fall in production.
- Abandoning the centralised planning system of management without setting up a market-based mechanism led to an undefined condition of the economies of these countries, which is something different from the Chinese transition.
- Liberalisation of imports resulted in suffocation of domestic production.
- Privatisation of state and public property—with a multitude of uncertainties—represents a long-term process which blocked investment and slowed down the existing production.
- After the disintegration of the COMECON system, the socialist countries lost a huge market (Avramović 1994).

A well-developed entrepreneurial sector provides all the benefits to an economy, like in mature market economies (Aidis 2005a, b), which means that there is no difference between the role of entrepreneurship and characteristics of small enterprises in relation to the level of economic development (Smallbone and Welter 2001). The role and characteristics of entrepreneurship on development are identical, but different types and phases of entrepreneurship may impact economic growth differently in different stage of economic development (Sternberg and Wennekers 2005). The state is also responsible for the creation of a favourable economic environment at all levels (Smallbone et al. 2010), under the obligation to provide an appropriate institutional, legal, and cultural framework, as the external environment is one of the essential preconditions for the development of entrepreneurship both in transition countries and in countries of developed market economy (Smallbone and Welter 2001).

The basic tasks set before an economy in the process of transition to market economy stated by Russian and American professors in textbooks for academies and faculties of economics in Russia are the following:

- Separation from state and privatisation of economy, and development of entrepreneurship. Separation from state in this context implies releasing the state from the functions of direct governance of economy and their delegation to enterprises, but without change in the character of property
- Formation of market infrastructure, a new mechanism of establishing economic relations, including commodity markets

- Demonopolisation of economy, a highly important prerequisite for development of competition and achieving market balance
- Liberalisation of prices, removing the state control in price formation, transition to pricing based on supply and demand
- Financial and economic stabilisation through rigorous credit and monetary policies, by limiting the volume of money supply
- A strong welfare system, which would facilitate the adaptation of a part of population to the conditions of market economy
- Social reorientation of economy based on active structural investment policy towards a faster development of consumer goods and services, and increase in the flexibility of production and its adaptation in accordance with the changes in demand and technological advances (Gužalić 1999).

It is quite justified that the first place is taken up by privatisation and development of entrepreneurship as the essential task in carrying out the transition process, if we remind ourselves that one of the main reasons for the crisis and inefficiency of the socialist system was the issue of property. Entrepreneurship and privatisation are mutually conditioned and connected factors. Privatisation is the first condition that needs to be met in order to provide the development of entrepreneurship and private initiative, while, on the other hand, entrepreneurship and establishing small enterprises encourages and accelerates the process of privatisation, restructuring of large enterprises, and building the market. Also, all the listed tasks of the transition process represent the required conditions for development of entrepreneurship as a factor of economic development.

The positions of the following prominent theoreticians may serve when defining the factors for development of entrepreneurship. Say argues that all an entrepreneur must possess is ability, while the necessary capital can be borrowed. Marshall fully agrees with this position, adding that entrepreneurial activity is much easier to organise if own capital is available. Schumpeter is the first author to distinguish between innovators and entrepreneurs and is therefore regarded as the "father of entrepreneurship". In his opinion, capital can be borrowed, entrepreneurship can be learned, and the only necessary element is motivation or will to become an entrepreneur. The contemporary approach to the entrepreneurship development factors does not rank factors by importance; they are all equally important, as start-up capital, entrepreneurial ability, and motivation to become an entrepreneur.

Undoubtedly, numerous recent articles in this area point out entrepreneurship and the SME sector as the most efficient instrument for the transformation of former socialist countries from centrally planned to market economies (Smallbone and Welter 2001). The discussion shows that entrepreneurship in a transition context is not unique, as the essential principles of individual behaviour are the same regardless of the environment. However, where the process of entrepreneurship is distinctive is with respect to the specific interplay between individual entrepreneur/firm behaviour and the external environment, which changes as the process of transition unfolds (Smallbone and Welter 2006).

2.2 Entrepreneurial Motives in Transitional Countries

Some of the so far presented models imply the existence of two different business processes based on and supported by the arguments of scholars in the area of entrepreneurship, predominantly of Austrian school, including Schumpeter (1934), Kirzner (1997), but other economists as well, who have recognised the role of entrepreneurship in economic development, such as Leibenstein (1968), Baumol (2002), and Acs and Storey (2004). The basis of both sets of conditions lies in the model of social, cultural, and political context, or as Leibenstein (1968) terms them, "socio-cultural and political limitations". These fundamental factors can imply national culture or universal values (Smith et al. 2002), national wealth in terms of the government's ability to support direct entrepreneurial environment, a kind of political economic system. Furthermore, these circumstances can refer to population growth (Levie and Hunt 2004) and economic growth rate (Lundström and Stevenson 2005).

Schumpeter's entrepreneur disrupts the state of economic balance through a process of innovation, whereas an alternative view of entrepreneurship and economic growth comes from another set of Austrian economists such as Ludwig von Mises (1949), Hayek and Hayek (1978), and Kirzner (1997), who point out the role of entrepreneur as the inventor of favourable market conditions, stating that "in any real and real-life economy, any participant is always an entrepreneur" (Mises 1949; Kirzner 1997). It follows from this that the basic question is not who entrepreneurs are, but what they do, within which conditions, and with which consequences (Murphy et al. 1996; Baumol 1996; Shane and Venkataraman 2000).

In a transition context, the Kirzner type of opportunities would be more apparent in later stages of transition, where markets have been developed and flows of information, ideas, and knowledge from mature market economies represent an important source of innovation for enterprises (Smallbone et al. 2002). It is reflected in empirical surveys in more advanced transition countries, where entrepreneurs complain about growing competition as one of their pressing business problems (e.g. Smallbone et al. 1999; Smallbone and Welter 2003). By contrast, in early-stage transition countries it is the lack of resources needed to realise an entrepreneur's business idea, together with a lack of institutional stability and unpredictability of institutional behaviour, that is emphasised (e.g. Smallbone et al. 2002; Welter et al. 2003). Moreover, because the pursuit of entrepreneurial opportunity is an evolutionary process in which people select out at many steps along the way, decisions made after the discovery of opportunities—to positively evaluate opportunities, to pursue resources, and to design the mechanisms of exploitation—also depend on the willingness of people to "play" the game (Shane et al. 2003). They also say that human motivations influence these decisions and that variance across people in these motivations will influence who pursues entrepreneurial opportunities, who assembles resources, and how people undertake the entrepreneurial process. Aldrich and Zimmer (1986), for example, write, "entrepreneurial activity can be conceptualized as a function of opportunity structures and motivated entrepreneurs with access to resources". All human action is the result of both motivational and cognitive factors, the latter including ability, intelligence, and skills (Locke 2000). We also assume that entrepreneurship is not solely the result of human action; external factors also play a role (e.g. the status of the economy, the availability of venture capital, the actions of competitors, and government regulations (Shane et al. 2003). Moreover, the incentives for innovation and efficiency were notoriously weak under communism (Hayek 1945) so reformers in the transition economies have been also greatly concerned with Schumpeterian entrepreneurship (Schumpeter 1934). Thus, the characteristics of entrepreneurs and their economic impact cannot be assumed to be the same as those in Western countries (Smallbone and Welter 2004).

Motives and personal characteristics distinguish first and foremost between needs-based and opportunity-driven entrepreneurship. The needs-based or survival motive induces people who set up a business to earn a living or a proper income where other forms of employment (and social welfare) are scarce. Opportunity-driven entrepreneurs follow more intrinsic motives such as to be independent, to implement an idea, a technology, or to make a contribution to society, and are more typical for developed countries. The Global Entrepreneurship Monitor (Reynolds et al. 2004) suggests that few entrepreneurs in Eastern Europe are driven by needs-based motives. In contrast to GEM (Reynolds et al. 2004), Smallbone and Welter (2001) observe a large proportion of start-ups being motivated by push factors. Scase (2003) offers a different dichotomy, namely by entrepreneurs' commitment to business growth. He argues that, in transition economies, a large proportion of business owners are "proprietors" who use profits for private consumption rather than reinvest into business. According to these authors, entrepreneurship is characterised by the reinvestment of business profits for the purpose of business growth and ultimately further capital accumulation, while proprietorship is characterised by the consumption of surpluses generated (Scase 2003). Thus even though SMEs numbers may be high, they do not necessarily constitute a growth engine, as their motivation is different from that of their West European counterparts (Estrin et al. 2006). Necessity versus opportunity (or push vs. pull) entrepreneurship is largely determined by the level of economic development in the long run and the actual state of the economy in the short run (Minniti et al. 2006; Audretsch et al. 2005). Necessity entrepreneurs predominate in the developing country context where lack of other alternatives pushes individuals to engage in entrepreneurial activity. In contrast, opportunity entrepreneurs are individuals who feel pulled into entrepreneurship due to the desire to apply a marketable idea or to apply their skills to starting a business venture (Aidis 2005a, b). However, Welter (2004) urges a more dynamic view be taken which recognises the learning capacity of individuals over time (particularly where considerable human capital is involved), as well as possible changes in external circumstances. Both can lead to changes in the aspirations of individuals and their ability to spot and exploit new business opportunities.

3 Data and Methodology

We shall analyse the sample of 55 countries classified in four subsamples in relation to the degree of development according to the methodology of the World Economic Forum: Group 1—factor-driven economies; Group 2—efficiency-driven economies; Group 3— innovation-driven economies; and Group 4—efficiency-driven transitional economies. The authors decided to form a subgroup within the framework of *efficiency-driven economies*, under the name of efficiency-driven transitional economies. It was done in order to carry out an analysis of selected features in relation to other groups. As the source for characteristics of GDP per capita in US$, we used the data from the International Monetary Fund, World Economic Outlook Database, October 2010. The criterion to select countries for the sample was data availability for every country according to chosen variables. The year to be observed was chosen according to the same criteria; in this case, it is 2011, because, as well as satisfying structure in subsamples, the number of 55 countries was provided in the sample in this year.

The observed variables, development degree represented as GDP per capita in US $, and motive of entrepreneurial behaviour are the features or variables. They make together the research space in this work. The development degree feature, represented as GDP per capita in US$ in relation to those for sample division, is the criterion feature.

These indicators are the result of methodology and research of the GEM project. In 2011, the GEM project included 55 countries which were included as the sample in this work, according to the established criteria. The database for chosen indicators, besides many others, which were also the result of this project, is GEM 2011 Adult Population Survey Country, version 3b. All these indicators are defined as percentage of adult population (18–64 years old) involved in some phase of the entrepreneurial process or activity being researched.

Hypothesis definition for applied procedures was carried out in the following way:

The hypothesis H0 was tested by the procedure of ANOVA:

H0 There is difference between subsamples (defined group of countries) according to motives of entrepreneurial behaviour.

The hypothesis H1 was tested by the procedure of multiple comparisons for observed characteristics/variables—Tukey HSD.

H1 Significant difference between some subsamples and motives is a direct consequence of the level of economic development.

4 Research Results and Discussion

As the result of the analysis relating to the prevailing motive of entrepreneurial behaviour, represented by selected variable, according to the degree of economic development, measured by GDP per capita in USD Purchasing Parity Power Basis, which represents a defined group of countries with specific observation of transitional group of countries, we got the results of ANOVA analyses presented in Table 1. From the analysis of received results, we can draw a conclusion relating to indicators of the motives of entrepreneurial behaviour that are a direct consequence of achieved level of economic development. It is expected that the indicators of opportunity motives and negative motives do not deviate from the logical to the now established tendency.

With the features TEA and opportunity motive, statistically significant difference is established at the level $p < 0.05$ between three groups of countries $F(3, 447.747) = 11.177, p = 0.000$, which means that there is a significant difference in means between groups. The real difference between medium values of groups is at the level of medium expressed by means of the indicator eta squared amounting to 0.4. The subsequent comparison by means of the value Tukey HSD test indicates that the group of countries named as factor-driven economies differs significantly from innovation-driven economies with positive difference. Group of countries with lower development levels have a bigger scope of entrepreneurial activities and also opportunity motive. We have the same situation between efficiency driven and innovation driven, and efficiency driven and transitional efficiency driven, which means that the transitional efficiency-driven countries have a higher level of economic development than other efficiency-driven countries. This factor causes differences in motives of entrepreneurial behaviour between defined and analysed group of countries.

With the features TEA and necessity motive, statistically significant difference is established at the level $p < 0.05$ between three groups of countries $F(3, 141.186) = 14.415, p = 0.000$, which means that there is a significant difference in means between groups. The real difference between medium values of groups is at the level of medium expressed by means of the indicator eta squared amounting to 0.46. The subsequent comparison by means of the value Tukey HSD test indicates that the group of countries named factor-driven economies differ significantly from innovation-driven economies with positive difference and with transitional efficiency-driven economies also with positive difference and then efficiency driven and innovation driven with positive difference. In this analysis, necessity motive of entrepreneurial behaviour has the same tendency as opportunity; we have one more cause for conclusion that the only factor of entrepreneurial behaviour is level of economic development of country but not features like transition of society.

With the features TEA and improvement-driven opportunity motive, statistically significant difference is established at the level $p < 0.05$ between three groups of countries $F(3, 3418.132) = 7.229, p = 0.000$, which means that there is a significant difference in means between groups. The real difference between medium values of

Table 1 ANOVA analysis for observed characteristics/variables

		Sum of squares	df	Mean square	F	Sig.
% 18–64 pop [7/10] TEA and opportunity motive	Between groups	447,747	3	149,249	11,177	0.000
	Within groups	681,015	51	13,353		
	Total	1,128,762	54			
% 18–64 pop [7/10] TEA and necessity motive (entr. because of no better choice for work)	Between groups	141,186	3	47,062	14,415	0.000
	Within groups	166,504	51	3265		
	Total	307,690	54			
% 18–64 pop [7/10] TEA and improvement-driven opportunity motive	Between groups	3,418,132	3	1,139,377	7229	0.000
	Within groups	8,037,736	51	157,603		
	Total	11,455,868	54			
% within TEA [7/10] opportunity motive: increase in income	Between groups	849,611	3	283,204	2939	0.042
	Within groups	4,914,352	51	96,360		
	Total	5,763,963	54			
% within TEA [7/10] opportunity motive: independence	Between groups	1,252,793	3	417,598	5537	0.002
	Within groups	3,846,054	51	75,413		
	Total	5,098,847	54			
% within TEA [7/10] non-opportunity motive: necessity/maintain income	Between groups	3,240,793	3	1,080,264	9046	0.000
	Within groups	6,090,654	51	119,425		
	Total	9,331,447	54			
% within TEAOPP [7/10] opportunity type: independence	Between groups	596,743	3	198,914	1282	0.291
	Within groups	7,757,171	50	155,143		
	Total	8,353,915	53			
% within TEAOPP [7/10] opportunity type: increase in Income	Between groups	1,910,859	3	636,953	4139	0.011
	Within groups	7,694,062	50	153,881		
	Total	9,604,920	53			
% within TEAOPP [7/10] opportunity type: maintain income	Between groups	183,626	3	61,209	1543	0.215
	Within groups	1,982,952	50	39,659		
	Total	2,166,578	53			

(continued)

Table 1 (continued)

		Sum of squares	df	Mean square	F	Sig.
% within TEAOPP [7/10] opportunity Type: other (incl. family business), no answer	Between groups	516,134	3	172,045	5691	0.002
	Within groups	1,511,520	50	30,230		
	Total	2,027,653	53			

Source: Authors' calculation

groups is at the level of small expressed by means of the indicator eta squared amounting to 0.30. The subsequent comparison by means of the value Tukey HSD test indicates that the group of countries named as innovation-driven economies differ significantly from all other observed groups of countries with positive difference. This variable represents specific and small part of opportunity motive and typical for higher development countries like opportunity motive: independence.

With the feature opportunity motive: increase in income, statistically significant difference is established at the level $p < 0.05$ between three groups of countries $F(3, 849.611) = 2.939, p = 0.042$, which means that there is a significant difference in means between groups. The real difference between medium values of groups is at the level of small expressed by means of the indicator eta squared amounting to 0.15.

With the feature opportunity motive: independence, statistically significant difference is established at the level $p < 0.05$ between three groups of countries $F(3, 1252.793) = 5.537, p = 0.002$, which means that there is a significant difference in means between groups. The real difference between medium values of groups is at the level of small expressed by means of the indicator eta square squared amounting to 0.25.

With the feature non-opportunity motive: necessity/maintain income, statistically significant difference is established at the level $p < 0.05$ between three groups of countries $F(3, 3240.793) = 9.046, p = 0.000$, which means that there is a significant difference in means between groups. The real difference between medium values of groups is at the level of medium expressed by means of the indicator eta squared amounting to 0.35. Here, we have more logical opposite results than before, in case of Factor-driven economies with all other groups of countries with positive difference.

With the feature opportunity type: independence, statistically significant difference is established at the level $p < 0.05$ between three groups of countries $F(3, 596.743) = 1.282, p = 0.291$, which means that there is no significant difference of mean values between groups.

With the feature opportunity type: increase in income, statistically significant difference is established at the level $p < 0.05$ between three groups of countries $F(3, 1910.859) = 4.139, p = 0.011$, which means that there is a significant difference in means between groups. The real difference between medium values of groups is at the level of small expressed by means of the indicator eta square which is 0.2.

With the feature opportunity type: maintain income, statistically significant difference is established at the level $p < 0.05$ between three groups of countries $F(3, 183.626) = 1.543, p = 0.215$, which means that there is no significant difference of mean between groups.

With the feature opportunity type: other (incl. family business), no answer, statistically significant difference is established at the level $p < 0.05$ between three groups of countries $F(3, 516.134) = 5.691, p = 0.002$, which means that there is a significant difference in means between groups. The real difference between medium values of groups is at the level of small expressed by means of the indicator eta square which is 0.25.

5 Summary

With all the analysed groups of countries, as well as with separated group of transitional countries within the framework of efficiency-driven economies, some specific features of all observed characteristics are identified. All the applied statistical procedures point to the previous assertion, by means of which we obtained the presented results with significant differences, precise limits of separation, characteristics and homogeneity of the groups of countries, as well as their mutual distances. It contributed to all observed characteristics at the level of economic development (as criterion), the scope and structure of entrepreneurial activities, and economic growth.

This means that we have achieved the following results in this study:

- From the analysis of received results, we can draw a conclusion, relating to indicators of the motives of entrepreneurial behaviour which are a direct consequence of achieved level of economic development. It is expected that the indicators of opportunity motives and necessity motives do not deviate from the logical to the now established tendency. Transition of society generates specific conditions and has some typical features, but there is not direct link with motive of entrepreneurial behaviour.

Thus, reached level of economic development measured by GDP per capita represents a very complex, strong, and reliable indicator of the social-economic potential of a country, regarding the capabilities for creating growth and development, as defined by the World Economic Forum methodology and the Global Competition Index. As entrepreneurship is also a social and economic phenomenon, it becomes the direct consequence of the previous conclusion.

Appendix: Multiple Comparisons for Observed Characteristics/Variables

Tukey HSD

Dependent variable	(I) Country group GCR report 4 CAT	(J) Country group GCR report 4 CAT	Mean difference (I–J)	Std. error	Sig.	95% Confidence interval Lower bound	Upper bound
% 18–64 pop [7/10] TEA and opportunity motive	Stage 1: factor driven (includes transition countries to phase 2)	Stage 2: efficiency driven	−1.87345	1.59980	0.648	−6.1222	2.3753
		Stage 3: innovation driven	4.42581*	1.51823	0.026	0.3937	8.4579
		Stage 2a: transitional efficiency driven	4.47567	1.69797	0.052	−0.0338	8.9851
	Stage 2: efficiency driven (includes transition countries to phase 3)	Stage 1: factor driven	1.87345	1.59980	0.648	−2.3753	6.1222
		Stage 3: innovation driven	6.29926*	1.23535	0.000	3.0184	9.5801
		Stage 2a: transitional efficiency driven	6.34912*	1.45057	0.000	2.4967	10.2016
	Stage 3: innovation driven	Stage 1: factor driven	−4.42581*	1.51823	0.026	−8.4579	−0.3937
		Stage 2: efficiency driven	−6.29926*	1.23535	0.000	−9.5801	−3.0184
		Stage 2a: transitional efficiency driven	0.04987	1.36007	1.000	−3.5622	3.6620
	Stage 2a: transitional efficiency driven	Stage 1: factor driven	−4.47567	1.69797	0.052	−8.9851	0.0338
		Stage 2: efficiency driven	−6.34912*	1.45057	0.000	−10.2016	−2.4967
		Stage 3: innovation driven	−0.04987	1.36007	1.000	−3.6620	3.5622

(continued)

Dependent variable	(I) Country group GCR report 4 CAT	(J) Country group GCR report 4 CAT	Mean difference (I–J)	Std. error	Sig.	95% Confidence interval Lower bound	95% Confidence interval Upper bound
% 18–64 pop [7/10] TEA and necessity motive (entrepreneurship because of no better choice for work)	Stage 1: factor driven (includes transition countries to phase 2)	Stage 2: efficiency driven	1.48905	0.79104	0.248	−0.6118	3.5899
		Stage 3: innovation driven	4.40438*	0.75071	0.000	2.4106	6.3981
		Stage 2a: transitional efficiency driven	2.76984*	0.83958	0.009	0.5401	4.9996
	Stage 2: efficiency driven (includes transition countries to phase 3)	Stage 1: factor driven	−1.48905	0.79104	0.248	−3.5899	0.6118
		Stage 3: innovation driven	2.91533*	0.61083	0.000	1.2931	4.5376
		Stage 2a: transitional efficiency driven	1.28079	0.71725	0.292	−0.6241	3.1857
	Stage 3: innovation driven	Stage 1: factor driven	−4.40438*	0.75071	0.000	−6.3981	−2.4106
		Stage 2: efficiency driven	−2.91533*	0.61083	0.000	−4.5376	−1.2931
		Stage 2a: transitional efficiency driven	−1.63453	0.67251	0.084	−3.4206	0.1515
	Stage 2a: transitional efficiency driven	Stage 1: factor driven	−2.76984*	0.83958	0.009	−4.9996	−0.5401
		Stage 2: efficiency driven	−1.28079	0.71725	0.292	−3.1857	0.6241
		Stage 3: innovation driven	1.63453	0.67251	0.084	−0.1515	3.4206
% 18–64 pop [7/10] TEA and improvement-driven opportunity motive	Stage 1: factor driven (includes transition countries to phase 2)	Stage 2: efficiency driven	−6.03878	5.49611	0.692	−20.6354	8.5578
		Stage 3: innovation driven	−17.65366*	5.21586	0.007	−31.5060	−3.8013
		Stage 2a: transitional efficiency driven	1.01144	5.83334	0.998	−14.4808	16.5037

(continued)

Dependent variable	(I) Country group GCR report 4 CAT	(J) Country group GCR report 4 CAT	Mean difference (I–J)	Std. error	Sig.	95% Confidence interval Lower bound	Upper bound
	Stage 2: efficiency driven (includes transition countries to phase 3)	Stage 1: factor driven	6.03878	5.49611	0.692	−8.5578	20.6354
		Stage 3: innovation driven	−11.61488*	4.24402	0.041	−22.8862	−0.3436
		Stage 2a: transitional efficiency driven	7.05022	4.98341	0.496	−6.1848	20.2852
	Stage 3: innovation driven	Stage 1: factor driven	17.65366*	5.21586	0.007	3.8013	31.5060
		Stage 2: efficiency driven	11.61488*	4.24402	0.041	0.3436	22.8862
		Stage 2a: transitional efficiency driven	18.66510*	4.67252	0.001	6.2558	31.0744
	Stage 2a: transitional efficiency driven	Stage 1: factor driven	−1.01144	5.83334	0.998	−16.5037	14.4808
		Stage 2: efficiency driven	−7.05022	4.98341	0.496	−20.2852	6.1848
		Stage 3: innovation driven	−18.66510*	4.67252	0.001	−31.0744	−6.2558
% within TEA [7/10] opportunity motive: increase income	Stage 1: factor driven (includes transition countries to phase 2)	Stage 2: efficiency driven	−3.53656	4.29755	0.843	−14.9500	7.8769
		Stage 3: innovation driven	−6.89122	4.07842	0.340	−17.7227	3.9403
		Stage 2a: transitional efficiency driven	3.43698	4.56125	0.875	−8.6768	15.5508
	Stage 2: efficiency driven (includes transition countries to phase 3)	Stage 1: factor driven	3.53656	4.29755	0.843	−7.8769	14.9500
		Stage 3: innovation driven	−3.35465	3.31852	0.744	−12.1680	5.4587
		Stage 2a: transitional efficiency driven	6.97354	3.89666	0.290	−3.3752	17.3223

(continued)

Dependent variable	(I) Country group GCR report 4 CAT	(J) Country group GCR report 4 CAT	Mean difference (I–J)	Std. error	Sig.	95% Confidence interval Lower bound	Upper bound
	Stage 3: innovation driven	Stage 1: factor driven	6.89122	4.07842	0.340	−3.9403	17.7227
		Stage 2: efficiency driven	3.35465	3.31852	0.744	−5.4587	12.1680
		Stage 2a: transitional efficiency driven	10.32820*	3.65357	0.033	0.6250	20.0314
	Stage 2a: transitional efficiency driven	Stage 1: factor driven	−3.43698	4.56125	0.875	−15.5508	8.6768
		Stage 2: efficiency driven	−6.97354	3.89666	0.290	−17.3223	3.3752
		Stage 3: innovation driven	−10.32820*	3.65357	0.033	−20.0314	−0.6250
% within TEA [7/10] opportunity motive: independence	Stage 1: factor driven (includes transition countries to phase 2)	Stage 2: efficiency driven	−2.95063	3.80186	0.865	−13.0476	7.1464
		Stage 3: innovation driven	−11.51298*	3.60800	0.013	−21.0951	−1.9308
		Stage 2a: transitional efficiency driven	−1.75619	4.03514	0.972	−12.4727	8.9604
	Stage 2: efficiency driven (includes transition countries to phase 3)	Stage 1: factor driven	2.95063	3.80186	0.865	−7.1464	13.0476
		Stage 3: innovation driven	−8.56235*	2.93575	0.026	−16.3591	−0.7656
		Stage 2a: transitional efficiency driven	1.19444	3.44721	0.986	−7.9607	10.3496
	Stage 3: innovation driven	Stage 1: factor driven	11.51298*	3.60800	0.013	1.9308	21.0951
		Stage 2: efficiency driven	8.56235*	2.93575	0.026	0.7656	16.3591
		Stage 2a: transitional efficiency driven	9.75679*	3.23215	0.020	1.1728	18.3408

(continued)

Dependent variable	(I) Country group GCR report 4 CAT	(J) Country group GCR report 4 CAT	Mean difference (I–J)	Std. error	Sig.	95% Confidence interval Lower bound	95% Confidence interval Upper bound
	Stage 2a: transitional efficiency driven	Stage 1: factor driven	1.75619	4.03514	0.972	−8.9604	12.4727
		Stage 2: efficiency driven	−1.19444	3.44721	0.986	−10.3496	7.9607
		Stage 3: innovation driven	−9.75679*	3.23215	0.020	−18.3408	−1.1728
% within TEA [7/10] non-opportunity motive: necessity/ maintain income	Stage 1: factor driven (includes transition countries to phase 2)	Stage 2: efficiency driven	15.66780*	4.78432	0.010	2.9616	28.3740
		Stage 3: innovation driven	20.45328*	4.54037	0.000	8.3949	32.5116
		Stage 2a: transitional efficiency driven	5.50866	5.07788	0.700	−7.9772	18.9945
	Stage 2: efficiency driven (includes transition countries to phase 3)	Stage 1: factor driven	−15.66780*	4.78432	0.010	−28.3740	−2.9616
		Stage 3: innovation driven	4.78548	3.69439	0.570	−5.0261	14.5971
		Stage 2a: transitional efficiency driven	−10.15914	4.33802	0.102	−21.6801	1.3618
	Stage 3: innovation driven	Stage 1: factor driven	−20.45328*	4.54037	0.000	−32.5116	−8.3949
		Stage 2: efficiency driven	−4.78548	3.69439	0.570	−14.5971	5.0261
		Stage 2a: transitional efficiency driven	−14.94462*	4.06739	0.003	−25.7468	−4.1424
	Stage 2a: transitional efficiency driven	Stage 1: factor driven	−5.50866	5.07788	0.700	−18.9945	7.9772
		Stage 2: efficiency driven	10.15914	4.33802	0.102	−1.3618	21.6801
		Stage 3: innovation driven	14.94462*	4.06739	0.003	4.1424	25.7468

(continued)

Dependent variable	(I) Country group GCR report 4 CAT	(J) Country group GCR report 4 CAT	Mean difference (I–J)	Std. error	Sig.	95% Confidence interval Lower bound	Upper bound
% within TEAOPP [7/10] opportunity type: increase in income	Stage 1: factor driven (includes transition countries to phase 2)	Stage 2: efficiency driven	1.72673	5.49788	0.989	−12.8844	16.3378
		Stage 3: innovation driven	14.36825*	5.15391	0.036	0.6713	28.0652
		Stage 2a: transitional efficiency driven	8.24402	5.76406	0.487	−7.0745	23.5625
	Stage 2: efficiency driven (includes transition countries to phase 3)	Stage 1: factor driven	−1.72673	5.49788	0.989	−16.3378	12.8844
		Stage 3: innovation driven	12.64152*	4.28009	0.024	1.2668	24.0162
		Stage 2a: transitional efficiency driven	6.51729	4.99807	0.565	−6.7655	19.8001
	Stage 3: innovation driven	Stage 1: factor driven	−14.36825*	5.15391	0.036	−28.0652	−0.6713
		Stage 2: efficiency driven	−12.64152*	4.28009	0.024	−24.0162	−1.2668
		Stage 2a: transitional efficiency driven	−6.12423	4.61702	0.551	−18.3944	6.1459
	Stage 2a: transitional efficiency driven	Stage 1: factor driven	−8.24402	5.76406	0.487	−23.5625	7.0745
		Stage 2: efficiency driven	−6.51729	4.99807	0.565	−19.8001	6.7655
		Stage 3: innovation driven	6.12423	4.61702	0.551	−6.1459	18.3944
% within TEAOPP [7/10] opportunity type: other (incl. family business), no answer	Stage 1: factor driven (includes transition countries to phase 2)	Stage 2: efficiency driven	−0.84153	2.43682	0.986	−7.3176	5.6345
		Stage 3: innovation driven	−7.38271*	2.28437	0.011	−13.4536	−1.3118
		Stage 2a: transitional efficiency driven	−2.87733	2.55480	0.675	−9.6669	3.9123

(continued)

Dependent variable	(I) Country group GCR report 4 CAT	(J) Country group GCR report 4 CAT	Mean difference (I–J)	Std. error	Sig.	95% Confidence interval Lower bound	Upper bound
	Stage 2: efficiency driven (includes transition countries to phase 3)	Stage 1: factor driven	0.84153	2.43682	0.986	−5.6345	7.3176
		Stage 3: innovation driven	−6.54118*	1.89707	0.006	−11.5828	−1.4996
		Stage 2a: transitional efficiency driven	−2.03580	2.21529	0.795	−7.9231	3.8515
	Stage 3: innovation driven	Stage 1: factor driven	7.38271*	2.28437	0.011	1.3118	13.4536
		Stage 2: efficiency driven	6.54118*	1.89707	0.006	1.4996	11.5828
		Stage 2a: transitional efficiency driven	4.50538	2.04640	0.137	−0.9331	9.9439
	Stage 2a: transitional efficiency driven	Stage 1: factor driven	2.87733	2.55480	0.675	−3.9123	9.6669
		Stage 2: efficiency driven	2.03580	2.21529	0.795	−3.8515	7.9231
		Stage 3: innovation driven	−4.50538	2.04640	0.137	−9.9439	0.9331

Source: Author's calculation
*The mean difference is significant at the 0.05 level

References

Acs, Z., & Storey, D. (2004). Introduction: Entrepreneurship and economic development. *Regional Studies, 38*(8), 871–877.

Aidis, R. (2005a). Institutional barriers to small- and medium-sized enterprise operations in transition countries. *Small Business Economics, 25*, 305–318.

Aidis, R. (2005b). *Entrepreneurship in transition countries: A review.*

Aldrich, H., & Zimmer, C. (1986). Entrepreneurship through social networks. In D. Sexton & R. Smilor (Eds.), *The art and science of entrepreneurship* (pp. 3–23). Cambridge, MA: Ballinger.

Audretsch, D. B., Carree, M. A., Thurik, R., & Van Stel, A. J. (2005). *Does self-employment reduce unemployment?*

Avramović, D. (1994). *Transition in Eastern Europe.* Beograd: ECPD.

Baumol, W. J. (1996). Entrepreneurship: Productive, unproductive, and destructive. *Journal of Business Venturing, 11*(1), 3–22.

Baumol, W. J. (2002). *The free-market innovation machine: Analyzing the growth miracle of capitalism*. Princeton, NJ: Princeton University Press.
Drnovsek, M. (2002). Job creation process in transition economy. *Small Business Economics, 23*, 179–188.
Estrin, S., Meyer, K. E., & Bytchkova, M. (2006). Entrepreneurship in transition economies. The *Oxford Handbook of Entrepreneurship*. Oxford: Oxford University Press.
Gužalić, M. (1999). *Preduzetnik – preduzetništvo i biznis*, Beograd.
Hayek, F. A. (1945). The use of knowledge in society. *The American economic review, 35*(4), 519–530.
Hayek, F. A., & Hayek, F. A. (1978). *Denationalisation of money: The argument refined* (pp. 119–120). London: Institute of Economic Affairs.
Jojić, R. (1973). Preduzetništvo dileme i zablude jugoslovenske teorije i prakse upravljanja. specijalni prilog časopisa, *Direktor*, Niro, Beograd.
Kejns, D. M. (1937). *Ekonomski eseji*. Belgrade: Matica srpska.
Kirzner, I. M. (1997). Entrepreneurial discovery and the competitive market process: An Austrian approach. *Journal of Economic Literature, 35*, 60–85.
Leibenstein, H. (1968). Entrepreneurship and development. *The American Economic Review, 58*, 72–83.
Levie, J., & Hunt, S. (2004). Culture, institutions and new business activity: Evidence from global entrepreneurship monitor. In A. Zahra, C. G. Brush, P. Davidsson, J. Fiet, P. G. Meyer, J. Sohl, & A. Zacharakis (Eds.), *Frontiers of entrepreneurship research*. Babson Park, MA: Babson College.
Locke, E. A. (2000). Motivation, cognition and action: An analysis of studies of task goals and knowledge. *Applied Psychology: An International Review, 49*, 408–429.
Lundström, A., & Stevenson, L. (2005). *Entrepreneurship policy: Theory and practice*. New York: Springer Science+Business Media.
McMillan, J., & Woodruff, C. (2002). The central role of entrepreneurs in transition economies. *Journal of Economic Perspectives, 16*(3), 153–170.
Minniti, M., Bygrave, W., & Autio, E. (2006). *Global entrepreneurship monitor—2005 Executive report*. Wellesley, MA/London: Babson College and London Business School.
Mises, L. V. (1949). *Human action*. Auburn: Ludwig von Mises Institute.
Murphy, G. B., Trailer, J. W., & Hill, R. C. (1996). Measuring performance in entrepreneurship research. *Journal of Business Research, 36*, 15–23.
Reynolds, P. D., Bygrave, W. D., Autio, E., & Arenius, P. (2004). *GEM 2003 global report*. Wellesley: Babson College.
Scase, R. (2003). Entrepreneurship and proprietorship in transition: Policy implications for the SME sector. In R. McIntyre & R. Dallago (Eds.), *Small and medium enterprises in transitional economies*. Houndsmill: Palgrave Macmillan.
Schumpeter, J. A. (1934). *The theory of economic development*. Cambridge, MA: Harvard University Press.
Shane, S., & Venkataraman, S. (2000). The promise of entrepreneurship as a field of research. *Academy of Management Review, 25*(1), 217–226.
Shane, S., Locke, E. A., & Collins, C. J. (2003). Entrepreneurial motivation. *Human Resource Management Review, 13*(2), 257–279.
Smallbone, D., & Welter, F. (2001). The role of government in SMEs development in transition economies. *International Small Business Journal, 19*, 63–77.
Smallbone, D., & Welter, F. (2003) 'Institutional development and the policy context for entrepreneurship in the transition economies of central and eastern Europe and the former Soviet Union. *Paper presented at the World Conference of the International Council for Small Business (ICSB)*, Belfast, June.
Smallbone, D., & Welter, F. (2004). *Entrepreneurship in transition economies: Necessity or opportunity driven*. Babson Park, MA: Babson College-Kaufmann Foundation, Babson College. Accessed November 9, 2010, from https://www.researchgate.net/publication/235966724_Entrepreneurship_in_transition_economies_Necessity_or_opportunity_driven

Smallbone, D., & Welter, F. (2006). Conceptualising entrepreneurship in a transition context. *International Journal of Entrepreneurship and Small Business, 3*(2), 190–206.

Smallbone, D., Welter, F., Isakova, N., Klochko, Y., Aculai, E., & Slonimski, A. (1999) *The support needs of small enterprises in the Ukraine, Belarus and Moldova: Developing a policy agenda*. Final Report to TACIS (ACE) Committee (Contract no. T95 4139R).

Smallbone, D., Welter, F., Voytovich, A., & Egorov, I. (2002). Innovation and the role of small businesses in the business services sector in Ukraine. *Paper presented at Rent XVI*, Barcelona, Spain, 21–22 November.

Smallbone, D., Welter, F., Voytovich, A., & Egorov, I. (2010). Government and entrepreneurship in transition economies: The case of small firms in business services in Ukraine. *The Service Industries Journal, 5*, 655–670.

Smith, P. B., Peterson, M. F., & Schwartz, S. H. (2002). Cultural values, sources of guidance, and their relevance to managerial behaviour A 47-nation study. *Journal of Cross-Cultural Psychology, 33*(2), 188–208.

Sternberg, R., & Wennekers, A. R. M. (2005). The determinants and effects of new business creation using global entrepreneurship monitor data. *Small Business Economics, 24*(3), 193–203.

Welter, F. (2004). The environment for female entrepreneurship in Germany. *Journal of Small Business and Enterprise Development, 11*(2), 212–221.

Welter, F., Smallbone, D., Aculai, E., Isakova, N., & Schakirova, N. (2003). Female entrepreneurship in post Soviet countries. In J. Butler (Ed.), *New perspectives on women entrepreneurs, research series in entrepreneurship and management* (Vol. 3, pp. 243–270). Greenwich: Information Age.

Zlatković, Ž. (1994). *Strategijska vizija razvoja zemlje u tranziciji*. Niš.

The Distinctiveness of Female Entrepreneurship in Post-Transition Countries: The Case of Central Europe and the Baltic States

Jelena Petrović and Snežana Radukić

1 Introduction

The Economic independence of women is one of the oldest gender-sensitive objectives of the European Union that has made significant progress over time (European Commission 2009; Goldin 2006). This progress is the result of long-term structural changes in the economy and society, and policy interventions. One of the means for promoting the economic independence of women in transition economies is the establishment of more supportive environments for the development of female entrepreneurship (Brodolini 2012). Indeed, female and male entrepreneurs might even be perceived as building the basis of communities—and communities are the building blocks of society (McKeever et al. 2014).

In developed economies, gender equality improves opportunities for women to become entrepreneurs or to find employment, whereas in transition countries, gender inequality impedes women's economic contribution to both starting a business and find employment (Sarfaraz et al. 2014). Women in developed economies are more likely to start businesses out of opportunity, while those in transition economies are mostly motivated by the necessity (Brush and Cooper 2012).

Norms and values learned and adopted during the socialist period still remain rooted and largely unchanged (Williams and Vorley 2015). In transition economies, informal institutions have substituted rather than complemented changes in the formal institutions (Estrin and Prevezer 2011). Within transitional economies, women experience many kinds of disadvantages in employment, family life, politics, and society. Although women in transition economies face similar problems in the

---

J. Petrović (✉)
Faculty of Science and Mathematics, University of Niš, Niš, Serbia
e-mail: jelena25@pmf.ni.ac.rs

S. Radukić
Faculty of Economics, University of Niš, Niš, Serbia

society and the labor market, there are significant differences in the position of women in these countries (Aidis et al. 2007).

The national-level data on female entrepreneurship indicate significant variance of female entrepreneurial activity rates across countries (Elam and Terjesen 2010; Estrin and Mickiewicz 2011; Kelly et al. 2010). For example, rates of women's entrepreneurial activity are observed to vary between 4.25% in Slovenia and 10.10% in Latvia (Singer et al. 2015). Understanding variance in rates of female entrepreneurial activity across countries is incomplete due to tendencies in the existing research. Some of the explanations of variance in total and female entrepreneurial activity emphasize individual-level factors, while other explanations emphasize national-level or macro-level factors. Relatively, few studies have investigated female entrepreneurship at the macro level. Although these studies provide useful insight into the impact of each factor (technological development, per capita income, unemployment, etc.) on female and male entrepreneurship, the present study develops a full model, explaining different female activity rates in transition countries, in which interplay of technological, economic, demographic, institutional, and cultural factors is accounted for. The main purpose of this chapter is to compare female entrepreneurial activities in transition economies. A comparison of female entrepreneurship in Central Europe and the Baltic States is interesting because, although they are transition countries and the members of the European Union, their development paths in the late twentieth century were quite different. This has affected the economic, technological, and social development of these countries. This chapter aims to draw conclusion from the way in which macro-level factors explain the differences of female entrepreneurship in Central Europe and the Baltic States. The basic hypotheses used as the starting point of this research are the following:

H1 Female entrepreneurial activity in transition countries depends on macro-level factors.

H2 Cultural factors have a dominant influence on the female entrepreneurial activity in transition countries in relation to other factors (technological development factors, economic factors, demographic factors, institutional factors, and government intervention).

The structure of this chapter is as follows. In Sect. 2, we explain variables that are derived from two streams of literature. A first stream of literature investigates female entrepreneurship in transition context. Secondly, there is the literature on the macro-level factors of female entrepreneurship.

Section 3 gives a description of the dependent and independent variables used in the empirical analysis, including their sources. The main source is the Global Entrepreneurship Monitor database for 2014. Using Global Entrepreneurship Monitor (GEM) date, we compare female entrepreneurial activity rates in transition countries. The female entrepreneurial activity rate is defined as the percentage of female or male 18–64 population of either nascent entrepreneurs or owners–managers of new businesses. Independent variables are technological development factors, economic factors, demographic factors, institutional factors, and government intervention and represent the external environment of female entrepreneurship.

In Sect. 4, the hypotheses are investigated using method for determining attribute weight based on the subjective and the objective integrated approach, VIKOR (Multi-criteria Compromise ranking) method, and correlation analysis. In order to analyze the impact of macro-level factors on female entrepreneurship, VIKOR method is applied, which allows us to reduce the impact of all factors on female entrepreneurship in a country in transition to one value. In this way, we can apply the analysis of correlation between factors at the national level and female entrepreneurial activity. VIKOR method represents a method of a multi-criteria optimization, which makes a decision regarding the choice of the best constructive based on the given final set of alternatives (Opricović and Tzeng 2007). This method introduces an aggregating function representing the distance from the ideal solution, considering the relative importance of all criteria (San Cristóbal 2011). In our case, transition countries are alternatives, and the independent variables, i.e., macro-factors, are the criteria for ranking alternatives.

The application of VIKOR method requires the determination of weight coefficients. Weight coefficients represent the numbers that can be calculated by using objective and subjective methods—CRITIC method, weighted least squares method, ENTROPY method, AHP method, etc. (Alemi-Ardakani et al. 2016; Kaminski and Ossowski 2014; Hazama and Kano 2015; Yu et al. 2015).

The chapter applies the method proposed by Fan (1996) in his dissertation. Short description of the method is given by Ma and his associates (1999). Ma et al. (1999) proposed an integrated approach to determine attribute weights in multiple attribute decision-making problems. The integrated approach is based on the subjective approach, i.e., weighted least square method, of Chu et al. (1979) and the objective approach of Fan (1996).

2 Theoretical Framework

2.1 *Female Entrepreneurship in Transition Context*

Entrepreneurship achieves its reaffirmation and full creativity in transition economies that are returning to the open market economy (Djankov et al. 2006; Smallbone and Welter 2009; Puffer et al. 2010). The transitional economies in the European Union have attained different levels of entrepreneurial engagement; such activity is critical for transition economies to accelerate economic growth and ameliorate the effects of structural economic change through self-employment and associated job creation. Within transitional economies, entrepreneurship is a mechanism for privatizing and restructuring state-owned enterprises; thus, it transforms distorted and monopolistic centrally planned economies and establishes a private enterprise sector (Stojanović and Vasić 2002; Smallbone and Welter 2006). It is, therefore, essential that transition countries pay special attention to the factors affecting the development of entrepreneurship to ensure their fair and efficient operation. Welter et al. (2004) note that the development of female entrepreneurship has great significance for transition countries, as women entrepreneurs mainly employ other women, thus reducing the effects of gender discrimination on the labor market and reducing the number of unemployed women.

While most studies examine the effects of person-specific resources and capabilities on entrepreneurship in transition economies, empirical evidence points to the fact that the external environment has a significant impact on the nature and pace of entrepreneurship in transition economies (Smallbone and Welter 2006; Welter and Smallbone 2008; Radukić et al. 2015). Research conducted in developed countries shows that the mixture of individual as well as social and cultural characteristics accounts for the difference between female and male entrepreneurship (McManus 2001). When comparing female entrepreneurship in transition economies, it is important to bear in mind not just different cultural and religious influences, but also different historical paths and the current position of women in the economy and society (Welter et al. 2003).

Many models and frameworks for the analysis of impediments entrepreneurs face in market economies can be found in entrepreneurial scientific reference. In transition environments, such models and frameworks are useful for the analysis of different impediments entrepreneurs face in different phases of market development (Smallbone and Welter 2006). Transition environment is characterized by a high level of uncertainty, rapid changes of external conditions, and institutional deficiencies (Smallbone and Welter 2001b).

In that sense, the concept of formal and informal institutions, i.e., the institutional theory proposed by Douglass North (1990), is an adequate theoretical framework for the analyses of entrepreneurship in transition economies. His theoretical framework points to the influences of external political, economic, and societal factors on entrepreneurial behavior, discussing them in terms of formal and informal institutions. Douglass North differentiates formal from informal institutions, stressing the fact that "the rules of the game" in formal institutions are visible, whereas those in the informal institutions are not. As an example of invisible rules, North (1990) states the role of women in the society.

Welter et al. (2003) apply the institutional theory in the analysis of female entrepreneurship development in transition economies, pointing to the fact that gender can be additional dimension in the analysis of the impact of formal and especially informal institutions on entrepreneurial development. In transition context, "the institutions might also ascribe housebound roles to women, which would conflict with entrepreneurial activities" (Aidis et al. 2007, p. 160). Estrin and Mickiewicz (2011) explain how institutional variations affect the entrepreneurship, i.e., whether they exert different influence on female and on male entrepreneurship in 55 developed and developing economies. Welter (2011) explores the impact of various contexts (business, institutional, spatial, and social) on entrepreneurship, with special attention to gender aspects in the spatial context, emphasizing the significant impact of gender stereotypes on the economic activities of women and the development of female entrepreneurship in transition countries (Welter 2011).

2.2 Determinants of Female Entrepreneurship in Transition Countries

According to Delmar (2003, p. 6): "women entrepreneurship is therefore closely related to the general framework conditions for entrepreneurship in a specific economy." To explain the differences regarding female entrepreneurship in transition countries, this research deals with a range of determinants of entrepreneurship categorized according to the following five groups: technological development factors, economic factors, demographic factors, institutional factors and government intervention, and cultural factors (Verheul et al. 2002, 2006).

"Modern conditions form a new competitive environment, where increasingly important role belongs to the ICT, which affects the improvement of business processes, stimulates the emergence and development of innovation, and increases the competitiveness of enterprises and national economies" (Petrović et al. 2016, pp. 4–5). Innovation is the critical factor for successful entrepreneurship. Although women often rely on the existing technology (Minniti et al. 2005), the level of development and application of technology is different in transition countries and can be expected to have a significant impact on female entrepreneurship.

Since transition countries significantly differ in per capita income, have a different structure of the economy and the unemployment rate, and are at different stages in the transition process, special attention is drawn to economic factors, namely per capita income, the share of the service sector, female unemployment, and economic transition. On the basis of a large number of studies, it can be concluded that the impact of economic development on self-employment and entrepreneurship depends on the level of per capita income (Schultz 1990; Bregger 1996; Carree et al. 2002). In countries with low per capita income, economic development has a negative effect on entrepreneurship, while in the countries where per capita income surpasses a certain level, economic development has a positive impact on entrepreneurship. Also, in economically highly developed countries, growing income and wealth enhance consumer demand for variety (Jackson 1984), creating new market niches for small businesses (Wennekers et al. 2005). Relying on several databases on entrepreneurship, Carree et al. (2002) and Wennekers et al. (2005) provide empirical evidence of U-shaped relationship between per capita income and entrepreneurship.

In developing and transition countries, there has been an increase of the service sector's share in the national income and in the total employment (The World Bank). Central European and Baltic states record an increase in female employment in the service sector at the average annual rate of around 1.5% (The World Bank). An expansion of the service sector tends to positively influence entrepreneurship (Verheul et al. 2006). Since women more dominantly participate in the service sector, and given that transition countries have a different structure of the economy, it can be expected that the share of the service sector will affect the differences regarding female entrepreneurship in transition countries.

Both theory and practice show that unemployment encourages entrepreneurship (Verheul et al. 2006; Carree et al. 2007; Startiene and Remeikiene 2009). Thus, the numbers of business start-ups decrease as a growing number of people are able to find stable employment (Minniti and Nardone 2007). It can be expected that in transition countries that face a higher unemployment rate of women, women are more directed towards starting their business.

The countries with formerly centrally planned economy origins display significantly lower levels of entrepreneurial development (Desai et al. 2003). Depending upon the reformation pace and the different stage of transformation to market-based economy, the impact of transition on total and female entrepreneurship is likely to differ between transition economies (Smallbone and Welter 2001a).

While female entrepreneurs from different transition economies face many common problems, some important differences can also be perceived. This emphasizes the need to recognize the diversity among transition economies, reflecting different inheritance and differences in the pace of change during the transition period (Aidis et al. 2007).

One increasingly important policy domain for promoting the congruence of formal and informal institutions is education, by shaping the culture, norms, and values of the population (Williams and Vorley 2015). In transition economies, the education system can aid reformation of informal institutions over time (Williams and Vorley 2015).

The entrepreneurship education represents one of the key instruments of increasing the entrepreneurial attitudes of people (Potter 2008). It can be used for the encouragement of commercial awareness, raising the social standing of the entrepreneur and the development of necessary entrepreneurial skills (Gavron et al. 1998).

Not every young woman will become an entrepreneur just because she is exposed to entrepreneurship education. However, it could sensitize women to the existence of opportunities in their environment (Fuduric 2009). Education provides female entrepreneurs with more financial resources and raises their self-confidence (Fuller-Love 2009).

"The clear conclusion is that underperformance is not a function of skills shortage or lack of competence in managing the business, but is directly attributable to unequal levels of starting capitalization" (Marlow et al. 2009, pp. 142–143). Unlike men, women start their businesses with less capital (Fuller-Love 2009), use less start-up credits (Harding 2007), rely on more available sources of finance, and face greater impediments when trying to provide financing through regular channels (Verheul and Thurik 2001). Previous studies related to the problems faced by women in securing funding are focused on the comparative analysis between women and men entrepreneurs. With this in mind, and given the fact that women face the same, but also some other problems in financing their business in the transition countries, the present chapter examines the following institutional factors: gap for market-supporting institutions to finance micro, small and medium-sized enterprises, gender gap in the availability of financial resources, and gender gap related to labor policy and maternity leave coverage.

The findings with regard to maternity leave policies are rather mixed: negative relationship between maternity leave and the start-up activities of women

(Kovalainen et al. 2002); positive relationship between paid maternity leave and self-employment of women (Tonoyan et al. 2010); and no significant relationship between parental leave benefits and female entrepreneurship (Thebaud 2011; Verheul et al. 2005). Suprinovič et al. (2015) find that "utilization of statutory parental leave decreases women's probability to switch into self-employment."

Informal institutions are widely accepted as a critical factor in explaining different levels of entrepreneurial activities (Frederking 2004). In order to understand the society's perception of a female entrepreneur, it is important to understand informal institutions, culture, norms, and values for better development of female entrepreneurship and entrepreneurship in general (Puffer et al. 2010). Cultural and social norms help in shaping the way into female entrepreneurship (Welter et al. 2003), but they may restrict the nature and extent of female entrepreneurial activity in transition economies (Welter and Smallbone 2008; Welter 2011).

In transition countries with a high density of entrepreneurial activity, examples of successful new venture creation offer role models people can conform to: "If he/she can do it, I can" (Veciana 1999). "Demonstration" of this principle applies to the following: the more female entrepreneurs, the higher the exposure of women to entrepreneurship, the higher the acceptance of entrepreneurship as an alternative to wage employment and the higher the likelihood of other women becoming self-employed.

3 Data: Determining Criteria for the Initial Decision Matrix

Table 1 presents in total, both female and male entrepreneurial activity rates for Central European and the Baltic countries participating in the 2014 Global Entrepreneurship Monitor. Transition countries with high female entrepreneurial activity also tend to be characterized by high total and male entrepreneurial activity.

Table 1 Total, female and male entrepreneurial activity rates in Central European and Baltic countries

Country	Total entrepreneurial activity	Female entrepreneurial activity	Male entrepreneurial activity
Croatia	7.97	4.75	11.28
Estonia	9.43	7.71	11.21
Hungary	9.33	5.29	13.48
Latvia	13.30	10.10	16.60
Lithuania	11.32	6.78	16.19
Poland	9.21	5.95	12.50
Slovak Republic	10.90	7.41	14.37
Slovenia	6.33	4.25	8.29

Source: Global Entrepreneurship Report 2014, http://www.gemconsortium.org/data

Table 2 Technical and technological development and economic factors

Country	Research and development investment—R&D investments (% of GDP)	GNI per capita, Atlas method (current US $)	Services (% of GDP)	Unemployment, female (% of female labor force)	EBRD transition indicator score—average transition score
Croatia	0.75	13,020	68.57	16.80	3.83
Estonia	2.18	18,530	67.46	8.30	4.05
Hungary	1.30	13,470	65.41	10.20	3.88
Latvia	0.66	15,660	74.05	10.50	3.94
Lithuania	0.90	15,380	68.72	10.50	3.94
Poland	0.90	13,730	63.45	11.10	4.00
Slovak Republic	0.82	17,810	62.73	14.50	3.94
Slovenia	2.80	23,220	65.85	11.20	3.66

Source: World Bank, http://data.worldbank.org/indicator; EBRD Transition Report 2014, http://www.ebrd.com/news/publications/transition-report/transition-report-2014.html/; Global Entrepreneurship Report 2014, http://www.gemconsortium.org/report

Table 3 Entrepreneurial education as demographic factor

	Entrepreneurship education	
Country	At basic school	At post-secondary levels
Croatia	1.68	2.35
Estonia	2.63	2.99
Hungary	1.68	2.82
Latvia	2.51	3.17
Lithuania	2.37	3.07
Poland	1.75	2.54
Slovak Republic	2.21	2.98
Slovenia	1.77	2.23

Global Entrepreneurship Report 2014, http://www.gemconsortium.org/report

Slovenia, which has the highest per capita income, assigns the largest percentage of income to research and development. The greatest participation of the tertiary sector in Gross Domestic Product (GDP) is perceived in Latvia and the smallest in Slovakia. The largest female unemployment rate is perceived in Croatia and the smallest in Estonia (Table 2).

Entrepreneurial education at the basic level, i.e., in primary and secondary schools, is considered rather unfavorable in many countries, except in Denmark, Singapore, the Philippines, and the Netherlands (Global Entrepreneurship Report 2014). Out of the countries that were the subject of this research, the lowest marks on the 1–5 scale were given to Croatia and Hungary, while the highest were given to Estonia. When it comes to the entrepreneurial education at universities, the highest mark was given to Latvia and the lowest to Slovenia (Table 3).

Table 4 Institutional and cultural factors

Country	Market-supporting institutions—MSME finance	Inclusion gaps for gender - Access to finance	Labor policy	Maternity leave coverage	Cultural and social norms
Croatia	Medium	Small	Medium	16.8	2.02
Estonia	Small	Medium	Small	16	3.39
Hungary	Small	Medium	Negligible	18	2.32
Latvia	Small	Small	Small	20	2.85
Lithuania	Small	Medium	Small	15.4	3.09
Poland	Small	Medium	Small	15	2.96
Slovak Republic	Negligible	Medium	Small	26	2.40
Slovenia	Small	Small	Small	20	2.06

Source: EBRD Transition Report 2014, http://www.ebrd.com/news/publications/transition-report/transition-report-2014.html/; EBRD Economic statistics and forecasts. http://www.ebrd.org. Online Database; Global Entrepreneurship Report 2014, http://www.gemconsortium.org/report; International Labour Organization, http://www.ilo.org/dyn/sesame/IFPSES.SocialDatabase

Difficult economic and sociopolitical environments have also revealed a number of structural challenges in micro, small, and medium-sized enterprises (MSMEs), private equity, and capital market sectors. Table 4 shows the data on institutional factors. In data on gap for market-supporting institutions to micro, small, and medium-sized enterprises, "large" indicates a major transition gap, while "negligible" indicates standards and performance typical of advanced developed economies. Out of the countries that were the subject of this research, the largest gap is perceived in Croatia. In Slovakia, the level of development of market-supporting institutions for financing MSMEs corresponds to the data on highly developed countries. The rest of the countries reveal a small gap.

In addition to the aforesaid institutional factor, the following factors were also examined in the chapter: gender gap related to the availability of the source of finance and gender gap related to labor policy and maternity leave coverage.

When it comes to the accessibility of finances, some gender-related inequalities in accessing finances are perceived in Croatia, Latvia, and Slovenia, while considerably higher inequality is perceived in other researched countries. The greatest gender inequality in the labor policy is perceived in Croatia, while it is somewhat lower in other researched countries, with the exception of Hungary, where gender equality in labor policy is fully reached. Maternity leave coverage is a product of a predefined percentage of a net salary and time during which maternity benefits are paid in weeks, divided by 100. The largest maternity leave coverage is perceived in Slovakia and the smallest in Poland.

In the 2014 Global Entrepreneurship Monitor report, 72 countries were assessed from the aspect of cultural and social norms that encourage or allow actions leading to new business methods or activities that can potentially increase personal wealth and income. Based on the data presented in Table 4, the highest mark was given to Estonia and the lowest to Slovenia.

4 Results and Discussion

Results of the application of VIKOR method and method for determining attribute weight based on the subjective and objective integrated approach are given in Table 5. According to all criteria in respect of QS, QR, and Q_i ($v = 0.5$), the best alternative is A_4 (Latvia). Latvia has the most supportive macro-level factors, i.e., external environment for female entrepreneurship of all the examined transition countries. At the same time, this country has the highest female entrepreneurial activity. Latvia allocates the lowest percentage of GDP for research and development investment, as compared to other transition countries. At the same time, it records lower per capita income, in comparison to Slovenia, Estonia, and the Slovak Republic, and higher share of the service sector in GDP in relation to other transition countries. It has the most supportive external environment due to cultural factors and entrepreneurship education.

The least supportive environment for female entrepreneurship is perceived in Slovenia, which has lower female entrepreneurial activity rates than other transition countries. Slovenia allocates the highest percentage of GDP for research and development investment, and records the highest per capita income, compared to other transition countries. At the same time, it records a significant share of the service sector in GDP and gender equality in respect of labor policy and access to finance. However, cultural factors restrict the extent of female entrepreneurial activity in Slovenia. The development of entrepreneurship education would influence cultural changes towards increasing female entrepreneurial activity rates in Slovenia.

Based on the Pearson correlation coefficient (Table 6), it can be concluded that correlation between external environment and female entrepreneurial activity is statistically significant, because Sig. is lower than 0.05. Since the transition economies, which showed the lowest value of Q_i ($v = 0.5$) (Table 5), offer the most

Table 5 Ranking transition countries based on macro-level factors

Alternatives	QS	QR	Q ($v = 0.5$)	Q ($v = 0.25$)	Q ($v = 0.75$)	Rank
Croatia	1.0000	0.5408	0.7704	0.6556	0.8852	7
Estonia	0.0482	0.1939	0.1211	0.1575	0.0847	2
Hungary	0.5998	0.1326	0.3662	0.2494	0.4830	5
Latvia	0.0000	0.0000	0.0000	0.0000	0.0000	1
Lithuania	0.3152	0.0189	0.1671	0.0930	0.2411	4
Poland	0.6729	0.1979	0.4354	0.3167	0.5542	6
Slovak Republic	0.1561	0.1632	0.1597	0.1615	0.1579	3
Slovenia	0.7243	1.0000	0.8622	0.9311	0.7933	8

Source: Author's calculation based on Microsoft Office Excel 2007

Table 6 Correlations between the macro-level factors (the external environment) and female entrepreneurial activity rates

		Q_i ($v = 0.5$)	Female entrepreneurial activity
Q_i ($v = 0.5$)	Pearson correlation	1	−0.891
	Sig. (2-tailed)		0.003
	N	8	8
Female entrepreneurial activity	Pearson Correlation	−0.891	1
	Sig. (2-tailed)	0.003	
	N	8	8

Source: Authors' calculations based on SPSS-20

supportive environment for female entrepreneurship, the correlation coefficient shows that there is a strong correlation between the macro-level factors and female entrepreneurial activity rates. It can be concluded that female entrepreneurship in transition countries depends on macro-level factors.

5 Conclusion

This chapter has an important conceptual and empirical contribution, in particular since there are relatively few studies focusing upon the macro-level factors of female entrepreneurial activity in transition countries. From a conceptual perspective, the present chapter brings together several streams of literature and discusses the influence of a large range of factors on female entrepreneurship that are classified into following five groups: technological, economic, demographic, institutional, and cultural factors. From an empirical viewpoint, the study shows the methodological implications of studying the macro-level factors of female entrepreneurial activity.

The present chapter has compared female entrepreneurial activity in transition countries; therefore, it contributes to better understanding significant variance in rates of female entrepreneurship across transition countries. Unlike previous researches that analyzed which macro-level factors describe differences of female and male entrepreneurial activity rates, the present research analyzes which macro-level factors describe differences of female entrepreneurial activity rates in transition countries.

The analyses of the impact of all the macro-level factors on female entrepreneurship is performed by means of VIKOR method (Opricović and Tzeng 2007) that proves to be a successful tool for getting the insight and analyzing the macro-level factors from the point of supporting the female entrepreneurship in transition countries. Moreover, developing a multi-criteria model where the all macro-level factors is accounted for may be more suitable for understanding the differences of female entrepreneurship in transition countries than merely investigating the direct correlation between each macro-level factor and female entrepreneurship activity rates.

It can be concluded that Latvia as the transition economy with the most supportive environment for female entrepreneurship has the highest female entrepreneurial activity rates. Using the VIKOR method and correlation analysis, the present study finds significant effects on female entrepreneurial activity rates of macro-level factors. The high correlation between the external environment and female entrepreneurial activity fully supports Hypothesis 1.

An additional advantage of this modeling procedure is that it offers a conclusion that the female entrepreneurial activity is influenced by different external environment of a specific economy (Delmar 2003), i.e., transition economy. At the same time, research result has shown that the external environment has a significant impact on entrepreneurial development (Smallbone and Welter 2006; Welter and Smallbone 2008), i.e., female entrepreneurship in transition economies.

Although Slovenia has supportive economic, technological, and institutional conditions for female entrepreneurship, it is ranked last of the researched transition economies, according to their supportive environment that consists of all macro-level factors. Research findings show a significant impact of cultural factors on the female entrepreneurial activity in Slovenia and other transition countries.

Cultural factors help with the development of female entrepreneurship in Latvia, Lithuania, and Estonia, but they restrict the female entrepreneurship (Welter and Smallbone 2008; Welter 2011) in Slovenia and Croatia. Informal institutions are widely accepted as a critical factor in explaining different levels of entrepreneurial activities (Frederking 2004), and they represent a critical factor for the explanation of variance in female entrepreneurial activity rates in transition countries. Hypothesis 2 is supported.

By raising entrepreneurial education in primary and secondary schools, and especially in universities, to a higher level, attitudes of the population would change, which would create new employment opportunities and affect the development of female entrepreneurship in transition countries. In that way entrepreneurial education would help the reformation of informal institutions in transition economies (Williams and Vorley 2015) especially in Slovenia.

With respect to the link between theory and the empirical analysis, it should be noted that most of the literature we refer to in this study focuses upon transition countries, while our data set also covers transition countries in the European Union. This limits the extent to which the literature survey explains developments of female entrepreneurial activity in transition countries. Considering the limited number of observations (i.e., transition countries in the European Union) in our data set and the selection of explanatory variables, the present study should be seen as an exploratory study, guiding future studies in this area. Future research should try and include more countries in the analysis and investigating more explanatory factors. Factors influencing female entrepreneurship in transition countries, that are not members of the European Union, may be different from those in transition countries in the European Union. It is necessary to identify and analyze the critical factors for the explanation of variance in female entrepreneurial activity rates in transition countries that are not members of the European Union. It should be examined whether cultural factors are a critical factor, or if, in addition to cultural factors, i.e., informal institutions, formal institutions are also the critical factor for the explanation of variance in female entrepreneurial activity rates in transition countries that are not members of the European Union.

References

Aidis, R., Welter, F., Smallbone, D., & Isakova, N. (2007). Female entrepreneurship in transition economies: The case of Lithuania and Ukraine. *Feminist Economics, 13*(2), 157–183. https://doi.org/10.1080/13545700601184831

Alemi-Ardakani, M., Milani, A. S., Yannacopoulos, S., & Shokouhi, G. (2016). On the effect of subjective, objective and combinative weighting in multiple criteria decision making: A case study on impact optimization of composites. *Expert Systems with Applications, 46*(15), 426–438. https://doi.org/10.1016/j.eswa.2015.11.003

Bregger, J. E. (1996). Measuring self-employment in the United States. *Monthly Labor Review, 119*(1), 3–9.

Brodolini, F. G. (2012). *The multi-annual financial framework 2014–2020 from a gender equality perspective*. The European Parliament, Brussels. Accessed December 27, 2016, from http://www.europarl.europa.eu/studies

Brush, C., & Cooper, S. (2012). Female entrepreneurship and economic development: An international perspective. *Entrepreneurship & Regional Development, 24*(1–2), 1–6. https://doi.org/10.1080/08985626.2012.637340

Carree, M. A., Van Stel, A. J., Thurik, A. R., & Wennekers, A. R. M. (2002). Economic development and business ownership: An analysis using data of 23 OECD countries in the period 1976–1996. *Small Business Economics, 19*(3), 271–290.

Carree, M. A., Van Stel, A. J., Thurik, A. R., & Audretsch, D. B. (2007). Does self-employment reduce unemployment? *Discussion Papers on Entrepreneurship, Growth and Public Policy, 1*(18), 1613–8333.

Chu, A. T. W., Kalaba, R. E., & Spingarn, K. (1979). A comparison of two methods for determining the weights of belonging to fuzzy sets. *Journal of Optimization Theory and Applications, 27*, 531–538.

Delmar, F. (2003). Women entrepreneurship: Assessing data availability and future needs. In *Paper for the workshop on Improving Statistics on SMEs and Entrepreneurship*. OECD, Paris. Accessed June 12, 2015, from http://www.oecd.org/std/business-stats/14723090.pdf

Desai, M., Gompers, P., & Lerner, J. (2003). Institutions, capital constraints and entrepreneurial firm dynamics: Evidence from Europe. Harvard Negotiation, Organizations and Markets Research Papers No 10165. National Bureau of Economic Research, Cambridge.

Djankov, S., Qian, Y., Roland, G., & Zhuravskaya, E. (2006). Entrepreneurship in China and Russia compared. *Journal of the European Economic Association, 4*(2–3), 352–365. https://doi.org/10.1162/jeea.2006.4.2-3.352

EBRD. (2014). Transition Report 2014. Accessed February 25, 2017, from http://www.ebrd.com/news/publications/transition-report/transition-report-2014.html/

EBRD. (2016). Economic statistics and forecasts. Accessed 20 February 2017, from http://www.ebrd.org

Elam, A. B., & Terjesen, S. (2010). Gendered-institutions and cross-national patterns of business creation for men and women. *European Journal of Development Research, 22*(3), 331–348. https://doi.org/10.1057/ejdr.2010.19

Estrin, S., & Mickiewicz, T. (2011). Institutions and female entrepreneurship. *Small Business Economics, 37*(4), 397–415. https://doi.org/10.1007/s11187-011-9373-0

Estrin, S., & Prevezer, M. (2011). The role of informal institutions in corporate governance: Brazil, Russia, India, and China compared. *Asia Pacific Journal of Management, 28*(1), 41–67.

European Commission. (2009). Equality between women and men. Accessed December 25, 2016, from http://eur-lex.europa.eu/LexUriServ/LexUriServ.do?uri=COM:2009:0694:FIN:EN:PDF

Fan, Z. P. (1996). *Complicated multiple attribute decision making: Theory and applications.* Dissertation, Northeastern University.

Frederking, L. C. (2004). A cross-national study of culture, organization and entrepreneurship in three neighbourhoods. *Entrepreneurship & Regional Development, 16*(3), 197–215. https://doi.org/10.1080/0898562042000197126

Fuduric, N. (2009). Formal institutions & environmental factors framing entrepreneurship in Croatia. Dissertation, Aalborg University.

Fuller-Love, N. (2009). Female entrepreneurship. In M.-Á. Galindo, J. Guzman, & D. Ribeiro (Eds.), *Entrepreneurship and business – A regional perspective*. Berlin: Springer-Verlag.

Gavron, R., Cowling, M., Holtham, G., & Westall, A. (1998). *The entrepreneurial society*. London: Institute for Public Policy Research.

Goldin, C. (2006). The quiet revolution that transformed women's employment, education and family. *American Economic Review, 96*(2), 1–21.

Harding, R. (2007). *Stairways to growth: Supporting the ascent of women's enterprise in the UK*. Norwich: Prowess.

Hazama, K., & Kano, M. (2015). Covariance-based locally weighted partial least squares for high-performance adaptive modeling. *Chemometrics and Intelligent Laboratory, 146*(15), 55–62. https://doi.org/10.1016/j.chemolab.2015.05.007

International Labour Organization. Accessed December 25, 2016., from http://www.ilo.org/dyn/sesame/IFPSES.SocialDatabase

Jackson, L. F. (1984). Hierarchic demand and the engel curve for variety. *Review of Economics and Statistics, 66*(1), 8–15. https://doi.org/10.2307/1924690

Kaminski, M., & Ossowski, N. (2014). Stokes problems with random coefficients by the weighted least squares technique stochastic finite volume method. *Archives of Civil and Mechanical Engineering, 14*(4), 745–756. https://doi.org/10.1016/j.acme.2013.12.004

Kelly, D. J., Brush, C. G., Greene, P. G., & Litovsky, Y. (2010). *Global entrepreneurship monitor (GEM) 2010 women's report*. Babson Park, MA. Accessed June 7, 2015, from www.babson.edu/cwl

Kovalainen, A., Arenius, P., & Galloway, L. (2002). Entrepreneurial activity of women in the global economy: Analysis of data from 29 countries. Paper presented at The Babson Kauffman Entrepreneurship Research Conference, Boulder, Colorado, 5–9 June 2002.

Ma, J., Fan, Z. P., & Huang, L. H. (1999). A subjective and objective integrated approach to determine attribute weights. *European Journal of Operations Research, 112*(2), 397–404. https://doi.org/10.1016/S0377-2217(98)00141-6

Marlow, S., Colette, H., & Carter, S. (2009). Exploring the impact of gender upon women's business ownership: Introduction. *International Small Business Journal, 27*(2), 139–148.

McKeever, E., Anderson, A., & Jack, S. (2014). Entrepreneurship and mutuality: Social capital in processes and practices. *Entrepreneurship & Regional Development, 26*(5–6), 453–477.

McManus, P. (2001). Women's participation in self-employment in western industrialized nations. *International Journal of Sociology, 31*(2), 70–97.

Minniti, M., & Nardone, C. (2007). Being in someone else's shoes: The role of gender in nascent entrepreneurship. *Small Business Economics, 28*(2), 223–238.

Minniti, M., Arenius, P., & Langowitz, N. (2005). *Global entrepreneurship monitor 2004 report on women and entrepreneurship*. The Centre for Women's Leadership and London Business School, Babson College.

North, D. C. (1990). *Institutions, institutional change and economic performance*. Cambridge: Cambridge University Press.

Opricović, S., & Tzeng, G. (2007). Extended VIKOR method in comparison with outranking methods. *European Journal of Operational Research, 178*(2), 514–529. https://doi.org/10.1016/j.ejor.2006.01.020

Petrović, J., Milićević, S., & Đeri, L. (2016). The information and communications technology as a factor of destination competitiveness in transition countries in European Union. *Tourism Economics, 7*, 1–9. https://doi.org/10.1177/135481661665329

Potter, J. (2008). *Entrepreneurship and higher education*. Paris: OECD—Local Economic and Employment Development (LEED).

Puffer, S. M., McCarthy, D. J., & Boisot, M. (2010). Entrepreneurship in Russia and China: The impact of formal institutional voids. *Entrepreneurship Theory and Practice, 34*(3), 441–467. https://doi.org/10.1111/j.1540-6520.2009.00353.x

Radukić, S., Petrović, J., & Popović, Ž. (2015). Comparative analysis of factors of economic growth in transition countries after economic crisis: The case of Southeast and Central Europe and the Baltic countries. In J. Ateljević & J. Trivić (Eds.), *Researching Economic Development and Enterpreneurship in Transitional Economies: Assessment of the last 25 years, going beyond the 'transition', REDETE 2015* (pp. 165–177), Faculty of Economics, University of Banja Luka, Republic of Srpska, BIH, Graz, Austria. Accessed February 25, 2017, from http://www.redete.org/doc/Fourth-REDETE-Conference_web.pdf

San Cristóbal, J. R. (2011). Multi-criteria decision-making in the selection of a renewable energy project in Spain: The Vikor method. *Renewable Energy, 36*(2), 498–502. https://doi.org/10.1016/j.renene.2010.07.031

Sarfaraz, L., Faghih, N., & Majd, A. A. (2014). The relationship between women entrepreneurship and gender equality. *Journal of Global Entrepreneurship Research, 2*(6), 1–11. https://doi.org/10.1186/2251-7316-2-6

Schultz, T. P. (1990). Women's changing participation in the labor force: A world perspective. *Economic Development and Cultural Change, 38*(3), 457–488.

Singer, S., Amoros, J. E., & Arreola, D. M. (2015). *Global entrepreneurship report 2014*. Global Entrepreneurship Research Association, London. Accessed January 15, 2017, from http://www.gemconsortium.org/data

Smallbone, D., & Welter, F. (2001a). The distinctiveness of entrepreneurship in transition economies. *Small Business Economics, 16*(4), 249–262.

Smallbone, D., & Welter, F. (2001b). The role of government in SME development in transition countries. *International Small Business Journal, 19*(4), 63–77.

Smallbone, D., & Welter, F. (2006). Conceptualising entrepreneurship in a transition context. *International Journal of Entrepreneurship and Small Business, 3*(2), 190–206. https://doi.org/10.1504/IJESB.2006.008928

Smallbone, D., & Welter, F. (2009). *Entrepreneurship and small business development in post socialist economies*. London: Routledge.

Startiene, G., & Remeikiene, R. (2009). The influence of demographical factors on the interaction between entrepreneurship and unemployment. *Inzinerine Ekonomika, 64*(4), 60–70.

Stojanović, B., & Vasić, S. (2002). Structural reforms in the transition countries in the globalization process. In *Transition in Central and Eastern Europe – Challenges of 21st Century* (pp. 607–614). Faculty of Economics, University of Sarajevo, BIH.

Suprinovič, O., Schneck, S., & Kay, R. (2015). *Family-related employment interruptions and self-employment of women: Does policy matter?* Bonn: Institut für Mittelstandsforschung.

The World Bank. (2016). Accessed December 29, 2016, from http://data.worldbank.org/indicator

Thebaud, S. (2011). Social policies and entrepreneurship: Institutional foundations of gender gaps across 24 countries. *Academy of Management Best Paper Proceedings*, (1), 1–6. https://doi.org/10.5465/AMBPP.2011.65869493

Tonoyan, V., Budig, M., & Strohmeyer, R. (2010). Exploring the heterogeneity of women's entrepreneurship: The impact of family structure and family policies in Europe and the US. In A. de Bruin, C. G. Brush, E. J. Gatewood, & C. Henry (Eds.), *Women entrepreneurs and the global environment for growth* (pp. 137–162). Cheltenham: Edward Elgar Publishing.

Veciana, J. M. (1999). Entrepreneurship as a scientific research programme. *European Journal of Business Economics, 8*(3), 2–10.

Verheul, I., & Thurik, A. R. (2001). Start-up capital: Does gender matter? *Small Business Economics, 16*(4), 329–345.

Verheul, I., Wennekers, A. R. M., Audretsch, D. B., & Thurik, A. R. (2002). An eclectic theory of entrepreneurship, policies, institutions and culture. In D. B. Audretsch, R. Thurik, I. Verheul, et al. (Eds.), *Entrepreneurship: Determinants and policy in a European-US comparison* (pp. 11–81). New York: Springer.

Verheul, I., Stel, A. J., & Thurik, A. R. (2005). Explaining female and male entrepreneurship at the country level. In: Intern rapport, ERIM Research in Management, no ERS-2005-089-ORG. ERIM, Rotterdam.

Verheul, I., Stel, A. V., & Thurik, A. R. (2006). Explaining female and male entrepreneurship at the country level. *Entrepreneurship and Regional Development, 18*(2), 151–183. https://doi.org/10.1080/08985620500532053

Welter, F. (2011). Contextualizing entrepreneurship—Conceptual challenges and ways forward. *Entrepreneurship Theory and Practice, 35*(1), 165–184. https://doi.org/10.1111/j.1540-6520.2010.00427.x

Welter, F., & Smallbone, D. (2008). Women's entrepreneurship from an institutional perspective: The case of Uzbekistan. *International Entrepreneurship and Management Journal, 4*(4), 505–520. https://doi.org/10.1007/s11365-008-0087-y

Welter, F., Smallbone, D., Aculai, E., Isakova, N., & Schakirova, N. (2003). Female entrepreneurship in Post Soviet countries. In J. Butler (Ed.), *New perspectives on women entrepreneurs* (pp. 243–269). Greenwich: Information Age.

Welter, F., Smallbone, D., Isakova, N., Aculai, E., & Schakirova, N. (2004). Female entrepreneurship in the Ukraine, Moldova and Uzbekistan: Characteristics, barriers and enabling factors and policy issues. In UNECE (Eds.), Access to financing and ICT: Women entrepreneurs in the ECE region (pp. 52–93). Geneva: United Nations.

Wennekers, S., Stel, A., Thurik, R., & Reynolds, P. (2005). Nascent Entrepreneurship and the level of economic development. *Small Business Economics, 24*(3), 293–309. https://doi.org/10.1007/s11187-005-1994-8

Williams, N., & Vorley, T. (2015). Institutional asymmetry: How formal and informal institutions affect entrepreneurship in Bulgaria. *International Small Business Journal, 33*(8), 840–861. https://doi.org/10.1177/0266242614534280

Yu, W., Li, B., Yang, X., & Wang, Q. (2015). A development of a rating method and weighting system for green store buildings in China. *Renewable Energy, 73*, 123–129. https://doi.org/10.1016/j.renene.2014.06.013

The Local Economic Impact of Universities: An International Comparative Analysis (France and Hungary)

Balázs Kotosz, Marie-France Gaunard-Anderson, and Miklós Lukovics

1 Introduction

Nowadays, the realization that certain economic units, universities, or other entities have an impact on the economy of their region has come more and more into prominence. A growing demand appears to generate more precise studies regarding the quantification of the economic impact of these entities. The topic of the examination of economic impact is especially interesting and exciting when we can compare regions with different levels of development, yet both with the presence of an internationally successful university (e.g. here the University of Lorraine in France and the University of Szeged in Hungary).

The roles of universities are also changing with time. As Wissema (2009) suggested, there are three generations of universities, while Pawlowski (2009) already mentioned fourth-generation universities. The characteristics of these universities are summarized in Table 1.

University generations are often mixed up with university missions, as education is considered the first mission, research the second, and developing the economy and enhancing competitiveness as the third mission (Zuti and Lukovics 2014).

The local economic impact of a large tertiary education institution such as a university is an issue which has attracted considerable attention in the literature. The different methods used in the literature make the results difficult to compare; *we use the same method to investigate universities in different countries:* lacking regional input–output matrices, a multiplier-based approach was used for the first and second missions (education and research).

B. Kotosz (✉) · M. Lukovics
University of Szeged, Szeged, Hungary
e-mail: kotosz@eco.u-szeged.hu

M.-F. Gaunard-Anderson
University of Lorraine, Metz, France

Table 1 Characteristics of first-, second-, third-, and fourth-generation universities (based on Lukovics and Zuti 2013, 2014)

Aspect	First-generation universities	Second-generation universities	Third-generation universities	Fourth-generation universities
Goal	Education	Education and research	Education, research, and utilization of knowledge	Education, research, R+D+I, utilization of knowledge, and proactive economic development
Role	Protection of truth	The cognition of nature	Creation of added value	Local economic accelerator, strategy determination
Output	Professionals	Professionals and scientists	Professionals, scientists, and entrepreneurs	Professionals, scientists, entrepreneurs, and competitive local economy
Language	Latin	National	English	Multilingual (national and English)
Management	Chancellor	Part-time scientists	Professional management	Professional management and local experts

Generally, there are four substantial problems in data collection and analysis. First, the definition of impact, second, measuring and estimating first-round expenditures and avoiding double counting, third, estimating the correct value of the multiplier, and fourth, the quantification of the third mission activities.

> The economic impact study has become a standard tool used by Western universities to persuade state legislatures of the importance of expenditures on higher education. As economic impact studies become a political tool in the review of education, conservative assumptions and methods should be used to promote objectivity in the research process. (Brown and Heaney 1997)

The main goal of this chapter is to compare the local economic impact of universities in two university towns, one in a relatively rich and the other in a relatively poor region of Europe. To avoid bias, we applied the same methodology based on the available data. As public universities guard their budget data as confidential information and do not permit outsiders to survey students, only the employers of the authors were possible targets of the research (see also Alves et al. 2015).

The structure of the chapter is the following. After this introduction, in the second part, we take a theoretical overview of the impact of universities. In the third part, we focus on measurement methods, solutions, and problems. The empirical evidence for the two universities is shown in Sect. 4, followed by a conclusion including a summary of open questions.

Table 2 Classification of regional/local impacts of universities (Florax 1992; Garrido-Yserte and Gallo-Rivera 2010)

Impact on	Example
Politics	Changes in the political structure, an increase in citizen participation, improvement in the organization of political processes
Demography	Impacts upon population growth, population structure, and mobility
Economy	Impacts upon regional/local income, industrial structure, job market, labour mobility
Infrastructure	Impacts upon housing, traffic, healthcare services, retail
Culture	Greater offers in cultural goods, influence upon cultural environment
Attractiveness	Influence upon the region's (local) image, regional (local) identity
Education	Impact upon participation rate, changes in its quality
Social aspects	Impact upon the quality of life, the influence of the students, influence upon the region's (local) image and regional (local) identity

2 Theoretical Overview

Beck et al. (1995) define economic impact as "the difference between existing economic activity in a region given the presence of the institution and the level that would have been present if the institution did not exist."

Florax (1992), and with modifications, Garrido-Yserte and Gallo-Rivera (2010), showed that the regional and local effects of a university can be observed in many fields beyond the economy (see Table 2).

Dusek (2003) sorts the impact into input and output side effects (with students on both sides, see Tables 3 and 4). He highlights the role of budget links as an important (economic) factor; the main financial source of the university is the government budget. These classifications are not far from the Segarra I Blasco (2004) model, who separated backward and forward effects. Among the forward effects are localization factors (instead of attractiveness), and he also mentions foreign investment and high-tech companies (that are typical actors of technopolis-type clusters).

Huggins and Cooke (1997) transferred the keywords into drivers and outcomes, and in their approach, one cannot find hard measures on the driver side, while there are hardly any soft outcomes.

Brown and Heaney (1997) concluded that the input size effects may be better measured than output side effects, while the third mission of universities, knowledge transfer, has mainly social impacts. Notwithstanding this, Beck et al. (1995) argue that social (human capital) factors must be heeded, unless the major part of impacts would not be incorporated. We agree that even if the volume of the third mission activities is difficult to recognize, the measurement of their impact on the local economy can be correctly arrived at only through complex dynamic economic models.

Pellenbarg (2005) modified Lambooy's table to achieve a complete list of economic impacts (see Table 5). However, this classification is a wide mixture of

Table 3 Regional/local impacts of universities on the input side (Dusek 2003)

Actor	Changes
Households	+ Income + Employment + Consumption
Local authority	+ Tax base + Services
Business	+ Volume of business

Table 4 Regional/local impacts of universities on the output side (Dusek and Kovács 2009)

Factor	Changes
Human capital	+ Qualification + New firms + Migration
Knowledge	+ University–business relations + Extensive use of resources
Attractiveness	+ Location choice of households and firms + Cultural and social possibilities
Business	+ Research and development, exhibitions

Table 5 Regional/local economic impacts of universities (Pellenbarg 2005)

Economic impacts of a university	Example
Employment at the university	The number of university jobs and related institutions
University income	State contributions, fees, benefits arising from entrepreneur activity, etc.
University expenditure	Purchase of goods and services by the university
Income and expenditures of the university employees	Wages and salaries, social security costs
Effects on the job market	Qualified job provision effect upon productivity; flexible workforce supply of the students
Generation of business	Companies created by university students and employees, with or without employment knowledge and technology
Knowledge marketing	The sale of knowledge in a variety of ways: from ideas, courses, and patents

impacts of the three main missions of universities (education, research, and university–enterprise cooperation) and has many doubly counted factors.

Lengyel (2008) gives a more complex system of economic effects, including many elements of the previous literature (see Fig. 1).

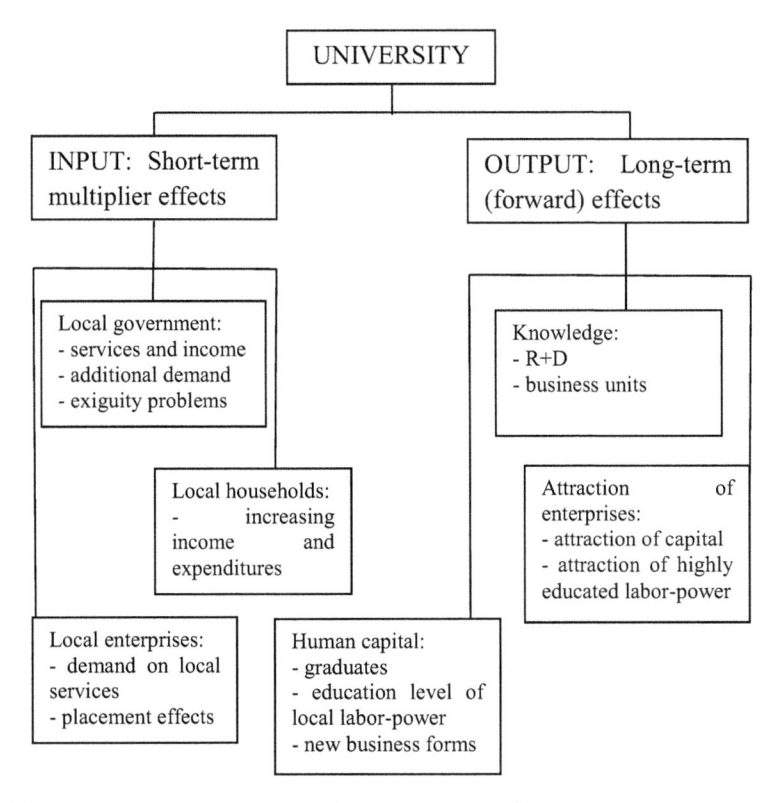

Fig. 1 Local economic effects of universities. Source: Lengyel (2008)

Table 6 Classification of the economic impacts of the universities (Garrido-Yserte and Gallo-Rivera 2010)

Impacts upon	Short term	Long term	
Expenditures	Increase of the regional GDP Salaries Employment Taxes	Steady increase of regional GDP Investments on equipment	
Knowledge	Changes in the job market Development of human capital	*Subjective* Externalities Workers' productivity Increase of income throughout life	*Objective* Patents Research and development

Garrido-Yserte and Gallo-Rivera (2010) also attached importance to the separation of short- and long-term effects and constructed a matrix of impacts (see Table 6). This version is the most complex rethinking of impacts and consideration of the economic impact of originally social phenomena.

Brown and Heaney (1997) compare two approaches to the computation: the skill-based approach and the economic-based approach. These approaches are close to the logic of the knowledge- and expenditures-based classification.

Johnson (1994) argues for separating local and non-local (determined by the choice of territorial scope), direct and indirect impacts (see later), but he also attends to various negative impacts of universities and to the necessity of a net approach (i.e. individuals could spend more if the government did not tax them to be able to pay the expenditures of universities—the double net question would be that people from somewhere are taxed to pay the expenditures of the given university). The question of gross or net impact can be analysed from many starting points. Generally, gross impact is easier to define and compute, as such questions arise in case of the lack of the university:

- What and where the staff would work,
- Where would students would pursue their studies (if at all),
- How large would the difference of knowledge in the local economy would be
- What would be the difference in housing prices?

We cannot forget that these questions are also linked to the choice of territorial level. The process can be observed when newly founded universities are investigated: e.g. most of the academic staff is coming from other (national) universities, while non-academic staff can be hired locally. Local housing prices change slowly, so only a complex comparative analysis (e.g. a panel regression analysis) can detect the differences due to the presence of a university.

The classification of impacts from the point of view of how directly the impact is related to the activity of the university is widely varied in the literature. We can find twofold, threefold, and fourfold classifications. The common point is the separation of direct and indirect impacts, where direct impacts include the expenditures of the university, the staff, and the students. In a larger classification, we have induced impacts (Klophaus 2008), while in the fourfold version, one can also find catalytic impacts [for these impacts, see Lukovics and Dusek (2014a, b) for university-related research, or Dusek and Lukovics (2011) for business service]. The modified version of these classifications (see Fig. 2) represents the impacts of universities as:

- Direct impact: output, income, and workplaces created on-site owing to the investments and operation of the university
- Indirect impact: income and employment generated in the companies providing inputs for the university
- Induced impact: income and employment generated with the multiplier impact owing to spending the incomes
- Catalytic impact: productivity growth achieved through the operation of the university, the income and employment created through the companies settling because of the university, and the spending of the visitors arriving because of the university

The contradictory and sometimes misleading mélange of the impacts can be well shown by juxtaposing (see Table 7) those of the Garrido-Yserte and Gallo-Rivera (2010)

```
                    ┌─────────────────────────┐
                    │     Direct impact       │
                    │ Production and income at│
                    │      the university     │
                    └─────────────────────────┘
                      ↙         │         ↘
┌──────────────────────────┐    │    ┌──────────────────────────┐
│    Indirect impact       │    │    │    Catalytic impact      │
│ Production and income at │    │    │ Production and income at │
│ companies providing inputs│──→│    │ companies arrived or founded│
│    to the university     │    │    │  because of the university│
└──────────────────────────┘    │    └──────────────────────────┘
                      ↘         ↓         ↙
                    ┌─────────────────────────┐
                    │     Induced impact      │
                    │ Production and income by│
                    │ the consumption of direct│
                    │  and indirect income    │
                    └─────────────────────────┘
```

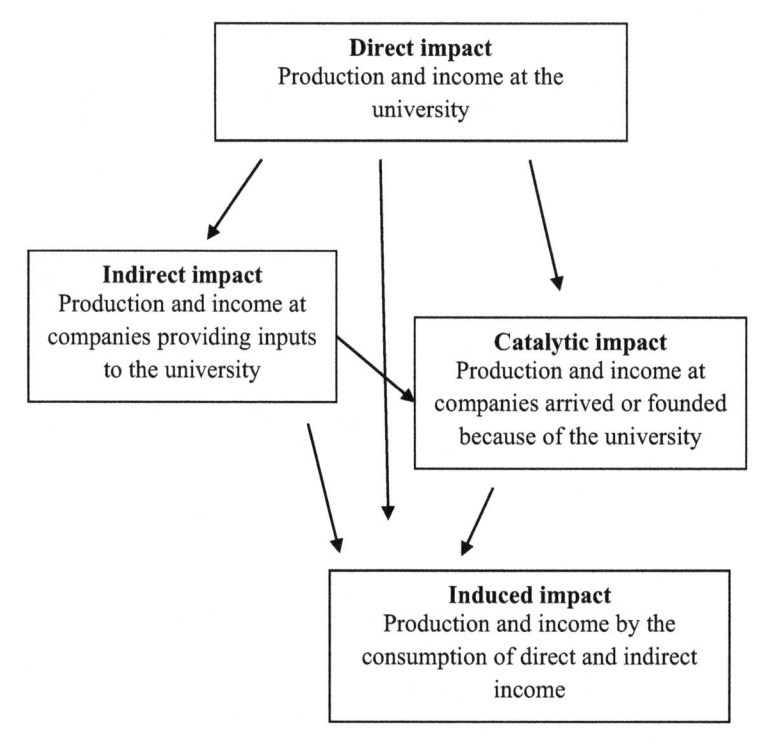

Fig. 2 Direct, indirect, induced, and catalytic effects. Source: Based on the idea of Dusek and Lukovics (2011)

Table 7 Regional/local economic impacts of universities (Garrido-Yserte and Gallo-Rivera 2010; Gagnol and Héraud 2001)

	Meaning	
Impact	*Garrido-Yserte–Gallo-Rivera*	*Gagnol-Héraud*
Direct	Related to the local expenditures of the university, staff, and students of the university	Consumption of the university, staff, and students of the university
Indirect	*Multiplied* income (each euro spent at the location by the university community (university, staff, and students) generates indirect transactions in the location linked to businesses that do not have a direct relation to the university	Impact through education of the workforce, development of synergies of R&D with regional enterprises
Induced	The expenditures of the people that visit the university, the effects upon financial institutions, the effects upon property value, and the impact upon location of new companies and so on	*Multiplier* effect

and the French school represented by Gagnol and Héraud (2001) and Baslé and Le Boulch (1999).

In this confusion, we would recommend using induced impact for all effects that are generated by the multiplication process. In the Lukovics and Dusek classification, the separation of direct and indirect impacts is artificial (practically, we separate personal expenses from the purchase of assets and investment due to the local analysis: on-site created income is always local—nevertheless, not necessary locally spent). Thereby, the primary expression for direct and indirect impacts would be better established. The catalytic impact of Lukovics and Dusek, the indirect impact of Gagnol and Héraud, and the induced impact of Garrido-Yserte and Gallo-Rivera have almost the same content. While it is not widespread in the literature, the catalytic expression better describes the content of this category than indirect or induced (induced seeming to be the worst choice).

3 Methodology

The main methodological possibilities are the use of input/output matrix-based models or the Keynesian multiplier model family. As up-to-date local or at least regional level input/output matrices are not available (neither for France, nor for Hungary), we could not use the first type of models. The use of such models is typical in the USA where such matrices are accessible at the state level, but these models have a territorial scope at this level.

The territorial scope of our analysis was local. In Szeged, the university is dominantly in the city (with one small faculty outside the city), in France we had the possibility for the survey only in Metz, and so a regional estimation of the impact of one campus would not be meaningful. Using a larger territorial scope would increase the absolute gross impact, but per capita or per GDP impact may be smaller.

Whenever it was possible, we used data for 2014.

In Bleaney et al. (1992), we can find a mathematical deduction of the formula of the Keynesian regional multiplier. This method is the most often used one for computation, with a series of disadvantages and deficiencies. Its simplicity makes it so popular, as a relatively narrow scale of data is necessary. In our comparison, we will follow a version of the regional multiplier model. The method we applied in Figs. 3 and 4 is a modification of the Caffrey and Isaacs (1971) and Bridge (2005) models, which we can also call a simplified ACE model in the terminology of Garrido-Yserte and Gallo-Rivera. The original Bleaney model was modified at two points: (1) we use and apply local consumption habits (with a rough estimation of local marginal propensity to consume) and (2) we calculate primary production and consumption effect in two steps. The latter methodological background is described in Felsenstein (1995).

In our chapter, we followed the computations made in our earlier work (see Kotosz 2013 or Zuti and Lukovics 2015), using the same methodology, model, and primary research agenda, so our results are fully comparable.

```
┌─────────────────────────────┐                ┌──────────────────┐
│ University incomes          │                │  Local economy   │
│ Government (183 M EUR)      │                └──────────────────┘
│                             │
│ Operation income (47 M EUR) │      ┌────────────┐   ┌──────────────────────┐
│ non-profit                  │      │   Staff    │   │ Total impact         │
│ institutions                │      │ (76 M EUR) │   │ Production: 314 M EUR│
│ charity                     │      └────────────┘   │ Income: 219 M EUR    │
│ (terminal) fees             │                       └──────────────────────┘
│ adventure income            │
│ foreign assistance          │
│ capital income              │
│ other                       │
└─────────────────────────────┘                       ┌──────────────┐
                                                      │   Primary    │
                                                      │  production  │
                                                      │  and income  │
┌─────────────────────────────┐      ┌────────────┐   │    effect    │
│ University expenses         │      │  Students  │   └──────────────┘
│                             │      │ (34 M EUR) │
│ Staff costs (97 M EUR)      │      └────────────┘
│                             │                       ┌──────────────┐
│ Material type and operating │                       │   Regional   │
│ costs, and investment       │                       │ multiplier   │
│ (121 M EUR)                 │                       │   (1.315)    │
│                             │                       └──────────────┘
│ Fellowships and other grants│
│ (9 M EUR)                   │
└─────────────────────────────┘
                                                      ┌──────────────┐
┌─────────────────────────────┐                       │   Primary    │
│ External economy*           │        3 M EUR        │    effect    │
├─────────────────────────────┤                       └──────────────┘
│ Visitors**                  │
└─────────────────────────────┘
```

──────▶ *Cash-flow in local economy*   * Non-local economy

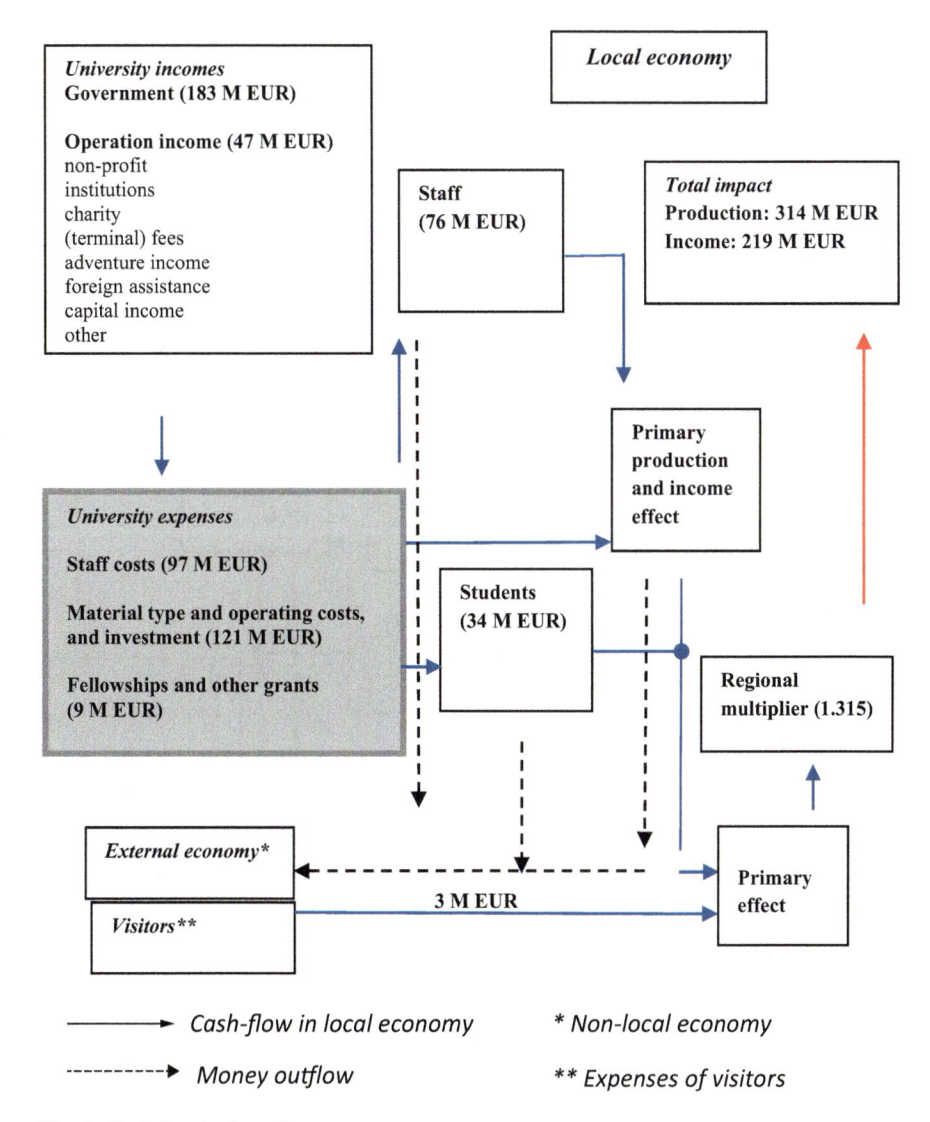

----------▶ *Money outflow*   ** Expenses of visitors

Fig. 3 Cash flow in Szeged

The multiplication effect is the function of the following factors:

- Personal income tax rate (average rate) [t]
- Value-added tax (average rate) [n]
- Marginal propensity to consume [c]
- Local consumption proportion of students [d]
- Local consumption proportion of employees [e]
- Local consumption proportion of the university [b]
- Local consumption proportion of the local economy [f]

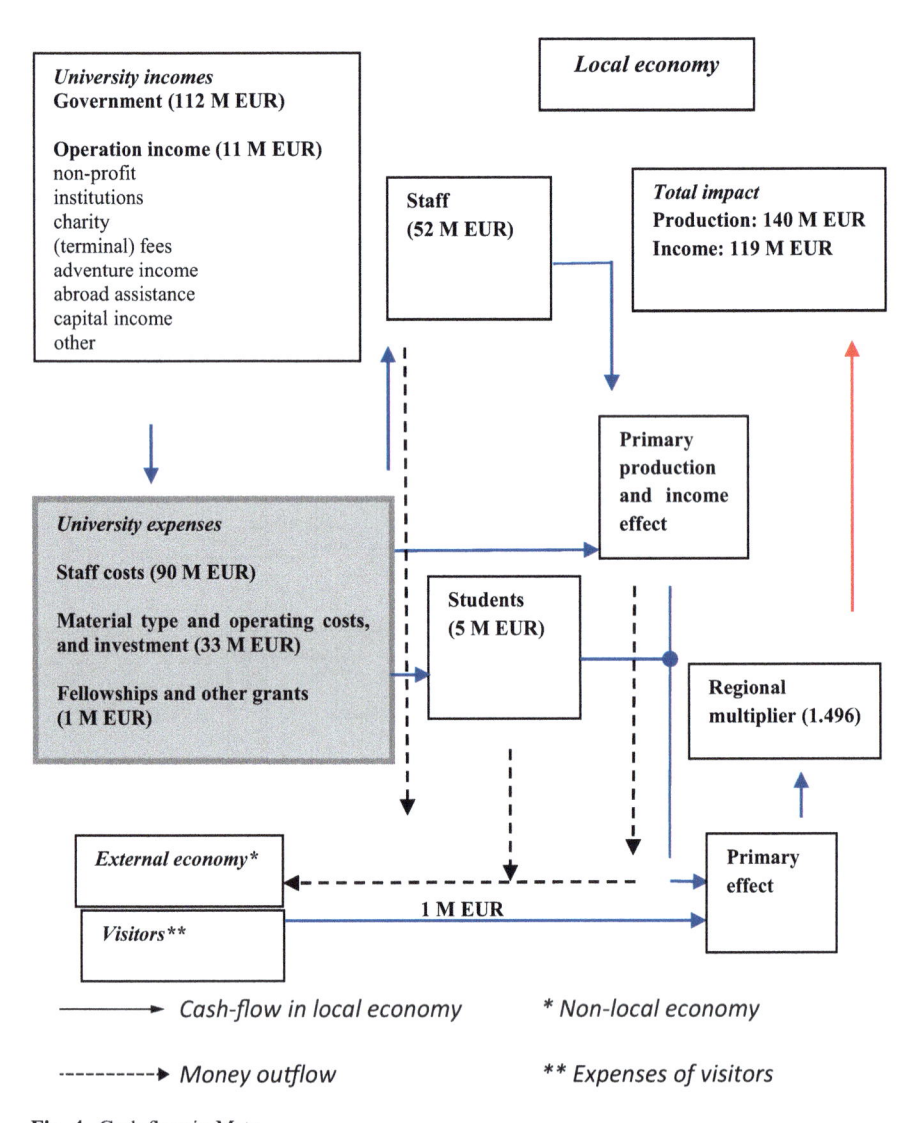

Fig. 4 Cash flow in Metz

Armstrong and Taylor (2000) and Lengyel and Rechnitzer (2004) supposed a fixed amount of spending of visitors and an equivalent local consumption proportion of students, employees, and the university. Instead of this, we applied a two-step estimation, so different proportions could be used. Thereby the formula of the multiplier is:

$$\frac{1}{1 - f \cdot c \cdot (1 - t) \cdot (1 - n)} \tag{1}$$

Expenditure data of the universities can be accessed from public information (profit and loss statements). In the case of multi-campus institutions, the allocation of expenditures by campus has been based on our estimation (when expenditures cannot be definitely allocated, we used keys related to relevant activities: the number of students, number of academic/non-academic staff, area, etc.). We supposed that employees have an additional income of 20% over their salary at the university. Estimation of visitors' expenditures is based on conferences and other events attracting visitors. Otherwise, visitors barely affect the total economic effect.

To map expenditures of students, we asked them to fill in a questionnaire (in 2014 in Szeged, and in 2015 in Metz). This element was based on a representative sample, and we multiplied the sample mean by the number of students enrolled at the university/campus.

To estimate the locally valid consumption function, we can follow two different paths. From one part, we can use national statistics, as from empirical evidence (see Árvay and Menczel 2001; Vidor 2005) local and national functions are not significantly different. From the other part, local sample surveys can also serve as a starting point. Our computations also showed that national or regional cross-sectional and time series data give largely different results, between 0.45 and 0.7 in both countries. We have local, survey-based results only for students. While Dusek (2003) found a high marginal propensity to consume in his survey of students (over 0.7), our results in Hungary are below 0.5, while in France it is around 0.5. In the model, we use a unique marginal propensity to consume, and we applied the most reliable national and regional estimations with a consensus value of 0.6.

The lack of reliable geographical knowledge of students (in many cases, they did not know in which county the university was operating) moved us to choose the local level as the city where the university is located (Szeged and Metz). By extending the geographical area, the local consumption ratio increases but not proportionally with distance.

The local consumption proportion of students varied around 70–80% based on our survey data (in accordance with previous data from other surveys). This number is always higher than the rate of local students, which is around 30–40%. In our estimations, we used the value of 0.7 in Metz, and 0.8 in Szeged, as the results of the surveys.

The estimation of employees' local consumption proportion is one of the most problematic points of the process, as in neither city did we have the right to ask employees via a questionnaire similar to students' questionnaire. As a result of the suburbanization process, we supposed that the local consumption proportion is lower than the students', and we used 75% in Szeged, but only 60% in Metz.

The local consumption proportion of public universities in Europe is typically determined and restricted by national law. Well-known estimation problems arise with the limitation of the local level (see Székely 2013), but this question is beyond the goals of the chapter. We analysed the official documents of the universities and estimated these impacts by separating local and non-local items. We used a 70% value for Szeged and 80% for Metz.

For the average tax rates, we used recent estimations of the Hungarian National Bank for Hungary and Ministry of Finance data for France. While average VAT rates are similar (16% in France, and 20% in Hungary), the NUTS3 level average personal income tax rate is only 6% in Lorraine, while the national rate of Hungary was 20.1% (for the methodology, see Benczúr and Kátay 2010). This difference can be explained by the inclusion of some social security contributions.

Generally, in scientific papers on impact studies, there are detailed *theoretical* comparisons of previously applied methods, but we cannot find international comparative studies where invariable methods have been used. Even with this deficiency, we can internationally compare the impact of the analysed universities.

4 Empirical Evidence and Results

Even if the theoretical background is not uniform, but well known, estimation methods are carefully done and discussed (see Siegfried et al. 2006 for a general comparison), and many international empirical examples can be found in the literature (Armstrong 1993; Blackwell et al. 2002; Bleaney et al. 1992; Bridge 2005; Brownigg 1973; Caroll and Smith 2006; Cooke 1970; Huggins and Cooke 1997; Jabalameli et al. 2010; Lewis 1988; Love and McNicoll 1988; Ohme 2003; Pellenbarg 2005; Robert and Cooke 1997; Simha 2005; Tavoletti 2007), yet until 2010 only one finished case study was known for Hungary, the case of the university of Győr (Széchenyi István University) (Dusek and Kovács 2009). Some steps were also made in Pécs (Mezei 2005), but this research has not reached the level of having at least one numerical result. An intensive phase of research started after 2010, the first results having been published in Kotosz (2012, 2013) for small colleges, and in Zuti and Lukovics (2015) for the University of Szeged. In Dusek and Lukovics (2014), we can also find an example impact study of a research-oriented future entity.

In France, three scientific impact studies are known, the case of Strasbourg (Gagnol and Héraud 2001), Rennes (Baslé and Le Boulch 1999), and the University of Littoral (Mille 2004). These papers can only partially handle the questions, not having an expressed number of euros (francs) as impact (except for Baslé and Le Boulch 1999 where multiplier effects are also determined).

The higher education systems in the two countries are similar in the sense that originally they are based on state-owned/state-financed universities, complemented by smaller private schools where education is more accentuated than research. Due to the Soviet heritage in Hungary, an independent (from universities) academic research centre network has survived. In France, research centres are more integrated in the universities, often creating a matrix system of education and research. Education divisions may run under different names (faculties, education and research units, institutes). While in the Hungarian system faculty positions are also divided between lecturers and researchers, in France academic staff members are lecturer–researchers. These characteristics do not help the separation of education and research-related expenditures and incomes.

Higher education in Hungary went through significant changes in the 1990s, which on the whole had an impact on the entire Hungarian society. Since the regime change, the number of students has risen significantly, nearly quadrupling. This tendency was noticeable both in the OECD and in the EU countries over a longer period. However, in Hungary after the 2005/2006 academic year, a decrease is perceptible regarding the number of students. On the basis of 2008 data, Hungary lags behind all examined OECD countries concerning the number of state-funded students per million inhabitants. While this data in Hungary was 21,324 per million, in Germany it was 24,639, in Austria 28,974, and in Norway 38,409 per million (Harsányi and Vincze 2012). From the perspective of our study, it is essential to review the Hungarian higher education's system of institutions. Since 2011, in Hungary the administration of higher educational institutions has transformed appreciably, and with this the organizational and administrational autonomy of the institutions, too. First, the appointment of rectors and economic directors has come under the authority of the ministry, and after that, budget commissioners were ordered to the institutions. In 2014, the chancellery system was implemented.

The French higher education system did not experience such shocks, and the number of students has had a growing trend with more than 2.4 million students in 2014. The significantly higher wage level in France can be observed in the dominancy of personnel costs in the budget of public universities.

The University of Szeged was founded in 1872 and has about 25,000 students and 12 faculties. After various historic events, in 2000 it unified almost all faculties working in the city. The Faculty of Medicine integrates a clinical centre (hospital) with activities that cannot be separated (financially) from the university. Szeged has around 170,000 inhabitants in a region which is among the 20 poorest regions of the European Union (measured in per capita GDP).

The first university in Metz was founded in 1970 based on smaller higher education institutions already existing in the city. In 2012, the universities of the Lorraine region were unified to create the University of Lorraine, which is the second largest university of France (by the number of students). The university has more than 50,000 students, 13,000 of them located in Metz, where 6 faculties can be recognized. As our research concerns only the city of Metz, university budget items had to be divided by keys. The city of Metz has about 120,000 inhabitants, in a region less developed than the French average (but over the EU average).

A summary of indicators of the two territories can be found in Table 8.

The main findings of our research for Szeged and Metz can be summarized in Figs. 3 and 4, respectively.

These flowcharts display the main financial information of the universities, including the incomes and expenditures of the universities. While the amount of staff costs is equivalent at the two universities, in Szeged more is spent on investment and material costs (due to wage level differences in the two countries). Major differences can also be observed in the case of students' spending; the more local

Table 8 Main indicators of the territories in the study (based on the different statistical data of the French and Hungarian statistical offices and OECD Statistics for 2014, persons in thousands)

Measure	*Metz*	*Szeged*
Region NUTS 2	Lorraine	Dél-Alföld
Region NUTS 3	Moselle	Csongrád
Number of inhabitants in the city	120	163
Number of inhabitants in the NUTS 3 region	1045	406
Number of faculties at the university	10	12
Number of companies	29,200	13,700
Number of employees (at NUTS 3 level)	212	173
GDP per capita in PPP (2013)	27,400	15,000

attraction zone of the French institution caused important differences (housing costs are the most important costs for students, but if they live with their parents, it is considered zero). The strong international characteristic of the University of Szeged resulted in higher visitor income, while the disparity of the regional multiplier has been explained earlier by different tax rates.

5 Conclusion

In the level of comparable results, we can analyse the impact per student or the impact per regional GDP.

The total impact per student is in the range of 15–50 thousand euros in the USA and in the range of 10–20 thousand euros in Western Europe, while between 5 and 10 thousand euros in Eastern Europe by benchmark studies. For a detailed comparison of benchmark studies, see Kotosz and Lukovics (2017). The results of around 11 thousand euros in our target cities can be explained by the fact that the University of Szeged has a clinical centre where medical activities require greater expenditures than education and—non-clinical—research of the whole university.

In the percentage of the regional GDP, the impact in the USA is generally in the range of 0.1–3.0%, while in Europe only 0.02–0.10%. Our results of 4% in Szeged and 0.02% in Metz are extremes. This difference can be explained by three facts: First, the presence of the medical centre in Szeged (four times higher impact); second, the difference of regional GDP (eight times higher impact); and third, we investigated a local campus in Metz, yet the whole university in Szeged (five times higher impact). The deviation is not methodology dependent; if we could find appropriate data for input–output matrix-based analysis, it would endure.

It is important to see that the direct and multiplied (induced) income impacts of these universities are in the order of the sum of money invested by different levels of government. Thereby, their third mission activities and/or catalytic impacts are crucial in their local/regional added value (Jongbloed 2008). It has been proven by Varga (2001) that agglomeration matters; the impact of third mission activities is larger in large universities than it could be explained by their relative size. However, the estimation of the impact of third mission activities is not developed in the literature. The intensity of these activities can be measured by a set of indicators, but it is not clear how we can turn these numbers to euros of economic impact.

References

Alves, J., Carvalho, L., Carvalho, R., Correia, F., Cunha, J., Farinha, L., Fernandes, J., Ferreira, M., Lucas, E., Mourato, J., Nicolau, A., Nunes, S., Nunes, S., Oliveira, P., Pereira, C., Pinto, S., & Silva, J. (2015). The impact of polytechnic institutes on the local economy. *Tertiary Education and Management*, (2), 1–18.

Armstrong, H. W. (1993). The local income and employment impact of Lancaster University. *Urban Studies, 30*, 1653–1668.

Armstrong, H. W., & Taylor, J. (2000). *Regional economics and policy*. Oxford: Blackwell.

Árvay, Z., & Menczel, P. (2001). A magyar háztartások megtakarításai 1995 és 2000 között. *Közgazdasági Szemle, 47*, 93–113.

Baslé, M., & Le Boulch, J.-L. (1999). L'impact économique de l'enseignement supérieur et de la recherche publique sur une agglomération de Rennes. *Revue d'Economie Régionale & Urbaine, 1*, 115–134.

Beck, R., Elliott, D., Meisel, J., & Wagner, M. (1995). Economic impact studies of regional public colleges and universities. *Growth and Change*, 245–260.

Benczúr, P., & Kátay, G. (2010). Adóreformok hatása a magyar gazdaságra egy általános egyensúlyi modellben. Accessed March 24, 2011, from http://media.coauthors.net/konferencia/conferences/3/benczur_katay.pdf

Blackwell, M., Cobb, S., & Weinberg, D. (2002). The economic impact of educational institutions: Issues and methodology. *Economic Development Quarterly, 16*(1), 88–95.

Bleaney, M. F., Binks, M. R., Greenaway, D., Reed, G., & Whynes, D. K. (1992). What does a university add to its local economy? *Applied Economics, 24*, 305–311.

Bridge, M. (2005). Higher education economic impact studies: Accurate measures of economic impact? *Journal of College Teaching and Learning, 2*, 37–47.

Brown, K. H., & Heaney, M. T. (1997). A note on measuring the economic impact of institutions of higher education. *Research in Higher Education, 38*(2), 229–240.

Brownigg, M. (1973). The economic impact of a new university. *Scottish Journal of Political Economy, 20*, 123–129.

Caffrey, J., & Isaacs, H. H. (1971). *Estimating the impact of a College or University on the Local Economy*. Washington: American Council on Education.

Caroll, M. C., & Smith, B. W. (2006). Estimating the economic impact of universities: The case of bowling Green State University. *The Industrial Geographer, 3*(2), 1–12.

Cooke, E. (1970). Analysing university student contribution to the economic base of the community. *Annals of Regional Science, 4*, 146–153.

Dusek, T. (2003). A felsőoktatás lokális termelésre és jövedelmekre gyakorolt hatása. In J. Rechnitzer & T. Hardi (Eds.), *A Széchenyi István Egyetem hatása a régió fejlődésére* (pp. 60–71). Győr: Széchenyi István Egyetem Gazdaság- és Társadalomtudományi Intézet.

Dusek, T., & Kovács, N. (2009). A Széchenyi István Egyetem hatása a helyi munkaerőpiacra. In A Virtuális Intézet Közép-Európa Kutatására VIKEK Évkönyve, II (pp. 69–73). Régiók a Kárpát-medencén innen és túl konferencia tanulmányai, VIKEK, Szeged.

Dusek, T., & Lukovics, M. (2011). Analysis of the economic impact of the Budapest Airport on the local economy. 58th Annual North American Meetings of the Regional Science Association International (RSAI). RSAI, Miami, 9–11 November 2011.

Dusek, T., & Lukovics, M. (2014). Az ELI és az ELI Science Park gazdasági hatásvizsgálata. *Területi statisztika, 5*, 1–18.
Felsenstein, D. (1995). Dealing with induced migration in university impact studies. *Research in Higher Education, 36*, 457–472.
Florax, R. (1992). *The university: A regional booster?* Aldershot, UK: Avebury.
Gagnol, L., & Héraud, J.-A. (2001). Impact économique régional d'un pôle universitaire : Application au cas strasbourgeois. *Revue d'Economie Régionale & Urbaine, 2001*(4), 581–604.
Garrido-Yserte, R., & Gallo-Rivera, M. T. (2010). The impact of the university upon local economy: Three methods to estimate demand-side effects. *Annals of Regional Science, 44*, 39–67.
Harsányi, G., & Vincze, S. (2012). A magyar felsőoktatás néhány jellemzője nemzetközi tükörben. *Pénzügyi Szemle, 2012*(2), 226–245.
Huggins, R., & Cooke, P. (1997). The economic impact of Cardiff University: Innovation, learning and job generation. *GeoJournal, 41*(4), 325–337.
Jabalameli, F., Ahrari, M., & Khandan, M. (2010). The economic impact of University of Tehran on the Tehran district economy. *European Journal of Social Sciences, 13*(4), 643–652.
Johnson, T. M. (1994). *Estimating the economic impact of a college or university on a nonlocal economy*. PhD dissertation, Texas Tech University, Texas.
Jongbloed, B. (2008). Indicators for mapping university-regional interactions. In: *Paper for the ENID-PRIME Indicators Conference in Oslo*, 26–28 May 2008.
Klophaus, R. (2008). The impact of additional passengers on airport employment: The case of German airports. *Airport Management, 2*, 265–274.
Kotosz, B. (2012). Felsőoktatási intézmények regionális multiplikátor hatása. *Jelenkori társadalmi és gazdasági folyamatok, 7*(1-2), 7.
Kotosz, B. (2013). Local economic impact of universities. *Analecta Technica Szegedinensia, 2013* (1–2), 22–26.
Kotosz, B., & Lukovics, M. (2017). *Az egyetemek helyi gazdasági hatásainak mérése*. Saarbrücken: GlobeEdit.
Lengyel, I. (2008). "Távolság versus közelség" dilemma az ipari-egyetemi kapcsolatokon alapuló tudásalapú helyi gazdaságfejlesztésben. In A gazdasági környezet és a vállalati stratégiák (pp. 551–562). A IX. Ipar- es Vállalatgazdasági Konferencia előadásai, Szeged.
Lengyel, I., & Rechnitzer, J. (2004). *Regionális gazdaságtan*. Budapest-Pécs: Dialóg-Campus.
Lewis, J. A. (1988). Assessing the effect of the polytechnic, Wolverhampton on the local community. *Urban Studies, 25*, 25–31.
Love, J. H., & McNicoll, I. H. (1988). The regional economic impact of overseas students in the UK: A case study of three Scottish universities. *Regional Studies, 22*, 11–18.
Lukovics, M., & Dusek, T. (2014a). Economic impact analysis of the ELI R&D infrastructure and science park. *Journal Mittelforum and Next Europe, 1*, 72–85.
Lukovics, M., & Dusek, T. (2014b). The economic impact of the ELI R&D infrastructure and science park in the Szeged sub-region. Diverse regions: Building resilient communities and territories. Regional Studies Association Annual International Conference 2014, Izmir, Turkey.
Lukovics, M., & Zuti, B. (2013). Successful universities towards the improvement of regional competitiveness: "Fourth Generation" universities. In *European Regional Science Association (ERSA) 53th Congress "Regional Integration: Europe, the Mediterranean and the World economy"*, European Regional Science Association, Palermo, 27–31 August 2013.
Lukovics, M., & Zuti, B. (2014). Egyetemek a régiók versenyképességének javításáért: "negyedik generációs" egyetemek? *Tér és Társadalom, 4*, 77–96.
Mezei, K. (2005). *A Pécsi Tudományegyetem hatása a város gazdaságára. A magyar városok kulturális gazdasága*. Budapest: MTA Társadalomkutató Központ.
Mille, M. (2004). Université, externalités de connaissance et développement local: l'expérience d'une université nouvelle. *Politiques et gestion de l'enseignement supérieur, 16*(3), 89–113.
Ohme, A. M. (2003). *The economic impact of a university on its community and state: Examining trends four years later*. mimeo: University of Delaware.

Pawlowski, K. (2009). The 'fourth generation university' as a creator of the local and regional development. *Higher Education in Europe*, (1), 51–64.

Pellenbarg, P. H. (2005). How to calculate the impact of university on the regional economy. In *Conference on Knowledge and Regional Economic Development*, Barcelona, 9–11 June 2005.

Robert, H., & Cooke, P. (1997). The economic impact of Cardiff University: Innovation, learning and job generation. *GeoJournal, 41*(4), 325–337.

Segarra I Blasco, A. (2004). La universitat com a instrument de dinamització socioconómica del territori. *Coneixement i Societat, 3*, 78–101.

Siegfried, J. J., Sanderson, A. R., & McHenry, P. (2006). *The economic impact of colleges and universities* (Vanderbuilt University Working Paper No 06-W12).

Simha, O. R. (2005). The economic impact of eight research universities on the Boston region. *Tertiary Education and Management, 11*, 269–278.

Székely, A. (2013). Regionális multiplikáció a szegedi Árkád példáján. In J. Rechnitzer, P. E. Somlyódiné, & G. Kovács (Eds.), *A hely szelleme – a területi fejlesztések lokális dimenziói* (pp. 565–573). Győr: Széchenyi István Egyetem.

Tavoletti, E. (2007). Assessing the regional economic impact of higher education institutions: An application to the University of Cardiff. *Transition Studies Review, 14*(3), 507–522.

Varga, A. (2001). Universities and regional economic development: Does agglomeration matter? In B. Johannson, C. Karlsson, & R. Stough (Eds.), *Theories of endogenous regional growth*. Berlin: Springer.

Vidor, A. (2005). A megtakarítás-ösztönzők hatása: magyarországi tapasztalatok. PM Kutatási Füzetek. Accessed October 13, 2010, from http://www2.pm.gov.hu/

Wissema, J. G. (2009). *Towards the third generation university: Managing the university in transition*. Cheltenham: Edward Elgar.

Zuti, B., & Lukovics, M. (2014). "Fourth generation" universities and regional development. In R. Hamm & J Kopper (Eds.), *Higher education institutions and regional development* (pp. 14–31). Mönchengladbach.

Zuti, B., & Lukovics, M. (2015). How to measure the local economic impact of the universities' third mission activities? In P. Nijkamp, K. Kourtit, M. Buček, & O. Hudec (Eds.), *5th Central European Conference in Regional Science* (pp. 1209–1215). Technical University of Košice, Košice.

Part II
Small and Medium-Sized Entrepreneurship in the Balkans Region

The Impact of Tangible and Intangible Assets on the SMEs' Success: The Albanian Case

Ylvije Boriçi Kraja

1 Introduction

The globalization of the economy and the growth of competition brought forward tremendous challenges for small and medium enterprises. SMEs play a key role in Albania by generating employment, innovation, competition and creating economic wealth. SMEs have a significant role in the sustainable economic growth and improvement of the living standards. In Albania, a large number of firms are family owned businesses. The size of the firm is a focal factor for the business performance. As of now, SMEs are facing a lot of challenges. Successful SMEs and which are oriented towards growth are vital for the economy (Analoui and Karami 2003). According to Gordon et al., managing risk is a fundamental concern in today's dynamic global environment.

According to Barney (1991), tangible and intangible assets, combined with competences and controlled by the firm, make it possible to create and implement efficient strategies capable of producing organizational improvements in the long run. According to the Resource-Based View, the nature of the resources, competences and knowledge accumulated by firms are the major causes of variation in business performance (De Luca et al. 2014). Hoog (2008) sees intangible assets as property without physical substance, the useful life of which tends to be subjective, varying according to the rights resulting from ownership and the associated competitive advantages and profits, which may be acquired or developed internally. SMEs are the most important factor to understand the performance of a country.

Y. B. Kraja (✉)
Faculty of Economy, Department of Business Administration, University "LuigjGurakuqi", Shkoder, Albania
e-mail: ykraja@unishk.edu.al

Fig. 1 Conceptual model

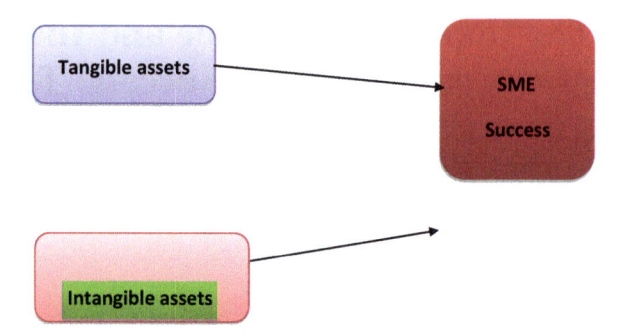

This chapter attempts to articulate the complications faced by SMEs, by focusing on the Albanian case. This study assesses small and medium enterprises and particularly intangible and tangible assets and their involvement in the success of a business.

The purpose of this chapter is to emphasize the rising importance of intangible assets on a firm's success by considering the great potential of both intangible and tangible assets on a SME's success. The researcher tries to extend our understanding and to shed light on the assessment of the impact of tangible and intangible assets in the existences of the SMEs in Albania.

Thus, the chapter is focused on the intangible factors such as: distinctive competencies, the abilities to evaluate and use culture, skills, work experience, capabilities to create qualitative products and services, to manage human resources, to use technologies, to generate business plans and to make clear how ideas can be turned into reality, as well as on the tangible assets like land, buildings, machinery, inventory, etc. Based on the fact that each firm is a unique combination of intangible and tangible assets, this chapter encourages the detection of ways in order to discover intangible assets that can be uncovered in relation to SMEs, identifying means to turn intangible assets into real values for businesses (Fig. 1).

In line with the above theoretical framework, derive the following hypotheses:

H1 SMEs are affected more by intangible assets than tangible assets.

H2 Intangible assets have more impact on the success of small and medium enterprises than tangible assets.

2 Literature Review

The legal identification of SMEs in Albania is regulated by law (Table 1). According to INSTAT, there were 112,537 active enterprises (enterprises include both legal entities and individuals that are engaged in an economic activity) in 2014, out of which 101,025 were enterprises with up to 4 people employed (Table 2).

Table 1 Legal SME definition in Albania

Size	No. of employees	Annual turnover or total assets
Micro	0–9	Up to ALL 10 million (or EUR 72,844)*
Small	10–49	Up to ALL 50 million (or EUR 364,219)*
Medium	50–249	Up to ALL 250 million (or EUR 1,821,096)*

Source: Law No. 1042 of 22.12.2008

Table 2 Breakdown of active enterprises by number of employed, 2010–2014

No. of employed	2014	2013	2012	2011	2010
Micro (1–4)	101,025	99,782	95,520	97,836	92,798
Small (5–9)	5387	5235	5636	5194	5018
Medium (10–49)	4647	4660	4439	4744	4078
SMEs	111,059	109,677	105,595	107,774	101,894
Large (50+)	1478	1406	1242	1265	1144
Total	112,537	111,083	106,837	109,039	103,038

Source: INSTAT, business register

The resource-based view of the firm (RBV) is an influential theoretical framework for understanding how competitive advantage within firms is achieved and how that advantage might be sustained over time (Barney 1991).

Resources of firms include all assets, capabilities, organizational processes, attributes of firms, information, and new knowledge, controlled by firms that know how to conceive and implement, to improve the efficiency and its effectiveness.[1] According to Coplin (2002), resources and products are two sides of the same coin. It is imperative to underline that more resources should be taken into account in the formulation of a strategy.

Resources are the centre of attention, and they can be financial, physical, human, technological or organizational (Barney 1991). When firms accumulate resources which are rare, difficult to imitate and non-replaceable, then they can be deemed to have achieved competitive advantage (Barney 1991). According to Analoui and Karami (2003), resources are assets, competencies, processes, capabilities and knowledge controlled by firms, which could be turned into strength if they could ensure competitive advantage. Company sources refer to the company's assets (Hill and Jones 2008).

Intangible assets like any other asset (a machine or a rental property) are a source of future benefits, but in contrast with tangible assets, intangible assets lack physical embodiment (Lev 2005) Intangible assets are resources and competences which may be combined to produce great success to SMEs. Iudícibus et al. (2013) point out that while tangible assets are visually identifiable and segregated items in accounting, intangible assets may not be considered as such. Intangibles differ from physical and

---

[1]Barney, J (1991). "Firm Resources and Sustained Competitive Advantage" Journal Management, 1991, Volume 17, N1, 99–120.

financial (stocks, bonds) assets in two important aspects by having considerable implications for management, valuation and financial reporting (Lev 2005).

A source can be used for different purposes, in different ways or in combination with other resources to create other services. Internal sources provide all the possibilities and limitations of firm growth. Barney (1991) pointed out that a firm's available resources might be a source of competitive advantage or of sustainable advantage.

Grant (1998) puts an emphasis on the importance of the resources and capabilities by suggesting five-step model in formulating a company's strategy:

1. Identifying and classifying the firm's resources.
2. Identifying skills and resources of input for each case.
3. Evaluating resources and capabilities in terms of their potential to create sustainable competitive advantage.
4. Choosing a strategy that best suits the firm's resources and environmental opportunities.
5. Identifying shortages of resources and investments in order to improve them.

Unique assets and capabilities of the firms are essential for optimizing the performance of such firms. The available resources of the firm, as well as their special characteristics, are considered the main reasons for having distinctive skills and consequently organizational growth. According to Hill and Jones (2008), capabilities refer to skills, competencies to coordinate resources and using them in an effective way. They stated that the competencies of the firms are products of organizational structure and control systems. A company may have resources and unique values, but if there is no ability to use actively these resources then the company may not be able to succeed over other competitors in the market.

Coff (1994) argues that human assets are a major source of sustainable advantage because of the ambiguity and systematic information, making them inimitable. Human capital could be the most important factor in order to be successful because it is difficult to imitate, says Guest.

The most important and strategic resources of SMEs are their employees (Analoui and Karami 2003). While John and Hill point out that there are a number of ways that human resources can help companies to create more value. If management believes in its employees and gives them a challenging appointment, says Guest,[2] employees in return will respond with high motivation and high performance. In order to generate healthy businesses, SMEs will need to initially comprehend their internal and external environment (Kraja and Osmani 2015).

Many studies have been undertaken with the intention of testing the relation between tangible and intangible assets. It is interesting to note that recent empirical studies show that the contribution of intangible assets is comparable to that of tangible assets as regarding to a wide range of countries. Corrado et al. (2005)

---

[2]Coff R.W. (1994) "Human Assets and organization control implication of the resource—based view" (Collis and Montgomery 1995; Hit and Ireland 1985; Littler 2005).

indicate that intangible assets have a greater impact on SMEs than tangible assets. As far as we know, it is not easy to manage intangible assets. Amongst the resources of a business, all the assets, capabilities, organizational processes, information, knowledge and other knowledge controlled by firms can be included, which help them to implement and improve efficiency and effectivity (Barney 1991).

In their paper on RBV, Collins and Mongomery (1995) have asserted that they perceive companies as diverse collections of physical assets, intangible assets and capabilities. As stated by them, companies are different because companies do not follow the same set of experiences or do not have the same organizational culture. Johansson (2008) in his study conveys the results of Grant et al. and according to him resources are an important factor and in particular knowledge is the most important source. While on the other hand in the literature (Porter 1980), good reputation is cited as source of competitive advantage. Studies show that organizational resources are as imperative as human resources. SMEs need to identify the resources that they possess, and they should endeavour to turn them into advantages for their business (Kraja and Osmani 2014).

Capabilities are the skills of individuals or groups to interact and to manage resources. Managing a source according to Barney (1991) is a resource in itself; it's an ability. Capabilities are more difficult to define than resources. When talking about the capabilities of a company, Hill and Jones (2008) refer to the abilities to coordinate resources and use them effectively. Capabilities are developed through a process of learning where employees of a firm repeatedly enhance their experiences in solving problems.

Sharma and Vredenburg (1998) stated that companies which possess the ability to use information will integrate knowledge into their businesses and will share this knowledge with different departments. They argued that, for example, oil companies of Sioux Buffalo have in place formal and informal meetings to share important information and discuss issues related to the intervention in the business environment and also related to the decision making and to the reduction of the environmental impacts of the company.

3 Research Methodology and Results

The methodology used in this research consists of a combination of qualitative and quantitative methods. The SMEs researched in this chapter were selected through a random sampling of 1120 participants throughout Albania. An empirical analysis was carried out based on the respondents that showed interest in completing the questionnaire. The population of the study consisted of a final sample of 475 small and medium enterprises from different SMEs in Albania. The collection of data for the study was carried out by using a questionnaire which included several from the seven-point Likert scale. The questionnaire was sent through electronic ways, but parts of them were filled in through face-to-face interaction. Most of the participants

Table 3 Factor analysis Cronbach alpha's = 0.93

Intangible assets	
1. The abilities to create the qualitative products and services	0.709
2. Distinctive competencies	0.659
3. Possession of skills to effectively communicate values and goals	0.747
4. Capabilities to evaluate and use culture	0.757
5. Being a flexible organizer	0.831
6. Capabilities to manage human resources	0.801
7. Capabilities in using the latest technology	0.757
8. Capabilities, skills, trainings and experience at work	0.802
9. Abilities in providing goods or services to satisfy the market	0.705
10. Capabilities to generate business plans and to make clear how ideas can be turned into reality	0.809
11. Skills to analyse and to forecast new possibilities	0.746
12. Good reputation and having brand names	0.763

Table 4 Factor analysis Cronbach alpha's = 0.713

Tangible assets	
Buildings and land	0.734
Inventory	0.815
Machinery	0.844

were from the sector of services, production, trade, construction, etc. For the generation of data, version 21of the SPSS was used (Table 3).

Questions are measured based on a Likert scale from 1 to 7 "Strongly Important" to "Strongly Unimportant".

"Intangible assets" measured as the average of thirteen questions. An exploratory factor analysis was carried out. One of the questions, "Difficulties to imitate", resulted with a factorial weight of 0.398, a figure lower than it is usually accepted as in accordance with Hair et al. (1998). Using the factorial analysis, the rest of the 12 questions resulted in a component which accounts for 57.42% of the total variance. In this case, the Varimax rotation analysis method was used. Cronbach's Alpha was computed to assess reliability. In our case, Cronbach's Alpha was 0.93, which is indeed a high value.

Based on the descriptive analysis, it was concluded that 34.5% of the participants were from the services sector, 29.3% from the production sector, 24.82% from trade, 5.4% from construction and the rest 5.98% from other different sectors.

"Tangible assets" were measured as the average of three questions. Factor analysis was carried out using the "Varimax rotation analysis" method. Reliability was measured by Cronbach Alpha. Questions resulted in a component, amounting for 63.81% of the total of the variance. In this case, Cronbach's Alpha was 0.713 (Table 4).

Questions are measured based on a Likert scale: 1–7 "Strongly Important" to "Strongly Unimportant".

Table 5 Descriptive statistics for variables "Intangible and tangible assets"

Variables	N	Mean	Std. deviation
Intangibles assets	474	5.5499	1.12373
Tangible assets	474	3.5886	1.01862

Table 6 Factor analysis Cronbach Alpha 0.745

Success	
ROI	0.822
Income	0.823
Market share	0.816

Firstly, in order to understand the distribution of these variables, there was a need to evaluate descriptive statistics of the tangible and intangible assets variables. For assessment purposes, Likert scale from 1 "not important" to 7 "extremely important" was used. These descriptive statistics are displayed in Table 5.

H1 $\mu_{\text{intangible assets}} > \mu_{\text{tangible assets}}$.

By means of comparing the averages of these two variables through T-test analysis (Paired-Sample Test), it resulted that the average of intangible resources is higher than the average of tangible resources. More precisely, they were, respectively, ($M = 5.5499$ and Std. Dev $= 1.12$) and ($M = 3.5886$ and Std. Dev $= 1.49$). However, it could be said that this difference of $\alpha = 0.05$ is significant because ($t (474) = 1.01862$, and $\alpha = 0.000$) consequently the H1 hypothesis was accepted, which means that:

$$\mu_{\text{intangible assets}} > \mu_{\text{tangibles assets}}.$$

Based on this result, we can say that intangible assets have greater impact on SMEs' tangible assets.

H2 Intangible assets have more impact on the success of small and medium enterprises than tangible assets.

Multiple regression analysis was used to examine this multiple. The dependent "success" variable was measured as the average of three questions. An exploratory factor analysis was carried out, Varimax rotation analysis method. These three questions resulted in a factor which explains 67.76% of the total variance. The results of this analysis are demonstrated in Table 6. The reliability coefficient was 0.745, which was adequate to continue with the analysis.

Questions are measured based on a Likert scale from 1 to 5 (disagree—very much agree).

A factor analyses was used to assess the factors. Multicollinearity refers to the correlation among independent variables (Hair et al. 1998) as shown in Table 7. The Pearson Correlation is satisfactory to continue with the regression analysis because the values are less than 0.7 (Table 8).

The R^2 squared correlation coefficient is 0.314, which is also referred to as the determination coefficient. This value indicates the percentage of total variation of Y explained by x_1 and x_2. The multiple regression equation in our case is as following.

Table 7 "Correlation", "intangible assets" and "tangible assets"

Variables	1	2
1. Pearson correlation Sig 2 tailed	1	
2. Pearson correlation Sig 2-tailed	0.233**	1

*Correlation 0.05 (2-tailed)
**Correlation is significant at 0.01 level (2-tailed)

Table 8 Multiple regression analysis for the "success of SME" dependent variable

Model	R^2	Adjusted R^2	t value	Sig.
	0.314	0.311		
(constant)			7.172	0.000
Intangible assets			11.978	0.000
Tangible assets			5.471	0.000

$$\widehat{Y} = \beta_0 + \beta_1 x_1 + \beta_2 x_2$$

where

$\widehat{Y}$ "success" dependent variable,
x_1 "intangible assets" predictor
x_2 "tangible assets" predictor

Using the unstandardized regression coefficient, or beta, the multiple regression equation can be illustrated as follows:

$$\text{"success"} = 1.329 + 0.363 \text{"intangible assets"} + 0.183 \text{"tangible assets"}$$

The coefficients of the "tangible assets" and *"intangible assets"* independent variables are positive, which entails that they have a positive impact on the SMEs' success. Based on the regression analysis, it resulted that the independents variables account for 31.4% of the variance of the "success" dependent variable, and this is not by chance. The unstandardized coefficients are ($B_1 = 0.363$) and ($B_2 = 0.183$). The results demonstrate that the regression model of the value $F(2.473) = 107.778$ becomes well matched for ($p = 0.00$), the significance level of (0.05), because in this case ($p = 0.000$) is less than (0.05). By using statistical testing of controlling the individual regression coefficient, the same results ($t_1 = 11.978$ and $p = 0.000$; $t_2 = 5.471$ and $p = 0.000$) were achieved. These coefficients are different from zero which means they contribute to this model. As it can be comprehended, both the unstandardized coefficient of intangible assets ($B_1 = 0.363$) and unstandardized coefficient of tangible assets ($B_2 = 0.183$) are positive, but B_1 has greater impact on the success. So, conclusion H2: is supported.

4 Limitations of the Study

As any empirical study, this study presented certain limitations:

- A limitation of the study is the fact that the application in different branches of industry can be dissimilar. Thus, many industries may have divergent success factors.
- Another limitation relates to the fact that the sampling has not included informal SMEs. This means that the population obtained in this chapter does not represent all SMEs operating in the districts. In other words, the sampling utilized for the research was limited to only formal SMEs. It would have been beneficial to extend the study through the entirety of the businesses in order to also reflect the views and practices of informal SMEs, which are not significant in number.

5 Conclusions

SMEs are considered generators of economic growth and of development of the country. Therefore, their role is becoming more and more important. Based on the information collected through the use of mixed methods, qualitative methods and quantitative methods, and based on the statistical data analysis as regarding to SMEs, exceedingly significant conclusions were reached. The study also revealed that tangible and intangible assets, which are very complex, unstable and sometimes uncertain, have a huge impact on the SMEs' success. The influence of the intangible assets on SMEs is especially substantial.

Organizations today are characterized by a complex relationship of different actors, so it is important to establish competitive advantages and create value by managing efficiently the missing resources in order to cope with fierce competition and to successfully confront the challenges faced by SMEs.

Access to information, provision of advice, training activities and participation in conferences, etc. help businesses to increase access regarding the use, processing, information dissemination and implementation of information analysis. In many SMEs, staff is the most essential asset.

Another objective of the study was to analyse the impact that intangible and tangible resources have on SMEs. The analysis concluded that intangible resources have more impact than tangible resources on SMEs.

It is evident from the study that intangible resources affect significantly the success of SMEs. The analysis revealed that success is positively related to intangible resources. This result is in the same track as the results and achievements reached by various studies that have shown a positive relationship existing between intangible resources and success such as the study of Bontis et al. (2000), which indicated positive links between the two.

6 Recommendations

The researcher recommends doing further research in this area, by studying and discovering further additional factors, apart from those taken into account, which may steer SMEs toward success.

This chapter ascertained that intangible resources have greater impact than tangible resources as in regard to the performance of SMEs. This does not exclude the impact of tangible resources, but it is a recommendation for the managers to pay respective and appropriate consideration to each and every element and aspect that contributes to the creation, growth and consolidation of tangible and intangible resources. This purports that managers, executives and owners of SMEs should be supported and should concentrate properly on the progression and consolidation of all the factors that are included in this study which ensued to be very crucial factors (factors that were taken to measure intangible resources) such as:

- Abilities to provide goods or services to satisfy the market.
- Transmitting knowledge.
- Reliance on the good reputation of the firm and in having the confidence to achieve more growth.
- Evaluating and using culture, in planned and flexible organization.
- Being able to adjust to new technologies and advanced software.
- Having the skills to communicate in an effective way appropriate values and goals.

References

Analoui, F., & Karami, A. (2003). *Strategic management. In small and medium enterprises.* London: Thomson Learning.

Barnes, Y. B., & William, S. H. (2010). *Strategic management and competitive advantage. Concepts and cases* (3rd ed., p. 10). Englewood Cliffs, NJ: Prentice Hall.

Barney, J. (1991). Firm resources and sustained competitive advantage. *Journal Management, 17*(N1), 99–120.

Barney, J. B., & Mackey, T. B. (2005). Testing resource-based theory. *Research Methodology in Strategy and Management, 2*, 1–13.

Bontis, N., Keow, W. C., & Richardson, S. (2000). Intellectual capital and business performance in Malaysian industries. *Journal of Intellectual Capital, 1*, 85–100.

Coff, R. W. (1994). *Human Assets and Organization control i of the resource based view.* St. Louis: School of Business, Washington University.

Collins, D. J., & Mongomery, C. A. (1995). Competing on resources: Strategy in the 1990s. *Harvard Business Review, 73*(4), 118–128.

Coplin, H. C. L. (2002). *Competitive advantage and the SME': The role of the distinctive competences as the determinants of success are there differences across gender, sector and size.* Spain.

Corrado, C., Hulten, C., & Sichel, D. (2005). Measuring capital and technology: An expanded framework. In *Measuring Capital in the New Economy.* University of Chicago Press.

Corrado, C., Hulten, C., & Sichel, D. (2009, September). Intangible capital and U.S. economic growth. *Review of Income and Wealth*, No. 3.

De Iudícibus, S., Martins, E., Gelbcke, E. R., & dos Santos, A. (2013). *Manual de contabilidadesocietária: aplicável a todas as sociedades de acordo com as normasinternacionais e do CPC* (2a ed.). São Paulo: Atla.

De Luca, M., Ribeiro Maia, A., Da Costa, V., De Vasconcelos, C., & Da Cunha, J. (2014). *Intangible assets and superior and sustained performance of innovative Brazilian firms*. http://www.anpad.org.br/bar

Grant, R. M. (1998). *Contemporary strategy analysis* (3rd ed.). Oxford: Wiley-Blackwell.

Hair, J. F., Anderson, R. E., Tatham, R. L., & Back, W. C. (1998). *Multivariate data analysis* (5th ed.). Englewood Cliffs, NJ: Prentice Hall.

Hill, C. W. L., & Jones, G. R. (2008). *Strategic management theory: An integrated approach* (9th ed.). Mason: South-Western/Cengage Learning.

Hoog, W. A. Z. (2008). *Fundo de comércio goodwill em: apuração de haveres, balanço patrimonial, danoemergente, lucrocessante, locaçãonãoresidencial*. Curitiba: JuruáEditora.

Johansson, J. (2008). *Essays on collaborative processes among SMEs for competitiveness development*. Doctoral Thesis (fq81).

Kraja, B. Y., & Osmani, E. (2014). The role of government policy in supporting SMEs. In *International Conference with the theme "Fostering sustainable development through creation of knowledge society"* Peje. Kosove.

Kraja, B. Y., & Osmani, E. (2015). Importance of external and internal environment in creating of competitive advantage to SMEs. *European Scientific Journal, 11*(13), 120–131.

Lev, B. (2005). *Intagible assets: Concepts and measurements. Encyclopedia of social measurement* (Vol. 2). New York: New York University.

Mackie, C. (2009). I*ntangible assets. Measuring and enhancing their contribution to corporate value and economic growth.* Summary of workshop. The National Academic Press. www.nap.edu

Penrose, E. T. (1959). *The theory of the growth of the firm*. New York: John Wiley.

Petkov, R. (2012). Competitive advantage from internally generated intangible assets measured at fair value fair value for Bulgarian small and medium sized enterprises (SME).

Porter, M. E. (1980). *Competitive advantage*. New York: Free Press.

Sharma, S., & Vredenburg, H. (1998). Proactive corporate environmental strategy and the development of competitively valuable organizational capabilities. *Strategic Management Journal, 19*(8), 729–753.

The Role of Networking in the Company's Growth Process

Anamarija Delić, Julia Perić, and Tihana Koprivnjak

1 Introduction

Small and medium-sized companies (SME) are the backbone of every economy. Croatia is no exception. But in every economy the focus should be on the growing companies, because only these companies will introduce new knowledge, invest in new technology, and employ. Unfortunately, in every economy growing companies are a minority. Croatia has only 8.2% of growing companies in total number of companies, according to the Global Entrepreneurship Monitor (GEM) results. In strategic documents, like the Strategy for Development of Entrepreneurship in the Republic of Croatia 2013–2020, Croatian Government has recognised their importance and outlined it as one of their goals. This strategic document is focused on strengthening entrepreneurial potential and improving entrepreneurial culture, and its programmes and projects are implemented through a wide infrastructure network of business support institutions. In addition to MINPO (Ministry of Entrepreneurship and Crafts) and HAMAG INVEST (Croatian Agency for SMEs, Innovations and Investments), as umbrella institutions of entrepreneurial infrastructure, entrepreneurs can rely on the support of 88 other institutions—21 regional development agencies, 10 local development agencies, 16 business incubators, 6 technology parks, and 35 entrepreneurship centres, which employ 700 people. Business support institutions support entrepreneurs by providing general advice and education, supporting new companies that are introducing new technology, assisting with completing project applications, and securing locations for industrial development with complete infrastructure. However, despite their number, according to the results of research conducted for the purpose of creating the Strategy for Development of Entrepreneurship in the Republic of Croatia 2013–2020, business support institutions do not

---

A. Delić (✉) · J. Perić · T. Koprivnjak
Faculty of Economics, Josip Juraj Strossmayer University of Osijek, Osijek, Croatia
e-mail: adelic@efos.hr; julia@efos.hr; tihana@efos.hr

© Springer International Publishing AG, part of Springer Nature 2018
J. Ateljević, J. Budak (eds.), *Entrepreneurship in Post-Communist Countries*,
https://doi.org/10.1007/978-3-319-75907-4_10

have appropriate products and services with which they would be able to help companies regardless of the stage of their development and life cycle. In other words, the owners of small and medium-sized companies in the Republic of Croatia lack knowledge of quality management, marketing knowledge, and project and finance management knowledge and are not fully aware of the advantages of association and protection of intellectual property. Owners of the Croatian small and medium-sized companies, although having lots of barriers, very rarely seek for professional advice. Despite their abundance and availability, according to the Croatia Consultancy Market Study as many as 78% of companies have not used the services of advisors or consultants in the last 3 years. But, even more worrying is the fact that as many as 68% of respondents have solved their problem independently, although the problems were complex and mostly of legal nature.

Barriers that prevent Croatian small and medium-sized companies to grow are studied by many researches and studies: GEM; World Bank's Doing Business; The Business Environment and Enterprise Performance Survey (BEEPS); Corruption Perceptions Index; Business, Corruption and Crime in Croatia; and The Global Competitiveness Report. The results of the aforementioned studies indicate the existence of a high level of agreement about the main characteristics of the business environment in Croatia: bad government policies and programmes, high levels of corruption, underdevelopment of informal sources of financing, hindered access to finance, inefficiency of the legal framework, high administrative barriers, and a poor focus on entrepreneurial education and transfer of knowledge from research institutions to the business sector. These characteristics of the business environment make doing business extremely complex and difficult, and administrative barriers require more time for obtaining permits and starting a business. In addition, the above barriers, particularly difficult access to financing sources, legal protection, and corruption, affect the small and medium-sized enterprise sector twice as much as the large companies.

Networks, which can be defined as "group of different organizations, with convergent goals, which share an identity and develop a singular definition of trust and power and pursue repeated exchange relations" (Braga 2004, p. 3), are becoming increasingly important to entrepreneurs. Entrepreneurs use networks for obtaining access to market, information, technology, and other resources (Robinson 2009). According to Taylor and Thorpe (2004), entrepreneurs, to some extent, depend on their networks of personal relationships when making decisions and solving problems. Networks can be a source of competitive advantage for companies (Melé 2009), enhance their chances of survival (Baum et al. 2000), and reduce the lender's expected cost of providing capital (Petersen and Rajan 1994). Small firms usually depend on financial intermediaries, particularly commercial banks, which makes asymmetric information a much more expressed problem (Berger and Udell 1995). Commercial banks tend to develop long-term relationships with SME owners in order to minimise these information problems. More information about the SMEs and their plans enables banks to offer better loan conditions and even lower collateral requirements. All SMEs need some external sources of finance while growing. In that phase, SME owners will heavily depend on dense networks (embedded relationships), often including a high proportion of family members (Klyver and Hindle 2007).

The research on the use of networking by owners of small and medium-sized companies when making decisions about the structure of capital, that is, selecting external source of financing, was conducted on 108 Croatian SMEs and was a part of the study on factors of decision-making on capital structure. Attitudes, thoughts, and decision-making methods of SME owners were collected through a questionnaire which consisted of 39 questions. The sample of companies on which the research was conducted was selected using the Business Croatia database, which has records of 750,000 business entities, but for the purposes of the research, owners of SMEs that can be contacted via email were selected. The response rate was 28.35%. The sample covers all activities and excludes companies that were present on the market for less than a year. Based on the characteristics of the business environment and the features of owners of small and medium-sized companies, a hypothesis was derived, which shows that when making decisions on capital structure, SME owners rely on their network of contacts (networking), which increases the level of indebtedness and allows financing the growth and development of their companies. Pearson correlation coefficient was used to test the hypothesis.

When financing company growth and development, owners of SMEs have most often used own funds, bank loans, and leasing. The funds were most often used for financing long-term assets, settling due liabilities, and crediting buyers. But, as many as 48.5% of respondents pointed out that creditors' demands were too large and that they lacked information on available sources of financing (27.5%). The research results are in line with previously identified barriers to growth of SMEs, where they have especially highlighted administrative barriers and access to sources of financing. Although there was no correlation between level of indebtedness and different sources of information or advice (network), companies that had better quality information and data, as well as politicians' "recommendations", obtained additional external financing and thus financed growth and development.

Corruption is, according to the opinion of Croatian entrepreneurs, the only way of solving problems, when government is not efficient in delivering services. Although companies can solve their problems significantly faster by resorting to corruption, it still cannot ensure long-term and sustainable growth. Companies that use that corruption as a way of solving problems remain small for a longer time. On national level, corruption will hinder sustainable growth of companies, as well as their competitiveness.

2 The Croatian Business Ecosystem

Small and medium-sized enterprises (SMEs) have a vital role in economic growth, especially in the creation of new jobs. According to Birch (1979), in the United States during the 1970s eight out of ten jobs were created in businesses with less than 100 employees. Based on research in 2014 by the European Commission, SMEs comprised 99.8% of all businesses in the EU-28 and employed 66.8% of all workers, while creating 57.9% of all added value. SMEs in the Republic of Croatia do not deviate statistically from the EU-28. In 2013, SMEs comprised 99.7% of all businesses and employed 68.40% of all workers.

In regard to SMEs, special attention is given to businesses experiencing growth. According to research by the Global Entrepreneurship Monitor (GEM), businesses experiencing growth typically undertake activities that strengthen their market competitiveness such as product development, creation of new jobs, technological modernisation of equipment and machinery, as well as constant work on internationalising their business. Enterprises experiencing growth are a minority in all national economies. GEM research indicates that in Croatia, such enterprises account for only 8.2% of all businesses. Increasing the number of enterprises experiencing growth is the goal determined in the 2013–2020 Strategy for the Development of Entrepreneurship in the Republic of Croatia. The strategy focuses on strengthening the potential and deepening a culture of entrepreneurship, with the programmes and projects conducted within a rich infrastructural network of supporting institutions. Besides the Ministry of Economy and the Croatian Agency for Small Entrepreneurship and Investments (HAMAG INVEST) as the main institution for entrepreneurial infrastructure, entrepreneurs also have at their disposal an additional 88 institutions, of which 21 are regional development agencies, 10 local development agencies, 16 entrepreneurial incubators, 6 technological parks, and 35 entrepreneurial centres, employing a total of 700 people.[1] Entrepreneurial support institutions "provide support to entrepreneurs by providing general advice, education, assistance to new businesses that are introducing new technologies, support in completing project applications and provide business premises for industrial development accompanied by a comprehensive infrastructure." According to research by GEM titled the *2015/2016 Global Report*, physical infrastructure is deemed the best contributing factor of a business environment, and in no way does it lag behind the average of all countries included in the research (Fig. 1).

This should also include the chambers, Croatian Chamber of Economics and the Croatian Chamber of Trades and Crafts, in which membership is mandatory for all businesses in Croatia. However, despite their numbers, and based on research results obtained in drafting the *2013–2020 Strategy for the Development of Entrepreneurship in the Republic of Croatia*, entrepreneurial supporting institutions do not have the appropriate products or services to assist enterprises regardless of the phase of their development and life cycle. In other words, owners of SMEs in Croatia lack knowledge in quality assurance management, marketing, managing projects and finance, and the benefits of joining consortiums as well as intellectual property rights. Moreover, neither do employees at the entrepreneurial supporting institutions possess adequate knowledge in resolving the mentioned requirements. The respective ministry, as well as HAMAG INVEST, implements projects and programmes that are mainly focused

---

[1] The Croatian SME Observatory Report 2012, https://poduzetnistvo.gov.hr/UserDocsImages/EU%20projekti/IPA%20IIIC/Pobolj%C5%A1anje%20administrativne%20u%C4%8Dinkovitosti%20na%20nacionalnoj%20razini/Izvjestaj%20opservatorija-2012.pdf

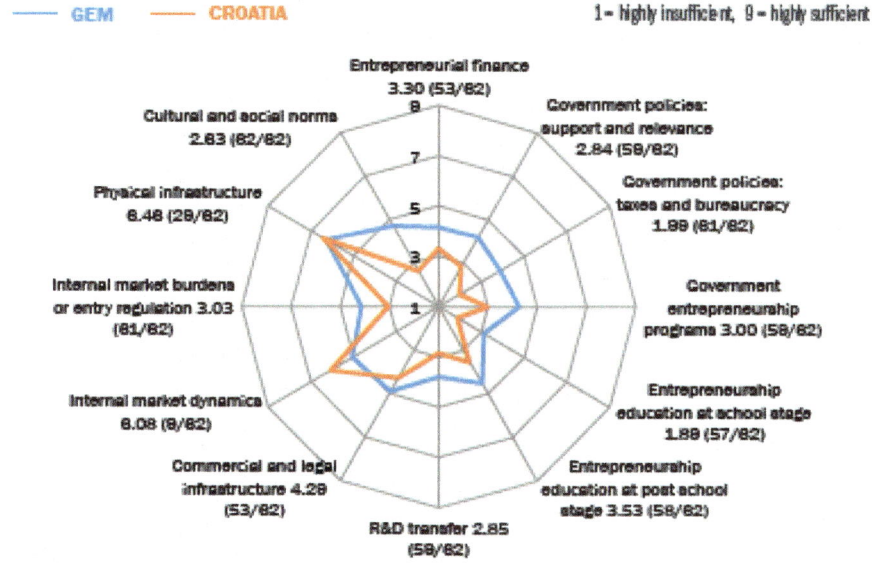

Fig. 1 Evaluation by experts for the business ecosystem in the Republic of Croatia with respect to GEM's country average. Source: Kelley D, Singer S, Herrington M (2016) Global Entrepreneurship Monitor: 2015/2016 Global Report, Babson College, USA, p 69. http://gemconsortium.org/report/49480. Accessed 12 July 2016

on start-ups. The Croatian Bank for Reconstruction and Development, which secures loans under favourable conditions for SMEs, is also mostly orientated towards novice entrepreneurs. This has resulted in owners of enterprises that experience growth turning towards business consultants. However, according to the *Study on Consultancy Services in the Republic of Croatia*, the perceived quality of consultancy services in the Republic of Croatia is lower than the average assessment given in GEM countries. The Republic of Croatia does not have a central register of available consultancy services, and the few attempts at certifying consultants and standardising consultancy services on the Croatian market have been unsuccessful. The main sources of business information are the 1415 companies registered for providing advisory and consultancy services. Despite their numbers and availability, according to the mentioned research, in the last 3 years 78% of business have not utilised the services of advisors or consultants despite encountering problems. However, what is more worrying is the fact that 68% of respondents resolved the problems they encountered on their own, even though the problems were complex and mostly of a legal nature (Fig. 2).

The reasons for this situation are to be sought in the level of trust by SME owners in business advisors and consultants, public administration institutions, where only 11.2% of SME owners trust state institutions, and possibly the existence of other channels and ways of resolving problems.

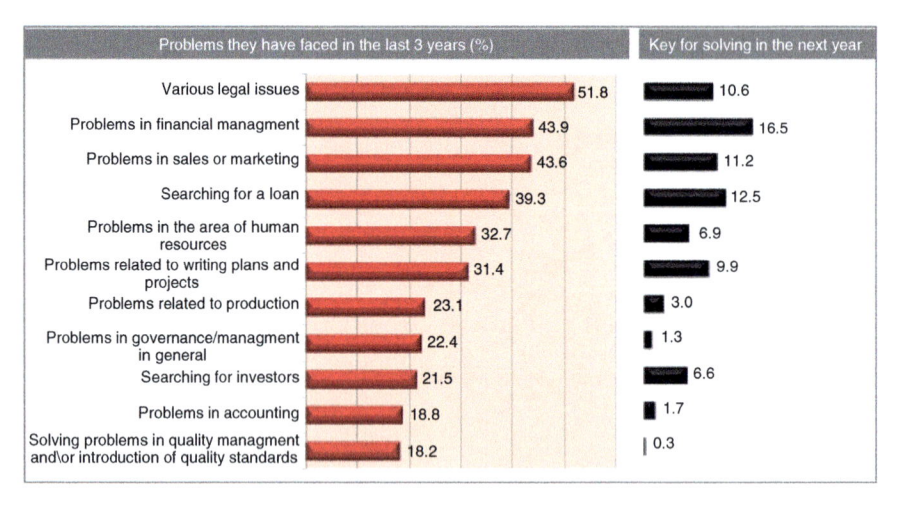

Problems they have faced in the last 3 years (%)		Key for solving in the next year
Various legal issues	51.8	10.6
Problems in financial managment	43.9	16.5
Problems in sales or marketing	43.6	11.2
Searching for a loan	39.3	12.5
Problems in the area of human resources	32.7	6.9
Problems related to writing plans and projects	31.4	9.9
Problems related to production	23.1	3.0
Problems in governance/managment in general	22.4	1.3
Searching for investors	21.5	6.6
Problems in accounting	18.8	1.7
Solving problems in quality managment and\or introduction of quality standards	18.2	0.3

Fig. 2 Types of problems faced by SMEs in Croatia. Source: Alpeza M, Mikrut M, Oberman Peterka S, Delić A (2014) Croatia Consultancy Market Study, European Bank for Reconstruction and Development, Zagreb, p. 81. http://www.cepor.hr/wp-content/uploads/2015/07/EN-Croatia-Consultancy-Market-Study.pdf. Accessed 12 July 2016

3 Barriers to Achieving Company Growth

To increase the proportion of enterprises experiencing growth in the Croatian economy, and to achieve growth of the Croatian economy, it becomes essential to eliminate barriers that hinder growth and development for enterprises and also increase the quality of the business environment. Some of the greatest barriers according to research by GEM and cited by SME owners are bureaucracy, legal and regulatory requirements, government measures and policies, and education, including cultural and social norms (Table 1).

Some of the best valued factors of a business environment are access to physical infrastructure, which also implies access to professional and business infrastructure, while access to commercial and professional structures lags behind the EU and the GEM average despite the fact that Croatia is continually investing in the development of entrepreneurial supporting institutions. Therefore, the conclusion is that it becomes necessary to reexamine current access to the development of the business environment "given that an extensive institutional presence does not guarantee adequate and good quality services." What is exceptionally important in strengthening the innovative capacity of enterprises is the transfer of knowledge from higher education and research institutions to SMEs. This factor of the business environment in Croatia lags significantly behind the EU and GEM average and is also one of the reasons for the non-competitiveness of Croatian enterprises on the EU-28 and international market. Among the business environment factors given, the lowest assessment is access to funds. Though the ability to get bank loans is adequate, other

Table 1 Average assessment of the business environment in Croatian and the EU average for 2015

Elements of the business environment	Croatia	EU average
Access to funds	2.0	2.7
State policies—priorities and support	1.8	2.5
State policies—promptness and ease of working in a regulatory framework	1.4	2.4
State programmes	2.0	2.7
Basic and mid-level education	1.3	2.1
Tertiary education	2.1	2.7
Transfer of research and development	1.8	2.5
Commercial and professional infrastructure	2.6	3.1
Market openness—speed of change	3.6	2.9
Market openness—barriers to entry	1.8	2.7
Access to physical infrastructure	3.8	3.8
Cultural and social norms	1.6	2.6

Sources: Singer S, Šarlija N, Pfeifer S, Oberman Peterka S (2016) What makes Croatia a (non) entrepreneurial country? GEM Croatia 2012–2015, SMEs and Entrepreneurship Policy Center, Zagreb. http://www.cepor.hr/izvjesce-o-malim-i-srednjim-poduzecima-u-hrvatskoj-2015/. Accessed 05 July 2016

forms of funding and products such as venture capital and IPOs are lacking, as well as funds directed to finance enterprises in their phase of intensive growth.

According to the World Bank's report *Doing Business 2016*, Croatia is ranked 40th of a total of 189 countries in the report. However, in categories relating to days required for commencing a business venture, obtaining construction permits, as well as getting loans, Croatia still needs more days and a greater number of permits on average than other countries covered in the research.

The Business Environment and Enterprise Performance Survey (BEEPS) carried out by the World Bank cites that the more important problems of a business environment are efficiency of the legal system, corruption, tax burden, and access to funds. The level of corruption, i.e. the problem of corruption, is also addressed in other research, such as the *Corruption Perceptions Index* carried out by Transparency International. Croatia is ranked 50th out of a total of 167 countries included in the research. The level of corruption in Croatia surpasses the global average. According to the opinions of enterprises that were gathered in the research on *Exposure of the Business Sector to Corruption and Criminal*, corruption is the third most important barrier to doing business and immediately follows high taxes and complex tax regulations. The research results indicate that businesses that have given bribes have done so a total of 8.8 times within a year. In Croatia, bribes are most often given to speed up procedures (in 43.1% of cases), ensuring better treatment (14.1%), and to complete administrative proceedings (12.6%). The main purpose of giving bribes is to gain an advantage over the competition, and the average bribe amounts to 396 €.

The *2015–2016 Report on Global Competitiveness* undertaken by the Global Economic Forum measures the national competitiveness of a country and is defined as a set of institutions, policies, and factors that determine the level of productivity of the business sector and affluence, i.e. the standard of living. Accordingly, the report states that in 2015 Croatia was ranked 77th (of 148 countries included in the report), where the main problems affecting low competitiveness are the costs of agricultural policies, the effects of taxes on investments, burdens imposed by government decisions, effectiveness of the legal framework in resolving disputes, and the legal framework for foreign investment.

The research results indicate a high correlation concerning the main characteristics of the business environment in Croatia: poor government decisions and programmes, high level of corruption, poorly development informal sources of financing, hindered access to funding, ineffective legal framework, high administrative barriers, and a poor focus on entrepreneurial education and transfer of knowledge from research institutions to the business sector. These characteristics create a complex business environment in which doing business becomes difficult, and administrative barriers require more time in obtaining permits and commencing business. Consequently, these barriers, especially experiencing hindered access to funding, legal protection, and level of corruption, are twice as likely to affect SMEs than large enterprises. This kind of business environments means that SMEs will continue to remain *small* longer and their growth and development will be hindered if not at times even prevented (Beck and Demirguc-Kunt 2006). To speed up administrative processes, SME owners tend to use available means when obtaining the necessary permits or seeking loan approvals and where such means have been proven to be effective in previous cases.

4 Networking to Minimise Barriers in the Business Ecosystem

Networks that can be defined as "a group of different organisations, with convergent goals, which share an identity and develop a singular definition of trust and power and pursue repeated exchange relations"[2] are becoming increasingly important to entrepreneurs. Entrepreneurs use networks to gain access to markets, information, technology, and other resources.[3] Other researchers have concluded that entrepreneurs, to some extent, depend on their networks of personal relationships when making decisions and solving problems (Taylor and Thorpe 2004). The networking of SME owners can be defined as "resources individuals obtain from knowing

---

[2]Braga V (2004) Business networking for SMEs as a means to promote regional competitiveness: A Theoretical Framework. 44th Congress of the European Regional Science Association: Regions and Fiscal Federalism, 25–29th August, Porto, Portugal, p 3.

[3]Robinson S (2009) Informal Social Networks of European Small Business Owners. Proceedings of the Academy for Studies in International Business 9(2):20–25.

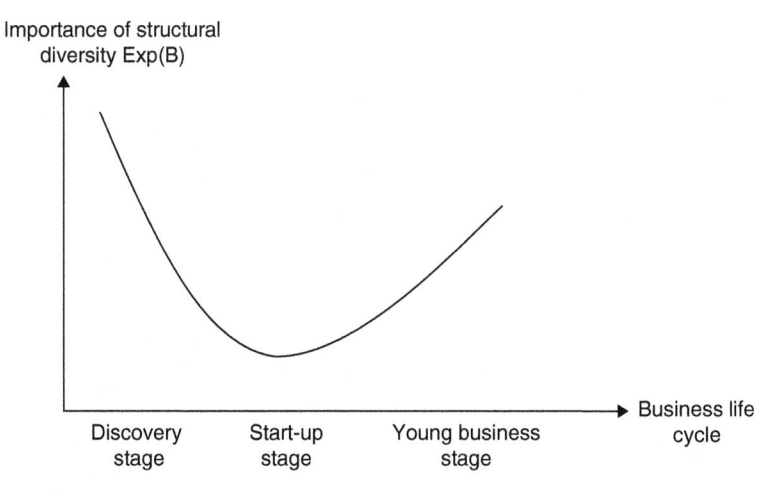

Fig. 3 The changing importance of structural diversity. Source: Klyver K, Hindle K (2007) The Role Of Social Networks At Different Stages Of Business Formation, Small Business Research 15 (1):22–38

others, being part of a network with them, or merely being known to them and having a good reputation."[4] Networks can be a competitive advantage for enterprises (Melé 2009), enhance their chances of survival (Baum et al. 2000), and reduce the lender's expected cost of providing capital (Petersen and Rajan 1994). Small enterprises usually depend on financial intermediaries, particularly commercial banks, which makes asymmetric information a much more expressed problem (Berger and Udell 1995). Commercial banks tend to develop long-term relationships with SME owners in order to minimise such informational problems. More information about an SME and its plans enables a bank to offer better loan conditions and even lower collateral requirements.

However, SME owners are reluctant to share information about their enterprises. According to Uzzi (1999), there are two types of networks that entrepreneurs use for obtaining information. The arm's-length relationship is used to obtain a wider range of resources, viewpoints, and different information, whereas embedded relationships are used for solving specific problems and sharing views and information that are of vital interest for an enterprise, such as choosing a source of external finance. The strength of the network depends mostly on the mutual trust of entrepreneurs and other members of the network.

In their growth phase, SMEs usually require some form of external finance. In such circumstances, SME owners heavily depend on dense networks (embedded relationships), which often includes a high proportion of family members (Klyver and Hindle 2007). The importance of diversity in social networks also changes during the business life cycle and follows the U-shape (Fig. 3).

---

[4]Ibidem, p. 21.

The ability to network seems to be one of the most important entrepreneurial skills as it enables entrepreneurs to "stay in touch with the latest developments, and also gain access to resources that would otherwise be inaccessible, or at least more costly."[5]

Networks and their structural diversity also vary with cultural and national differences. In some cultures, networks have a negative meaning and are often connected with some level of corruption. The typical examples found in the literature are *blat* in Russia and *guanxy* in China. However, in economies that suffer from "various types and levels of corruption and where such corruption may constitute various degrees of institutionalisation and embeddedness in the national culture"[6] it may also have an effect on the behaviour of market stakeholders. To solve such problems promptly, acquire the necessary resources, and gain access to sources of finance, entrepreneurs can utilise their networks to identify individuals or groups, usually with political power, that may "speed up a process" or "grease the wheels". This type of networking was identified by Melé (2009) as networking cronyism, where people with political power use their influence in one or several networks to obtain positions of influence for co-members, something that is contrary to the common good. According to Dobryninas and Zilinskiene (2004), a large majority of Lithuanian SMEs have been victims of bribery, and hardly any of the SMEs have reported it nor appealed for help. Some of the reasons SMEs cited for not reporting such activities were their lack of trust in institutions and they viewed bribery as an expected consequence of doing business and as a way of helping out a business.

The situation is almost the same in all developing countries. Batra et al. (2003) found that in many Central and Eastern European countries, SME owners reported that it was common in their line of business to have to pay some form of irregular, additional payment to get things done. Vorley and Williams (2015) concluded that "many Bulgarian entrepreneurs relied on "self-help" to navigate through an uncertain institutional environment", while in Romania the key challenge for entrepreneurs is with small-scale bribery.[7] Both countries are, according to *The Corruption Perceptions Index*,[8] ranked among the most corrupt countries in Europe. But, according to Franičević and Bartlett (2001), "Eastern Europe and still less South Eastern Europe should not be treated as a consistent regional bloc", because

---

[5]Robinson S (2009) Informal Social Networks of European Small Business Owners. Proceedings of the Academy for Studies in International Business 9(2):20–25.

[6]Dobryninas A, Zilinskiene L (2004) Map of Corruption in Lithuania: The Residents View, In: Organised Crime, Trafficking, Drugs: Selected papers presented at the Annual Conference on the European Society of Criminology, Helsinki, 2003. http://heuni.fi/material/attachments/heuni/reports/6KkbNhFWZ/First_part_42.pdf#page=43. Accessed 20 July 2016.

[7]Vorley T, Williams N (2015) Between petty corruption and criminal extortion: How entrepreneurs in Bulgaria and Romania operate within a devil/s circle. International Small Business Journal 34(6): p. 802.

[8]Transparency International (2014) Corruption Perceptions Indeks 2013. Berlin. Transparency International.

characteristics of SME sector in these countries suggest different ways for networking.[9] Bartlett (2016) pointed out that "a much more supportive institutional framework in Slovenia" helped in reducing social barriers and therefore secured lower levels of corruption.[10]

According to the report titled *Exposure of the Business Sector to Corruption and Crime*, the greatest instances of bribing public officials by enterprises in Croatia relate to officials working in cadastral offices (6.9%); municipal, city, and county officials (5.9%); and police officials (5.7%).[11] In the opinion of Croatian entrepreneurs, corruption becomes the only way of resolving problems when the government fails to deliver services efficiently. Consequently, businesses that do business mainly on the domestic market are most exposed to corruption and poorly written laws, whereas businesses that export their goods and services are less burdened by such situations.

In a very narrow sense, corruption as network cronyism may be viewed as a lubricator that speeds up things and helps entrepreneurs get on with wealth creation in specific instances (Aidt 2009); however, corruption hinders the development of the SMEs that can assume risks and secure the greatest possible return on invested capital. In other words, corruption leads to pure waste and misallocation of resources (Batra et al. 2003) and represents a significant hindrance for sustainable development.

5 Designing the Research

Research into utilisation of networking by owners of SMEs when deciding on the structure of capital or choosing an external form of financing was conducted on 108 Croatian SMEs. The attitudes, thoughts, and manner of making decisions by SME owners were collected through a questionnaire comprising 39 questions. The sample of enterprises which were the subject of the research was devised using the Business Croatia database containing records on 750,000 Croatian enterprises. For research purposes, only those SME owners that could be contacted via email were selected. The response rate was 28.35%. The gathering of data also included data on the entrepreneurial supporting infrastructure and its networking in order to facilitate approaching each owner and acquire internal financial information necessary for understanding the processes involved in making decisions on capital structures for SMEs (Delić 2012). Given that analysing the financial results was necessary for the research, all SMEs that failed to maintain double-entry bookkeeping were excluded

---

[9]Franičević V, Bartlett W (2001) Small Firm Networking and Economies in Transition: An Overview of Theories, Issues and Policies, International Review of Economics & Business 4(1): 80.

[10]Bartlett W (2016) Barriers to SME growth in Slovenia, MOCT-MOST Economic Policy in Transitional Economics 11(2):186.

[11]UNODC (2013) Business, Corruption and Crime in Croatia: The impact of bribery and other crime on private enterprise. The Institute of Economics Zagreb, Zagreb.

from the sample (craft and trade businesses as well as family agricultural businesses). Collecting secondary data necessary for decision-making, final financial reports (balance sheets and profit and loss statements) in the sample were carried out using the Register of Financial Statements (RGFI). The sample included all business activities with the exclusion of those businesses that had been operating on the market for a period of less than 1 year. In terms of number of employees, the sample comprised 58.3% of enterprises with less than 10 employees, 31.5% of enterprises with less than 50 employees, and 10.2% of enterprises that had up to 250 employees. The observed enterprises that included members of their families in business operations (family members had never worked in only 28.7% of enterprises) on a daily basis accounted for 38% of the enterprises.

The sample of observed enterprises mostly comprised owners 40–50 years of age and accounted for 37.5% of all owners, whereas those younger than 30 years of age accounted for 5.8%. While most have a secondary education (only 7.8% of owners have a tertiary education), only 29.8% regularly attend educational courses on management, whereas 23.1% cited that daily business operations left them no time for additional training. The greatest number of owners in the sample had 10 or more years of experience in managing a business (56.2%) which they declared to be exceptionally important in making decisions on capital structures. At the same time, 97.2% of owners pointed out that financial literacy was essential in making decisions on capital structures in SMEs. SME owners mostly relied on information from their accountants, and only 39.4% personally monitored the finances of their enterprises.

The market in the Republic of Croatia features a high level of barriers that hinder growth and development of enterprises, along with an exceptionally shallow financial market, meaning a very small number of financial products and little access to sources of funding. The greatest barriers that should be mentioned are administrative costs and requirements, ineffective court practices, as well as an ineffective assistance system that should be directed towards encouraging economic development, but also an inadequate level of financial literacy by SME owners. To overcome these mentioned barriers (costs of asymmetric information when applying for loans), SME owners tend to rely more on networking and internal sources of financing (Carlin and Mayer 1998; Rajan and Zingales 2001; Beck 2003).

Based on the characteristics of the business environment and SME owners, the hypothesis is that when making decisions on the structure of capital, SME owners tend to rely on their own network of contacts, and this networking in selecting sources of financing increases an enterprise's level of indebtedness, which in turn enables it to finance its growth and development.

The Pearson correlation coefficient was used to test the stated hypothesis.

6 Results

In financing growth and development of their enterprises, SME owners mostly rely on their own funds, bank loans, and leasing. The funds are most often used to finance fixed assets, settle due liabilities, and credit customers. However, a significant 48.5%

pointed out that the requirements of creditors were too rigorous and that they lacked additional information on available sources of funding (27.5%). The research results correlate with previously identified barriers to the growth of SMEs,[12] where special emphasis should be placed on administrative barriers and access to sources of funding. Entrepreneurs are very reluctant to divulge information on sources of funding as well as their enterprise's financial information. Access to information and trust by entrepreneurs is enjoyed only by a small circle of trusted confidants (friends and family members); hence, it comes as no surprise that the results indicate poor use of information from other persons outside of this circle of trusted persons. The results indicate that SME owners most often rely on advice from their families (28.8% often rely on advice from their families), which correlates with results from previous research. Advice from accountants is utilised by only 39.6% of owners and often by only 14.1% (Delić and Filakov (2016)). Interestingly enough, advice from bankers is used by 29.2% of entrepreneurs, and 8.3% do so on a regular basis which in turn prevents the development of long-term relationships and can reduce costs of providing capital.

Nonetheless, the results indicate, though only for the year 2010, a correlation between enterprises that frequently utilise information as well as advice from politicians at a national and local level and an indebtedness indicator. Specifically, enterprises that had better quality information and data, as well as "recommendations" from politicians, took on additional external loans to finance their enterprise's growth and development (Table 2).

As the economy gradually improves, the frequency of utilising politicians as contacts increases. In 2008 and 2009, the Republic of Croatia went through a recessionary period with a large proportion of bad loans in commercial banks and investments which were almost entirely extinguished. With the growth of GDP, the number of applications for external sources of funding also increased, and so too the "services" of politicians at the local and national level. Given that entrepreneurs exhibit a lack of trust in government officials and public institutions, entrepreneurs do not utilise advice from institutions created for the purpose of providing incentives for entrepreneurship when making decisions on selecting external sources of funding. Due to poorly organised and moreover inaccessible offers from business advisors and consultants to entrepreneurs, the correlation between the frequency of utilising their advice and the level of an enterprise's indebtedness has not been proven.

---

[12]Identified by Global Entrepreneurship Monitor Report (GEM), World Bank's report Doing Buiness and survey on Business Environment and Enterprise Performace (BEEPS).

Table 2 Results for correlation between frequency of using advice and leverage

Frequency of using personal contacts	Indebtedness indicator for the year 2008	Indebtedness indicator for the year 2009	Indebtedness indicator for the year 2010
Friends	$r = 0.013$	$r = 0.122$	$r = 0.157$
	$p = 0.901$	$p = 0.248$	$p = 0.143$
Other entrepreneurs	$r = 0.002$	$r = -0.056$	$r = -0.097$
	$p = 0.983$	$p = 0.589$	$p = 0.361$
Large clients and suppliers	$r = -0.001$	$r = 0.000$	$r = 0.001$
	$p = 0.995$	$p = 0.999$	$p = 0.990$
Consultants	$r = -0.088$	$r = 0.019$	$r = 0.025$
	$p = 0.415$	$p = 0.859$	$p = 0.816$
Accountants	$r = -0.054$	$r = 0.071$	$r = 0.119$
	$p = 0.620$	$p = 0.503$	$p = 0.269$
Bankers	$r = 0.156$	$r = 0.132$	$r = 0.153$
	$p = 0.158$	$p = 0.223$	$p = 0.165$
Politicians at the national and local level	$r = -0.003$	$r = 0.186$	$r = 0.237$
	$p = 0.978$	$p = 0.077$	$p = 0.026$
Support institutions	$r = -0.101$	$r = 0.083$	$r = 0.040$
	$p = 0.348$	$p = 0.430$	$p = 0.707$

Source: Analysis of data from conducted research

7 Conclusion and Recommendations for Further Research

Networking is one of the most important skills of an entrepreneur, regardless of an enterprise's life-cycle phase. Networking provides access to information, ideas, opinions, and also resources—raw materials, finances, and this consequently has an effect on an enterprise's competitiveness. Long-term relationships with commercial banks reduce costs associated with asymmetrical information, and this in turn makes it easier to obtain the necessary funds for growing and developing an enterprise. In their network of contacts, entrepreneurs most often rely on advice from family members. However, the actual network of contacts, its density, and the frequency of utilising advice from particular members of the network are very much linked to the cultural and national factors of particular economies. In some economies, networking has a negative tone, whereas in other cultures it is an unavoidable part of any enterprise's business operations. Markets and economies that are characterised by high barriers for starting a business prevent the sustainable growth and development of an enterprise, as well as its competitiveness. On such markets, a deviant form of networking often prevails, i.e. network cronyism, which is characterised by networking with persons who have political power and privileged information. Though this form of networking in the literature is considered a way of speeding up processes, it nonetheless is a form of corruption. This type of networking will prevent sustainable growth of enterprises as well as their competitiveness.

The consequence of this type of networking is the wasting of resources, and SMEs that remain in this phase fail to grow. Research undertaken for the purpose of this chapter has endeavoured to ascertain the degree to which a network of contacts can assist in overcoming the largest and most frequent barriers, i.e. access to sources of funding, and which contacts may assist SME owners the most in obtaining external sources of funding. Though SME owners covered by this research mostly utilised advice from family members, the results indicate that networking with politicians at the local and national level has the greatest impact on financial leverage and capital structure. Entrepreneurial infrastructure, into which Croatia has been investing a lot, and advice from business advisors and consultants, has not been viewed as important in making decisions on capital structure. Therefore, the emphasis of future research should focus on identifying the needs of entrepreneurs based on the entrepreneurial infrastructure and strengthening the capacity of public officials in such institutions. Insomuch as such institutions fail to contribute to growth of the SME sector, neither do they contribute in any way to growth of the national economy and sustainable development. Though corruption does resolve problems quicker, it nonetheless cannot ensure long-term and sustainable growth of enterprises.

References

Aidt, T. S. (2009). Corruption, institutions, and economic development. *Oxford Review of Economic Policy, 25*(2), 271–291.

Alpeza, M., Mikrut, M., Oberman Peterka, S., & Delić, A. (2014). *Croatia consultancy market study* (p. 81). European Bank for Reconstruction and Development. Accessed July 12, 2016, from http://www.cepor.hr/wp-content/uploads/2015/07/EN-Croatia-Consultancy-Market-Study.pdf

Bartlett, W. (2016). Barriers to SME growth in Slovenia. *MOCT-MOST Economic Policy in Transitional Economics, 11*(2), 177–195.

Batra, G., Kaufmann, D., & Stone, A. H. W. (2003). *The firms speak: What the world business environment survey tells us about constraints on private sector development*. World Bank.

Baum, A. C., Calabrese, T., & Silverman, S. (2000). Don't go it alone: Alliance network composition and startups' performance in Canadian biotechnology. *Strategic Management Journal, 21*(3), 267–294.

Beck, T. (2003). Financial dependence and international trade. *Review of International Economics, 11*(2), 296–316.

Beck, T., & Demirguc-Kunt, A. (2006). Small and medium-sized enterprises: Access to finance as a growth constraint. *Journal of Banking and Finance, 30*, 2931–2943.

Berger, A. N., & Udell, G. F. (1995). Relationship lending and lines of credit in small firm finance. *Journal of Business, 68*(3), 351–382.

Birch, D. G. W. (1979). *The job generation process*. MIT Program on Neighbourhood and Regional Change (32).

Braga, V. (2004). Business networking for SMEs as a means to promote regional competitiveness: A theoretical framework. In *44th Congress of the European Regional Science Association: Regions and Fiscal Federalism* (p. 3), 25–29th August, Porto.

Carlin, W., & Mayer, C. (1998). *Finance, investment and growth* (Working Paper). University College London, Accessed July 20, 2016, from http://www.ucl.ac.uk/~uctpa36/carlin%20mayer%20journal%20of%20financial%20economics.pdf

Delić, A. (2012). *Capital structure determinants in SMEs on underdeveloped financial market of the Republic Croatia*. Doctoral dissertation, Faculty of Economics in Osijek, Osijek.

Delić, A., & Filakov, L. (2016). Why not to use the service of business advisers? In: *Some evidence from Croatia, Proceedings from the 5th International Scientific Symposium Economy of Eastern Croatia-Vision and Growth* (pp. 891–900). Osijek: Faculty of Economics in Osijek.

Dobryninas, A., & Zilinskiene, L. (2004). Map of corruption in Lithuania: The residents view. In *Organised Crime, trafficking, drugs: Selected papers presented at the Annual Conference on the European Society of Criminology*, Helsinki, 2003. Accessed July 20, 2016, from http://heuni.fi/material/attachments/heuni/reports/6KkbNhFWZ/First_part_42.pdf#page=43

European Commission. (2014). *A partial and fragile recovery*. Annual Report on European SMEs 2013/2014, Final Report, July 2014.

Franičević, V., & Bartlett, W. (2001). Small firm networking and economies in transition: An overview of theories, issues and policies. *International Review of Economics & Business, 4*(1), 63–89.

Kelley, D., Singer, S., & Herrington, M. (2016). Global entrepreneurship monitor: 2015/2016 global report (p. 69). Babson College. Accessed July 12, 2016, from http://gemconsortium.org/report/49480

Klyver, K., & Hindle, K. (2007). The role of social networks at different stages of business formation. *Small Business Research, 15*(1), 22–38.

Melé, D. (2009). The practice of networking: An ethical approach. *Journal of Business Ethics, 90*, 487–503.

National Competitiveness Council. (2016). Presentation of results of the Global Competitiveness Report 2015–2016 for Croatia. Accessed July 13, 2016, from http://www.konkurentnost.hr/lgs.axd?t=16&id=550

Petersen, M. A., & Rajan, R. G. (1994). The benefits of lending relationships: Evidence from small business Dana. *The Journal of Finance, 49*(1), 3–37.

Rajan, R. G., & Zingales, L. (2001). Financial systems, industrial structure and growth. *Oxford Review of Economic Policy, 17*(4), 467–482.

Robinson, S. (2009). Informal social networks of European small business owners. *Proceedings of the Academy for Studies in International Business, 9*(2), 20–25.

Singer, S., Šarlija, N., Pfeifer, S., & Oberman Peterka, S. (2016). *What makes Croatia a (non) entrepreneurial country? GEM Croatia 2012–2015*. Zagreb: SMEs and Entrepreneurship Policy Center. Accessed July 05, 2016, from http://www.cepor.hr/izvjesce-o-malim-i-srednjim-poduzecima-u-hrvatskoj-2015/

Taylor, D. W., & Thorpe, R. (2004). Entrepreneurial learning: A process of co-participation. *Journal of Small Business and Enterprise Development, 11*(2), 203–211.

The Croatian SME. Observatory Report 2012., https://poduzetnistvo.gov.hr/UserDocsImages/EU%20projekti/IPA%20IIIC/Pobolj%C5%A1anje%20administrativne%20u%C4%8Dinkovitosti%20na%20nacionalnoj%20razini/Izvjestaj%20opservatorija-2012.pdf

The World Bank Group. (2016). Doing Business 2016: Measuring Regulatory Quality and Efficiency, International bank for Reconstruction and Development and The World Bank, USA. Accessed June 04, 2017, from http://www.doingbusiness.org/~/media/WBG/DoingBusiness/Documents/Annual-Reports/English/DB16-Full-Report.pdf

Transparency International. (2014). *Corruption perceptions index 2013*. Berlin: Transparency International.

UNODC. (2013). *Business, Corruption and Crime in Croatia: The impact of bribery and other crime on private enterprise*. Zagreb: The Institute of Economics Zagreb.

Uzzi, B. (1999). Embeddedness in the making of financial capital: How social relations and networks benefit firms seeking financing? *American Sociological Review, 64*, 481–505.

Vorley, T., & Williams, N. (2015). Between petty corruption and criminal extortion: How entrepreneurs in Bulgaria and Romania operate within a devil/s circle. *International Small Business Journal, 34*(6), 797–817.

The Effect of EU Membership on Public Procurement for SMEs in Post-Transition Countries

Sunčana Slijepčević, Jelena Budak, and Edo Rajh

1 Introduction

The size of public procurement markets worldwide is impressive. For developed economies, the ratio of government procurement markets to GDP is about 15–20% of GDP (OECD 2012), and in the European Union (EU) countries the share of public procurement is estimated to range between 10 and 25% (European Commission 2015). The government procurement markets in post-transition countries make a significant share of national economy, and seemingly its importance rises in the times of economic crisis. Previous research on public procurement and involvement of small and medium enterprises (SMEs) noted severe obstacles for companies to access public procurement markets, and the set of policies were established in the EU to promote SMEs' involvement in public procurement (European Commission 2010b). Here, most of the research is focused on the government procurers, i.e. the demand side of public procurement markets and its (in)efficiencies. The shift to the supply side makes the new stream of research in developed countries, yet comprehensive assessment of this process in transition economies is missing.

Public procurement in the post-transition context is rather underexplored. Most of available literature considers public procurement in the context of corruption (Grødeland and Aasland 2011 for post-communist states; Ateljević and Budak 2010 for Croatia; Pashev 2011 and Yalamov 2012 for Bulgaria; Ochrana and Pavel 2013 and Palguta 2015 for Czech Republic, and for other national studies see OECD 2005). Comparative studies as well as studies focused on the effects of EU-membership on public procurement are missing. Trybus (2006) described the legal effects of EU enlargement to the public procurement to the post-communist countries of Central and Eastern Europe; hence, at the time when his study was

---

S. Slijepčević · J. Budak (✉) · E. Rajh
Institute of Economics, Zagreb, Zagreb, Croatia
e-mail: jbudak@eizg.hr

made, only the 2004 wave of the EU enlargement was completed, and it was too early to evaluate any effects besides stating that accession required legal harmonization. However, he concludes that "there is reason to believe that the efficiency of the public procurement countries of the accession countries in Central, Eastern, and South Eastern Europe will have considerably improved after the enlargement process has been completed". (Trybus 2006, p. 425).

Besides legal aspects, other topics in public procurement call for attention such as strengthening the role of SMEs in the European economy (Loader 2013). The role of SMEs is particularly important in post-transition economies since over 90% of public procurement suppliers in post-transition economies are SMEs. Thus, this chapter aims to fulfil the gap in the literature by investigating the accession policy impact on the role of SMEs in post-transition countries. Based on the experience of companies in two post-transition countries, Croatia and Bosnia and Herzegovina (BiH), it analyses the role of the EU in public procurement generally and specifically the effect of EU membership on public procurement for SMEs. Furthermore, here it is explored if national policies are in line with EU standards of public procurement. Are there differences observed between two countries that might stem from the different EU membership status? This study contributes to the debate on the effects of the EU membership on public procurement to the SMEs in post-transition as a unique context. This comparative assessment fills the gap in the scarcity of parallel studies in public procurement noted in the literature by Preuss (2009).

In order to give plausible answers to these research questions, the empirical evidence collected by the surveying companies in BiH in 2014 and comparable data on Croatian companies surveyed in 2013 are used. The choice of these two countries in the region for a comparative assessment of SMEs in the public procurement was not done by incident. Historically, both Croatia and BiH are former republics of ex-Yugoslavia, which might have shaped the perceptions and attitudes of business people in the region. Two observed countries had similar problems in getting close to European standards where Croatia had successfully finished the EU accession process. Compliance with the EU acquis in the case of Croatia accession to the EU was in terms of legal framework relatively easy to achieve. The negotiation chapter 5: Public procurement was opened in December 2008 and closed in June 2010 and was considered one of the less complicated negotiation chapters Croatia closed in the long period of accession to the EU. The process took some time because Croatia had to prove the smooth implementation of the law.

The starting point of this assessment is narrative description of opinions collected in two country surveys. It compares specifically the opinion of managers and business people representing companies of the small and medium size on the competition and entry barriers. They were asked about the range and intensity of obstacles to participate at public procurement tenders, availability of resource, corruption risks, transparency and fairness of procedure, clarity of documentation, principles and standards achieved, price and other dimensions. The findings are put in the context of public procurement for SMEs in post-transition era, and the impact of EU membership on the public procurement for SMEs is discussed.

2 Literature Review

The chapter builds on existing EU studies and on preliminary research conducted for Croatia (Budak and Rajh 2014) that provided insights into the functionality of the system from the business sector perspective. Its findings have revealed new issues in the public procurement system in Croatia, a post-transition country and a new EU member state. Real experience, attitudes and practices of Croatian companies involved in public tenders showed to be encouraging, in particular regarding professional capacity and integrity of procurers and low level of informal payments and corruption risk in the process of public tenders. These topics were worth exploring further, especially in comparison to other similar countries. However, the most intriguing finding for Croatia was that the low participation of SMEs in the public procurement market is not an issue. Therefore, Slijepčević et al. (2015) in the first version of this research focused on the competitiveness at the national public procurement markets in Croatia and BiH. Here, the analysis is extended in order to examine other aspects of public procurement for SMEs and if the differences stand between similar but somewhat different post-transition economies.

Over 99% of the total number of enterprises in the EU is SMEs (Table 1). These enterprises create 67% of jobs and deliver 58% of the gross value added generated by private economy in the EU (European Commission 2014b), which clearly indicates the substantial economic role of SMEs.[1] Nevertheless, the number of authors claim that SMEs' participation in public procurement is very weak (Loader 2013; Vincze et al. 2010). Data revealing the actual involvement of SMEs in public procurement are quite limited, and no comparative and reliable evidence on SMEs in Croatia and BiH participating in public procurement is available. For illustration, European

Table 1 Number of enterprises by size in the EU-28, Croatia and BiH

Size	Number of enterprises			Share of SMEs in total number of enterprises, in %		
	EU-28	Croatia	BiH	EU-28	Croatia	BiH
Micro	19,969,338	134,091	24,512	92.4	91.7	75.1
Small	1,378,374	10,091	5841	6.4	6.9	17.9
Medium	223,648	1722	1981	1.0	1.2	6.1
SMEs	21,571,360	145,904	32,334	99.8	99.7	99.1
Large	43,517	388	300	0.2	0.3	0.9
Total	21,614,877	146,292	32,634	100.0	100.0	100.0

Note: Data for EU-28 and Croatia are for 2013–2014 based on Eurostat, and data for BiH are for 2014 based on national statistics
Source: For EU-28 and Croatia, Muller et al. (2014); for BiH Central Bureau of Statistics, http://www.bhas.ba/saopstenja/2014/SPR_2014_001_01-bh.pdf

---

[1] See, for example, Alpeza et al. (2015) report on Croatian SME sector or Vanjskopoliticka inicijativa BH 2013 report on small businesses in BiH.

Commission (2010b) data show that on average in EU-27, SMEs secured 38% of the value of public contracts and 61% of the number of successful bidders.[2]

The position of SMEs at the public procurement market in post-transition countries is not clear-cut. Scattered national studies suggest there are discouraging barriers for SMEs to access public contracts (see, for example, Mitran (2013) for Romania or Yakovlev and Demidova (2012) for Russia). New EU member states and ex-transition countries seem to stand worse when compared to old EU member states in terms of SMEs' participation at public procurement market. On the other hand, Vincze et al.'s (2010) evaluation of SMEs' access to public procurement market in different EU countries showed that SMEs have a stronger position in public procurement in smaller countries.

In this context, SMEs and public procurement in Croatia and BiH could be influenced by the recent economic crisis as well. The two observed countries went through a slow post-war recovery and were severely hit by the 2008 crisis that plunged national economies into the prolonged economic recession. In times of crisis, some scholars and practitioners advise public investment to boost recovery. In Croatia and BiH government, money and public sector are main generators of economic activity which consequently makes public procurement market even more appealing for SMEs; however, crisis might squeeze available resources of SMEs to compete. Although studies have suggested that SMEs were more resistant to the impact of the crisis compared to large enterprises, they also stress that they are recovering more slowly (European Commission 2014b) thus affecting the competition at the public procurement market where SMEs often act as subcontractors.

Contemporary public procurement practices incorporate three, often competitive strands of public procurement: commercial, regulatory and social strand (Erridge and McIlroy 2016), and policymakers seek to find the optimal combination between them. EU policies regarding SMEs and public procurement allow social consideration in contracting if such decisions comply with fundamental single market principles and freedoms (Kidalov 2011). Studies of scholarly research and practitioners showed a strong, two-way relation between public procurement and competition. The lack of free and fair competition among private and public agents both at the supply and demand side seriously threatens the level of competitiveness at public procurement market. Undesired level of competition could be the result of regulatory framework for public procurement, market characteristics, collusive behaviour of bidders or other factors (UNCTAD 2012). Free and fair competition might be limited by a set of factors, such as discriminatory regulations, preferential treatment in designing tender documentations and/or procedures applied and all kinds of entry barriers. One obstacle for fair competition frequently observed in post-transition countries is corruption (Ateljević and Budak 2010; Grødeland and Aasland 2011). In a wider context, it refers as well to the conflict of interest, cartel deals, trading

---

[2]Available data concern only successful bidders, but there is no data on actual attempts of SMEs to participate in public procurement process (both successfully and unsuccessfully).

information and other irregularities in tender and contracting procedures (OECD 2012). Safeguarding and enhancing competitiveness by opening public procurement markets to all potential participants (along with applying money for value criterion) contributes to rational usage of resources and increases efficiency of the public sector as a whole.

The literature observes factors influencing SMEs' access to participate in the public procurement tenders from a different perspective, but several factors influencing the level of their participation are commonly recognized. The large size of the contract is recognized to stand as the most important obstacle for SMEs to access the public procurement market (European Commission 2014a; OECD, European Commission, and ETF 2014; Loader 2005). SMEs are less involved in above-threshold contracts. Second, the share of contracts awarded to SMEs depends on the type of procurer and is larger in tenders of local authorities (Vincze et al. 2010; European Commission 2014a). Third factor is tender procedure which has an impact on SMEs' access to public contracts. SMEs' participation is larger in open procedure or restricted procedure than in negotiated procedure (European Commission 2014a). Furthermore, lack of time and financial and human resources are shown to be significant barriers for SMEs (Loader 2013).

Studies on the success of companies in public tenders found the company size to be the relevant factor. In the public procurement processes, medium-sized companies have proven to be more successful that micro-sized companies (European Commission 2010b). On average, SMEs in the EU have been performing well considering they secured 58% of public contracts in the period between 2006 and 2008. However, since the term includes various types of enterprises, it is necessary to analyse each type separately. Medium-sized enterprises performed well, making up between 15 and 19% of public procurement suppliers. Also, there are almost no differences between medium and large companies when it comes to securing public procurement contracts. On the other hand, small and micro-enterprises are lagging behind making up 10% and 5% of public procurement contracts, respectively (Vincze et al. 2010).

Public procurement is seen as an important mechanism to boost national economic activity. The share of public procurement in GDP was 12% in 2013 in Croatia (Directorate for the Public Procurement System 2014) and 13% in BiH in 2012 (Balkan Tender Watch 2015). Therefore, policymakers worldwide use public procurement to conduct economic policy measures, and the EU takes the lead in common market public procurement regulations and policies. For this purpose, EU standards and principles of public procurement have been agreed whereas special attention has been devoted to the inclusion of small and medium-sized companies. EU regulatory framework defines national public procurement regulations and delineates behaviour of agents in the EU member states or acceding countries. It means that EU directives apply in Croatia as a new EU member state and impose rules for the future development of public procurement system in BiH.

The importance of public procurement is recognized in EU strategic documents such as Europe 2020 Strategy for smart, sustainable and inclusive growth, and EU legislative acts that explicitly say that public procurement is one of the instruments based on market principles, used to achieve smart, sustainable and inclusive growth that enables the most efficient usage of public resources (European Commission 2010a). Considering the performance of SMEs,[3] and referring to the EU's best practice codex to facilitate SMEs' access to public procurement contracts (European Commission 2008), the EU upgraded the existing regulations in order to enable these enterprises to integrate more easily into the public procurement market. In the course of 2014, the new EU legislation relevant to public procurement has been adopted[4] (for review of the previous EU public procurement regulation, see Bovis 2012). The main goal of the new legislation is to improve competitiveness and reduce discrimination practices in general. The new framework will support the already ongoing initiatives like JEREMIE—Joint European Resources for Micro to Medium Enterprises that aim to improve the overall position of small and micro-companies.

Prior to the implementation of the new directives, awarding of contracts was regulated by the Directive 2004/18/EZ. Ramsey (2006) argues that EU public procurement directives failed to open up public contracts to competition and therefore did not enhance efficiency and market liberalization as expected. There are a lot of legal insecurities and entry barriers due to the lack of clear rules for awarding contracts. Such a legal environment elicits a lot of missed opportunities for SMEs. Since the rules in the old directive were open to interpretation, developing a new framework was necessary to raise the efficacy of public procurement. This has been achieved by replacing the old framework with the Directive 2014/24/EU.

Some of the problems regarding SMEs and public procurement calling for immediate actions were previously noted in the academic literature. Carpineti et al. (2006) opted for facilitating entry of SMEs to public procurement market by splitting contracts into lots. Equally, in its new directive, the European Commission recommends that public procurers split large contracts into several smaller lots thus enabling SMEs to take a part of the public procurement market pie. Splitting public procurement is expected to keep market competition alive and to lower entry barriers to SMEs. Special instructions on how to implement these recommendations are given in order to maintain fairness and non-discriminatory principles of public procurement.[5]

---

[3]Micro-enterprises are defined as enterprises that employ fewer than 10 persons and whose annual turnover or annual balance sheet total does not exceed 2 million euros; small enterprises are defined as enterprises that employ fewer than 50 persons and whose annual turnover or annual balance sheet total does not exceed 10 million euros; medium-sized enterprises are defined as enterprises that employ fewer than 250 persons and whose annual turnover or annual balance sheet total does not exceed 50 million euros. Large enterprises are above these thresholds. Commission Recommendation 2003/361/EC, http://ec.europa.eu/growth/smes/business-friendly-environment/sme-definition/index_en.htm

[4]Directive 2014/23/EU for concessions, Directive 2014/24/EU for public procurement in general, and Directive 2014/25/EU for public procurement in the water, energy, transportation sectors.

[5]For EU public procurement principles, see more in Aviani (2007).

One of the existing barriers for SMEs' participation in public procurement are complex requirements for SMEs to fulfil, disproportionate to their economic and financial capacities. The new directive, therefore, envisages three basic criteria in terms of professional, economic and financial and technical capacities that have to be proportional to the volume of the public contract. Although there are no unified practices on contract size reduction across EU countries (Kidalov 2011), the new EU directives recommend dividing contracts into smaller lots in order to make contracts suitable to business capabilities of SMEs.

Furthermore, in the EU, there is a tendency to collaborate with large enterprises in order to utilize the economies of scale. For that reason, it is necessary to monitor the centralization of public procurement purchases which in turn will ensure that SMEs have a representative share in securing public contracts.

Additional entry barriers in the EU are an administrative burden in public procurement procedures, in terms of mandatory submission of numerous documents, validation forms, certificates and licenses. The new unique procurement documentation system of the EU (e-Certis) would make the procedure simpler both for procurers and for suppliers.

Substantial changes in the Directive 2014/24/EU make subcontracting easier and more transparent, and the subcontracted payment could be effectuated directly from the procurer. This ensures a timely pay for SMEs engaged as subcontractors, and it lowers their operational costs and risk.

Technical specifications should not stand as unjustified barriers for market competition, and public procurers should use all available instruments to enhance competition at their tenders. The novelty in the Directive is the new definition of the awarding criteria that favour the best offer in economic terms instead of (widespread and easier to manage) lowest-price criterion.

Enhancing the competitiveness of SMEs which are participating at public procurement markets by, e.g. eliminating entry barriers, stands as a primary EU policy goal. The obstacles and policy responses that apply in that domain in two post-transition sample countries, Croatia and BiH, are assessed in the following analysis.

3 Methodology and Data

The empirical analysis is performed on the survey data of Croatian and BiH companies. The Croatian part of the study uses data on Croatian companies collected in a specially designed cross-sectional survey conducted in April 2013. The target population includes active businesses of all sizes. The stratified sampling procedure is applied with company size, region and business sector as control variables. There were three categories for company size (small, medium, large), six categories for region (Zagreb region, Northwest Croatia, Central and Mountainous Croatia, Slavonia, Dalmatia, Istria and Croatian Littoral) and 15 categories for business sector according to the NACE Rev. 2 classification, where sectors omitted from the sample were sectors considered not participating in public tenders. The total net sample size is 300 Croatian companies, where the share of SMEs is 90%. The stratified sampling procedure was combined with the quota sampling, with the additional control variable of participation/non-participation in public procurement tenders. Namely, the sampling was conducted by randomly selecting 200 companies and then filling the rest of the sample with 100 companies that had participated in public procurement tenders. The survey was administrated through telephone interviews (for details on Croatian survey, see Budak and Rajh 2014).

In BiH, two surveys have been conducted among the representatives of the business sector. The first large telephone survey in 2014 was conducted at the net sample of 2500 companies of all sizes and operating in all economic sectors over the entire BiH territory. The purpose of this survey was to identify the sample of companies with public procurement experience, i.e. the share of companies which have participated in public tenders in total business population. The subsample of 511 companies with public procurement experience was surveyed in detail by face-to-face interviews conducted in spring 2014 (for details on BiH survey, see Voloder 2015b). The data of both surveys conducted in BiH are used in different phases of the analysis.

In the first phase, preliminary findings of large surveys on the entire population in Croatia and BiH have been qualitatively assessed and compared (results presented in Table 3). The core analysis performed in the second phase refers to SMEs only. For that purpose, only SMEs in terms of number of employees were extracted in the survey databases: for BiH the data from face-to-face interviews with managers from companies with up to 249 employees were used, and for Croatia, large companies were removed from the survey database as well. In that way, of the original large survey databases, only small and medium enterprises in both countries were extracted to perform the detailed analysis, totalling 725 companies. The large sample of SMEs surveyed assures the reliability of the analysis. Summary statistics on sampled SMEs is presented in Table 2.

When it comes to the questionnaire items used in the analysis, all questions and answers from both national surveys were first explored and described (results presented in Table 3). For the next phase of the detailed analysis, eight questions that tackle different public procurement issues were selected from larger questionnaires. Questions were selected based on their content and their availability in both-country

Table 2 Sample characteristics, $n = 725$

Characteristics	%
Size (number of employees)	
Micro (1–9)	34.0
Small (10–49)	44.2
Medium (50–249)	21.8
Country	
Bosnia and Herzegovina	65.2
Croatia	34.8

Table 3 Survey results: a comparison between BiH and Croatia—summary

Comparison	BiH	Croatia
Questionnaire objective: subject of research	Candidate selection criteria, scoring of offers. Technical specifications, procedure types, tender documentation price, legal protection of suppliers, contract implementation, corruption perception, trust in public procurement system: three stages of procurement: pretender, tender, post-tender—contract implementation	Attitudes and experiences of business sector—suppliers about public procurement procedures, regulations, compliance with main principles of public procurement, achieved European standards and corruption risk levels in public procurement
Respondents	2500 companies general sample, 511 companies participating in public procurement	300 companies
Tender	Contracting authority sets up tender conditions in agreement with interest groups and/or with preferential suppliers	Restricted internal human and material resources of companies available for tender participation
• Information	Prompt and available	Prompt and available. Tender deadlines too short for 10% of respondents
• Qualification criteria	Subjectively appointed, often ambiguously defined and subject to different interpretations; restrictive	Clear and non-discriminatory. Companies prefer to be involved in public procurement as direct contractors
• Technical specifications	Clear, but restrictive	Clear and well prepared
• Procedure	Splitting of procurement into smaller amounts is a common occurrence, although forbidden by law. Urgency and other (un)justifiable reasons are too often misused to account for the choice of competitive dialog procedure instead of open procedure	Transparent
Supplier selection	Ambiguous assessment criteria. Prohibited deals among suppliers. Conflict of interest among participants in public procurement. However, half of the participants state that the most favourable offer is being chosen in a fair manner	Deals among suppliers present in subcontracting: subcontractors arrange collaborations with the main supplier in advance
Post-tender stage	Subsequent changes in contract conditions are a common occurrence More than half of all contracts are subject to supervision and revision	Contractors are least satisfied with the achieved price, but are very satisfied with contract deadlines
Appeals procedure	Appeals are resolved promptly, transparently and fairly. Distrust in legal system in BiH stated as main reason among those unsatisfied participants who did not appeal	A share of unsatisfied did not appeal so as to not spend additional resources on procedures, and a part of them do not believe appealing would change anything

(continued)

Table 3 (continued)

Comparison	BiH	Croatia
Costs	Generally, costs ordained by law are reduced	Public procurement increases business costs for contractors
• Participation in tender	Purchase of tender documentation and submitting proof not regarded as excessive expense by half of participants	–
• Appeals	Fee amount for initiation of appeal procedure not among the main reasons why companies do not appeal tender outcomes	Companies do not appeal tender outcomes because they do not want to spend additional resources
Corruption	Perception of corruption in public procurement is very high, 88% of respondents. Twenty percent of companies encounter corruption in public procurement. Half of respondents believe they were not awarded a contract because of corruption	High corruption perception in public procurement not confirmed by questionnaire (11% of respondents believe informal payments to be necessary to receive a contract). Only 1% of respondents believe not to have been awarded a contract because of corruption
Trust in the system	Fifty-eight percent of companies do not trust the system	Ten percent of respondents demonstrate distrust in public procurement

questionnaires.[6] Initial data format for all questions were recoded in order to prepare them for comparative analysis. Chi-square tests were employed to test differences between BiH and Croatia.

4 Results

Two national public procurement systems were assessed from the point of view of participants who provided authentic insiders' evidence on the characteristics of their system. Although two country surveys that are not identically matching and therefore not directly comparable were considered, qualitative narrative analysis of the main features of the two countries' public procurement systems was employed. It helped to identify main issues in both of them regarding the competition and entry barriers. Comparison was made in seven main areas of public procurement. Along the public procurement process, the issues in tender phase (application criteria for companies to participate and quality of tender information provided, technical specifications and procedures), selection of suppliers in terms of awarding criteria applied and suppliers' deals and post-tender stage referring to contracting practice were examined. Special sections refer to appeals and cost assessment. Corruption

---

[6]Questionnaires are available upon request.

risk and perceived trust in the public procurement system were compared as well. Summary of results is presented in Table 3.

In both countries, companies evaluate tender information as prompt and available and technical specifications as clear (although in BiH somewhat restrictive). The main variations in responses appear in tender qualification criteria applied (in Croatia they are considered clear and non-discriminatory, in BiH ambiguously defined and subjective) and procedures (considered transparent in Croatia and frequently misused in BiH). The major differences are noted in corruption and trust in the system. In BiH, perceptions of corruption in public procurement is very high and significantly more observed when compared to Croatia. In BiH, over half of the respondents expressed their distrust in the system, and in Croatia that was the case of one in ten respondents. Although companies in both countries observed making deals in the supplier selection process, it seems at the first sight that EU principles of fair and non-discriminatory procurement are better applied in Croatia than in BiH.

In Croatia, the situation seems to be different from the point of view of principal supplier and his subcontractors. Of Croatian companies that had experience in public procurement, more than one-third participated as a subcontractor. This indicates opening up to SMEs is already taking place in Croatia. Main entry barriers identified for Croatian companies in general were the lack of capacities and resources. One part of companies surveyed had no business interest to participate and some were reluctant to participate because of their distrust in the system, corruption, informal payments and other unfair deals in (sub)contracting. It is interesting to note that companies in Croatia evaluated the public procurement procedures better than one would expect and much better than companies in BiH.

Croatian respondents mainly do not agree that informal payments are necessary to get the public contract and find the system well designed and pretty effective in seizing the ever-existing corruption risk. The strengths of the Croatian system are seen in high transparency, well-prepared and clear tender documentation, and procurement is well managed by competent staff. Croatian companies see public procurement practices in other EU countries and at the EU level as better and consequently have high expectations that EU standards become fully implemented in Croatia as well. At the time of the survey, it was early for respondents to estimate the benefit of the EU membership since Croatia has been the new EU member state since July 1, 2013. The empirical analysis of the system at first sight indicated that SMEs in Croatia participate to a significant extent in the national public procurement market and that the development of SME sector is viable through public investment.

The main entry barriers to enhance competition at the public procurement market and to build the competitiveness of SMEs to participate at tenders are limited human and other resources of the companies, in particular considering direct contracting for large business deals. The entry barriers and problems for BiH are different. First of all, the EU public procurement standards and best practices are not fulfilled, in particular when it comes to non-discriminatory and fair practices applied to all participants. The lack of transparency and high corruption risk, poorly defined qualification and awarding criteria, cartel deals and conflict of interest jeopardize the efficiency and competitiveness on the BiH national public procurement market.

Over a half of the companies see corruption as "greasing the wheels"; companies gain competitive advantage by paying bribes, using political connections and making other unfair deals to get the public contract.

The level of competition at the public procurement market in BiH is exposed to many obstacles (Voloder 2015a). These are intentional misuse of the system in terms of cartel arrangements, deals between suppliers and public procurers in all phases of public tenders, restrictive terms of participating at tenders (e.g. high costs) and lack of competences at the public procurer side. Public procurers lack resources and knowledge for complex tenders and contracts and, therefore, prefer negotiation procedures directly with supplier(s) who have more expertise in the field. In line with this opinion, it is worth mentioning the general consensus among Croatian and BiH companies that policymakers should promote the criterion of an economically best offer instead of lowest price criterion that is easier to apply.

Based on these findings, the comparative analysis with focus on the SMEs only follows.

In the second phase of the analysis, eight areas of issues that both SMEs in Croatia and BiH are facing were identified. All issues are sorted by their estimated relevance for SMEs safeguarding competitiveness at the public procurement market (Table 4). Therefore, at the very top of the list is the degree of competition to which

Table 4 Issues SMEs are facing in public procurement, $n = 725$

Variable	BiH (%)	Croatia (%)	Chi-square test
Exposure to competition: Yes	12.6	92.6	Chi-square = 337.54, $p = 0.000$
Dissatisfaction with the achieved price: Yes	63.8	52.4	Chi-square = 5.42, $p = 0.020$
Satisfaction with tender deadlines: Yes	83.7	88.6	Chi-square = 2.15, $p = 0.143$
Transparency of tenders: Yes	84.7	87.3	Chi-square = 0.82, $p = 0.365$
Conflict of interest in public procurement: Yes	71.2	40.8	Chi-square = 52.37, $p = 0.000$
Trust in the system: Yes	47.5	17.0	Chi-square = 63.24, $p = 0.000$
Corruption risk in public procurement: Yes	90.8	82.8	Chi-square = 9.75, $p = 0.002$
Public contract awarded under the influence of corruption: Yes	60.1	28.0	Chi-square = 54.80, $p = 0.000$

SMEs are exposed when applying to public tender. The reported (dis)satisfaction with the achieved price of the public contract stands as a barrier for the company's future participation at tenders because of weak profit prospects. And if the contract price is publicly available, which is mostly the case, the unfavourable deal might deter other companies from participating in public tenders. Short tender deadlines seize competition at the public procurement tenders because if deadlines are too short, they may deter SMEs from applying. The EU principles of fairness and non-discriminatory treatment are reflected in the issues of transparency of tenders, perceived conflict of interest in public procurement and respondents' trust in the public procurement system. The last but not the least and according to the results, a very important issue in public procurement is the perceived corruption risk. However, the perceptions of how public procurement is prone to corruption may not match the real corruption incidence. For issues SMEs are facing in public procurement, we examined differences between SMEs by country and by size, i.e. among micro, small and medium companies.

In order to test the differences between BiH and Croatia, the share of companies that agree with various statements about public procurement issues was compared and tested with Chi-square tests (Table 4).

The results indicate that there are significant differences between BiH and Croatia at $p < 0.01$ level for the following variables: "exposure to competition", "conflict of interest in public procurement", "trust in the system" and "corruption risk in public procurement". Also, there are significant differences at $p < 0.05$ level for variable "dissatisfaction with the achieved price". There are no statistically significant differences for variables indicating "satisfaction with tender deadlines" and "transparency of tenders". "Dissatisfaction with the achieved price" in public procurement tenders is higher in BiH than in Croatia (64 vs. 52%).

Larger share of companies from Croatia, when compared with those from BiH, agrees that they are exposed to competition in public procurement tenders in their respective country (93 vs. 13%). On the other hand, a larger share of companies from BiH, when compared with those from Croatia, agrees that conflicts of interest exist in public procurement system of their respective country (71 vs. 41%). Also, larger share of companies from BiH agrees that public contracts were awarded under the influence of corruption (60 vs. 28% in Croatia). Although there are statistically significant differences between BiH and Croatia in the share of companies that agree that corruption risk exists in public procurement, both percentages are very high (91 vs. 83%). For Croatia, an intuitive assumption that SMEs are suffering from corruption more than other businesses is confirmed when compared to the low corruption perceptions of the overall sample (Table 3). Having in mind previous findings, the results for variable "trust in the system" might be considered somewhat contradictory. Although there seems to be more corruption and conflict of interest in public procurement system in BiH (based on companies' answers), at the same time the trust in such system is much higher in BiH than in Croatia (48 vs. 17%).

The analysis of differences among the sizes of SMEs comes next. Micro-companies up to 10 employees might have resources, business interests, negotiation power and other characteristics substantially different from medium-sized

Table 5 Company size and issues SMEs are facing in public procurement, $n = 725$

Variable	Micro (%)	Small (%)	Medium (%)	Chi-square test
Exposure to competition: Yes	11.4	37.6	57.1	Chi-square = 89.29 $p = 0.000$
Dissatisfaction with the achieved price: Yes	63.7	61.3	56.8	Chi-square = 1.57 $p = 0.455$
Satisfaction with tender deadlines: Yes	81.9	84.5	91.3	Chi-square = 5.91 $p = 0.052$
Transparency of tenders: Yes	80.9	87.0	89.9	Chi-square = 7.32 $p = 0.026$
Conflict of interest in public procurement: Yes	67.0	62.3	55.4	Chi-square = 4.83 $p = 0.089$
Trust in the system: Yes	40.2	39.4	30.6	Chi-square = 4.44 $p = 0.109$
Corruption risk in public procurement: Yes	91.0	88.1	83.5	Chi-square = 5.22 $p = 0.074$
Public contract awarded under the influence of corruption: Yes	58.6	49.7	37.7	Chi-square = 14.19 $p = 0.001$

companies up to 249 employees. The intuition of different entry barriers and challenges in front of micro-, small- and medium-sized companies competing at public procurement market is tested by an additional set of Chi-square tests (Table 5).

Statistically significant differences between companies of different sizes at $p < 0.01$ level for the variables "exposure to competition" and "public contract awarded under the influence of corruption" and at the $p < 0.05$ level for "transparency of tender" were found. Differences at $p < 0.1$ level were observed for "satisfaction with tender deadlines", "conflict of interest in public procurement" and "corruption risk in public procurement". There are no statistically significant differences for variables "dissatisfaction with the achieved price" and "trust in the system".

Largest differences between micro, small and medium companies are observed for variable "exposure to competition". More than half of all surveyed medium-sized companies agree that they are exposed to competition in public procurement tenders, while only one in ten micro-companies thinks the same (57 vs. 11%). Larger share of micro-sized companies when compared with small and medium-sized companies agrees with the statement that "public contracts are awarded under the influence of corruption" (59 vs. 50 and 38%). Small and medium-sized companies to a larger extent expressed their concern about the transparency of public procurement tenders, when compared with micro-sized companies (90 and 87 vs. 81%). On the other hand, micro- and small-sized companies are less satisfied with the tender deadlines when compared with medium-sized companies (82 and 85 vs. 91%). A different pattern could be observed for variable "corruption risk in public procurement", i.e. micro- and small-sized companies to a larger extent agree with the statement that there is a "corruption risk in public procurement", when compared with medium-sized companies (91 and 88 vs. 84%).

5 Conclusion and Discussion

Comparative assessment of entry barriers to public procurement market in Croatia and BiH yielded several results that are worth discussing further.

In Croatia, half of the participants at public procurement tenders surveyed were small companies with less than 50 employees. Companies of that size are important to Croatian economy (representing over 98% of companies in Croatia). Generally, SMEs with up to 249 employees are relatively big firms in the context of a small country of Croatia and the same applies for BiH.

For the overall sample of surveyed companies in both countries, the major differences in entry barriers are noted in corruption and low trust in the system. In BiH, perceptions of corruption in public procurement are much higher than in Croatia. Less conflicts of interest and less corruption in public contracting in Croatia compared to BiH might be explained by higher awareness of the Croatian business sector of corruption risk. Since the focus of this study is the position of SMEs in public procurement, this part of the analysis is discussed more in detail. Low trust of Croatian companies in the system might stem from many diverse business experiences.

When it comes to the SMEs only, a huge difference is found on the level of competition to which SMEs are exposed. The competition at the public procurement market for SMEs in Croatia is much higher than in BiH. This might stem from the Croatian EU membership that facilitates access to the market and establishes tendering procedures and practices by opening up bidding processes to a large number of businesses. Companies operating at the EU market should have gained more trust in the system, yet this was not the case observed in the analysis. One of the explaining reasons might be that survey in Croatia was performed at the very beginning of the EU membership period. Another possible reason which remains to be explored further is that EU membership per se does not change the quality of public administration, which is why business perceptions of national public procurement system remain low.

Considering the relative position of micro, small and medium subgroups of SMEs, the findings suggest that as the firm grows, the exposure to competition is higher as well. Maybe micro-companies are more engaged in small-scale public contracts of local provisioning of specific goods and services that are not interesting to other companies to bid for. Possible local and small public contracting might explain as well the higher perceptions of corruption of micro-firms in distinction to the perceptions of small and medium-sized companies. On the other hand, micro-firms have more trust in the public procurement system, which should not prevent them to continue applying to public bids. Other related issues were not claimed by micro-companies when compared to small and medium-sized companies.

Compared to issues often present in the literature as obstacles for SMEs to participate at public procurement market, SMEs in both observed countries do not experience barriers in terms of tender deadlines, transparency and level of achieved contract price. However, SMEs involved or potentially involved in public procurement are facing different obstacles when compared to the EU average.

Some authors argue that SMEs' performance depends on national and regional legislation (Vincze et al. 2010). SMEs perform better on the local level since those tenders usually do not require large suppliers. Also, they are less successful at securing tenders launched by the utilities sector and central government bodies. This would imply that: (1) the quality of local institutions plays a significant role in the success of SMEs; (2) central government institutions should take steps to facilitate SMEs' involvement in the procurement market. Further, contracts of higher value are less obtainable for smaller and micro-companies. This could be the reason why medium-sized enterprises perform better than smaller companies. In order to support smaller businesses, governments should introduce a practice of breaking down tenders. In this way, some unattainable tenders would become feasible opportunities and improve the position of micro and small companies on the public procurement market. Another solution would be to introduce a joint fulfilment allowing a few smaller companies to work together on a high-value tender.

One of the main goals of the new EU legislation is to ensure a better position for SMEs on the public procurement market. Croatia had a problem with corruption before the EU accession process was intensified, so it is intuitive to conclude that in the advanced EU accessing stage, BiH will overcome its current problems, i.e. resolve similar issues that Croatia was facing in the past. One could assume that BiH will attain a higher level of transparency, more competent public procurers, less corruption and, above all, a higher level of competition at some point in the future along its EU accession path. However, it is worth noting that despite introducing EU standards in public procurement (at least in terms of regulatory framework), Croatian companies still experience irregularities and lack confidence in the national public-procurement system, and these views are in line with Preuss (2009) pointing out the importance of supporting policies, organizational culture and strategies in implementing efficient public procurement practices. It is argued that there are no blank policies for post-transition countries. Instead of formal legislative prescription of EU regulations that may not be fully implemented, customized policies should be set up for every country, local government or type of public investment. However, high standards established through EU practices should stand as a higher rule in terms of rational allocation of public resources. Policy recommendations might be different for micro-, small- and medium-sized companies in the post-transition phase.

In this chapter, we shed light on the public procurement and SMEs in post-transition and opened new areas of the future research. However, the effects of the EU accession and membership for SMEs and public procurement need further investigation. As in Croatia and BiH SMEs are compared to the rest of business entities relatively big companies, SME policy that applies in the EU might not yield results in post-transition small countries as expected or foreseen by regulation. To illustrate the particularities, the thresholds applied in public procurement in Croatia and BiH are high with regard to the national GDP and economic power of companies. This is just one example how policies and regulations in the EU aiming to enhance SMEs are in the two post-transition countries referring to in fact large business entities. In the same time, micro-companies in the observed small economies face problems (entry barriers) similar to SMEs in the EU. So, what in the EU applies or is effective to the SMEs in the observed small post-transition economies? What EU policies are applicable to micro-companies, when in turn, Croatian and BiH SMEs are more alike large companies in the EU? What if it is not the EU regulation that matters but the mindset, or business culture or political context or something else? Do SMEs in these countries participate at the EU single market at all, and if not, could we conclude that EU regulation adopted and public procurement principles and policies implemented in Croatia and BiH did not produce expected effects. These and other questions wait for further investigation and perhaps the new theoretical study as well.

Official hard data on SMEs' involvement in public procurement for Croatia and BiH are missing, and this is valid for other post-transition nations as well. In this context, surveying the opinion of participating actors in public procurement is seen as valuable source of information. By acknowledging limitations of this study, the outline of future investigation is set. This work fills the gap in the scarce knowledge on SMEs and public procurement in Western Balkans region, and its findings and policy implications could be useful for other post-transition economies.

Acknowledgements The authors highly appreciate valuable comments of prof. Alistair Anderson. We would like to thank Transparency International Croatia for supporting the survey fieldwork conducted by the Promocija Plus agency which supplied us with the original database for Croatia. The original database for BiH survey was collected within the project Open Public Procurement in BiH funded by the EU and the British Government.

References

Alpeza, M., Biškupić, N., Eterović, D., Gucić, E. M., Oberman Peterka, S., Singer, S., & Šarlija, N. (2015). *Small and Medium Enterprises Report – Croatia 2014 including the results of GEM – Global Entrepreneurship Monitor research for Croatia for 2013*. Zagreb: CEPOR SMEs and Entrepreneurship Policy Center. Accessed September 22, 2015, from http://www.cepor.hr/wp-content/uploads/2015/03/Cepor-godisnje-izvjesce-ENG-web-2014.pdf

Ateljević, J., & Budak, J. (2010). Corruption and public procurement: Example from Croatia. *Journal of Balkan and Near Eastern Studies, 12*(4), 375–397.

Aviani, D. (2007). Temeljna opća načela u pravu europske zajednice relevantna za tržišno djelovanje javnopravnih tijela. *Zbornik radova Veleučilišta u Šibeniku, 1*(1–2), 38–49.

Balkan Tender Watch. (2015). *Public Procurement In Bosnia and Herzegovina, Montenegro, Macedonia and Serbia Comparative Analysis of Legal and Institutional Framework.* Accessed August 03, 2015, from http://balkantenderwatch.eu/btw/uploaded/Comparative/Comparative%20analysis%20of%20legal%20and%20instiutional%20framework.pdf

Bovis, C. H. (2012). Public procurement in the EU: Jurisprudence and conceptual directions. *Common Market Law Review, 49*(1), 247–289.

Budak, J., & Rajh, E. (2014). *The public procurement system: A business sector perspective.* Zagreb: The Institute of Economics.

Carpineti, L., Piga, G., & Zanza, M. (2006). The variety of procurement practice: Evidence from public procurement. In N. Dimitri, G. Piga, & G. Spagnolo (Eds.), *Handbook of procurement.* Cambridge: Cambridge University Press.

Directorate for the Public Procurement System. (2014). *Statističko izvješće o javnoj nabavi u Republici Hrvatskoj za 2013. godinu.* Zagreb: Ministry of Economy, Labour and Entrepreneurship.

Erridge, A., & McIlroy, J. (2016). Public procurement and supply management strategies. *Public Policy and Administration, 17*(1), 52–71.

European Commission. (2008). *European code of best practices facilitating access by SMEs to public procurement contracts.* Accessed August 03, 2015, from http://ec.europa.eu/internal_market/publicprocurement/docs/sme_code_of_best_practices_en.pdf

European Commission. (2010a). *Europe 2020: A strategy for smart, sustainable and inclusive growth.* Accessed August 04, 2015, from http://eur-lex.europa.eu/LexUriServ/LexUriServ.do?uri=COM:2010:2020:FIN:EN:PDF

European Commission. (2010b). *Evaluation of SMEs' access to public procurement markets in the EU*, Final Report. Accessed August 03, 2015, from http://ec.europa.eu/enterprise/policies/sme/business-environment/public-procurement/

European Commission. (2014a). *SMEs' access to public procurement markets and aggregation of demand in the EU.* Accessed August 03, 2015, from http://ec.europa.eu/internal_market/publicprocurement/docs/modernising_rules/smes-access-and-aggregation-of-demand_en.pdf

European Commission. (2014b). *Annual public procurement implementation review, 2013.* Accessed August 03, 2015, from http://ec.europa.eu/internal_market/publicprocurement/docs/implementation/20140820-staff-working-document_en.pdf

European Commission. (2015). *Public procurement.* Accessed August 03, 2015, from http://ec.europa.eu/trade/policy/accessing-markets/public-procurement

Grødeland, Å. B., & Aasland, A. (2011). Fighting corruption in public procurement in post-communist states: Obstacles and solutions. *Communist and Post-Communist Studies, 44*(1), 17–32.

Kidalov, M. V. (2011). Small business contracting in the United States and Europe: A comparative assessment. *Public Contract Law Journal, 40*(2), 443–510.

Loader, K. E. (2005). Supporting SMEs through government purchasing activity. *The International Journal of Enterpreneurship and Innovation, 6*(1), 17–26.

Loader, K. E. (2013). Is public procurement a successful small business support policy? A review of the evidence. *Environment and Planning C: Government and Policy, 31*(1), 39–55.

Mitran, D. (2013). Improving access of SMEs to the public procurement markets. *Internal Auditing and Risk Management, 8*(2), 244–251.

Muller, P., Gagliardi, D., Caliandro, C., Bohn, N. U., & Klitou, D. (2014). Annual Report on European SMEs 2013/2014-A Partial and Fragile Recovery. Accessed September 22, 2015, from http://ec.europa.eu/growth/smes/business-friendly-environment/performance-review/files/supporting-documents/2014/annual-report-smes-2014_en.pdf

Ochrana, F., & Pavel, J. (2013). Analysis of the impact of transparency, corruption, openness in competition and tender procedures on public procurement in the Czech Republic. *Central European Journal of Public Policy, 7*(2), 114–135.

OECD. (2005). *Fighting corruption and promoting integrity in public procurement*. Paris: OECD Publishing. https://doi.org/10.1787/9789264014008-en
OECD. (2012). *Recommendation of the Council of fighting bid rigging in public procurement*. Paris: OECD Publishing. Accessed August 04, 2015, from http://acts.oecd.org/Instruments/ShowInstrumentView.aspx?InstrumentID=284&InstrumentPID=299&Lang=en&Book=False
OECD, European Commission, and ETF. (2014). *Implementation of the "Small Business Act" for Europe in the Mediterranean Middle East and North Africa 2014*. Paris: OECD Publishing.
Palguta, J. (2015). *Political rent-seeking in public procurement: Evidence from the entry of political challengers at electoral thresholds* (Working Paper Series 549, CERGE-EI, Prague, September 2015).
Pashev, K. V. (2011). Corruption and accession. *Public Management Review, 13*(3), 409–432. https://doi.org/10.1080/14719037.2011.553270
Preuss, L. (2009). Addressing sustainable development through public procurement: The case of local government. *Supply Chain Management: An International Journal, 14*(3), 213–223.
Ramsey, L. E. (2006). The new public procurement directives: A partial solution to the problems of procurement compliance. *European Public Law, 12*(2), 275–294.
Slijepčević, S., Budak, J., & Rajh, E. (2015). *Challenging competition at public procurement markets: Are SMEs too big to fail? The case of BiH and Croatia*. EIZ-WP-1504 (October 2015) http://www.eizg.hr/en-US/New-edition-of-EIZ-Working-Papers-1542.aspx
Trybus, M. (2006). Improving the efficiency of public procurement systems in the context of the European Union enlargement process. *Public Contract Law Journal, 35*(3), 409–425.
UNCTAD. (2012). *Competition policy and public procurement*. United Nations Conference on Trade and Development. Accessed August 03, 2015, from http://unctad.org/meetings/en/SessionalDocuments/ciclpd14_en.pdf
Vanjskopolitička inicijativa BH. (2013). *Privredni razvoj – politike malih i srednjih poduzeća*. Accessed September 22, 2015, from http://www.vpi.ba/upload/documents/privredni_razvoj_bh.pdf
Vincze, M. P., Mathis, J., Dumitrescu, A., Erbilgic, A., Coscia, E., & Megliola, M. (2010). *Evaluation of SMEs' access to public procurement markets in the EU*. DG Enterprise and Industry, Final report. European Commission. Brussels. Accessed August 03, 2015, from http://ec.europa.eu/enterprise/policies/sme/business-environment/files/smes_access_to_public_procurement_final_report_2010_en.pdf
Voloder, N. (2015a). *Ključni problemi u javnim nabavkama u BiH: iskustva privrednih subjekata. Analitika Policy Brief 15*. Sarajevo: Analitika – Center for Social Research.
Voloder, N. (2015b). *Mapiranje ključnih prepreka za ravnopravno učešće privrednih subjekata u javnim nabavkama u Bosni i Hercegovini*. Sarajevo: Analitika – Center for Social Research.
Yakovlev, A., & Demidova, O. (2012). Access of firms to public procurement in Russia in the 2000s: Before and after radical reform of regulation. *International Journal of Economic Policy in Emerging Economies, 5*(2), 140–157.
Yalamov, T. (2012). Hiding, circumvention, public procurement, and shaping laws. *Eastern European Economics, 50*(5), 93–111.

The Effect of Market Liquidity on the Company Value

Tajana Serdar Raković

1 Introduction

Market liquidity, as an important factor of making investment decisions at the capital market, provides security for the investors and reduces the risk of not being able to close their positions without significant loss of financial assets. Considering the complexity of the liquidity term, there is more than one definition of liquidity. Generally, liquid market can be described as one where participants can quickly accomplish large transactions with no significant impact on the price. How can the liquidity on the capital market be measured?

One way to measure market liquidity is over the impact of the quantity of shares which were traded on the market price, as Pástor and Stambaugh (2003) demonstrated in their study. There is a correlation between market liquidity and shares yields (Amihud and Mendelson 1986). Liquidity variations are correlated with monetary policy and have an effect on shares and bonds (Chordia et al. 2005). The liquidity of capital markets is defined by four aspects (von Wyss 2004):

- *Trading time* (the ability to perform the transactions immediately and at the prevailing price)
- *Density* (capability of simultaneous purchase and sale at approximately equal price)
- *Depth* (possibility of buying or selling certain assets without affecting the price)
- *Elasticity* (the ability of simultaneous purchase or sale without a significant influence on the price, taking into account not only the volume but also the elasticity of supply and demand).

T. Serdar Raković (✉)
Faculty of Economics, University of Banja Luka, Banja Luka, Bosnia and Herzegovina
e-mail: tajana.serdar-rakovic@ef.unibl.org

These dimensions of liquidity can be observed at five different levels of liquidity:

- Trading possibility
- Possibility of buying and selling certain amount of securities with an impact on the price
- Possibility of buying and selling certain amount of securities without affecting the price
- Possibility of simultaneous buying and selling of securities at approximately equal price
- Possibility of immediate trading

Liquidity is considered a primary factor in the development of capital markets. Companies with shares listed on liquid markets and generally with more liquid shares generate higher returns on assets and have more equity in the capital structure. Researches done in the emerging markets showed that there is a correlation of 80% between the range of bid and offer prices and market liquidity (Levy Yeyati et al. 2007). With decrease in trading difficulties related to prices, volume, and market capitalization, the level of market liquidity increases (Lesmond 2005, p. 37). Thus, a liquid market is the one where participants can quickly accomplish large transactions with no significant impact on the price.

The chapter focuses on the hypothesis that market liquidity has a positive impact on the performance and operating profitability of the companies and thereby on the value of the companies. In order to confirm this hypothesis, the measures of market liquidity have been analysed, and the overview of previous research and studies of this subject has been given. Then we have specified the methodology for empirical analysis we used in our work, presented and discussed research results, and provided appropriate attitudes and conclusions of research topic. Empirical analysis proved that companies with more liquid shares, traded on more regular basis, had higher operating income which was increasing business value. Another basis for the growing performance of the companies with liquid shares is by increasing the incentive effects of managerial contract founded on performance on more liquid markets. Information feedback on the market price of shares that managers and other shareholders are getting is responsible for the better performance of companies whose shares are quoted on the more liquid capital markets. As the cash flow and control rights of the company are essentially determined by company shares, the marketability of shares will undoubtedly play a decisive role in corporate governance, assessing the value and performances of the company.

2 Measures of Market Liquidity

Liquidity measures can be classified into two categories: one-dimensional and multidimensional (as in Wyss 2004), depending on the number of variables covered. One-dimensional liquidity measures are divided into four groups regarding the size of company, volume, time, and spread (Benić and Franić 2008). Multidimensional measures (among others) are Amivest Liquidity Ratio (Benić and Franić 2008) and Amihud Illiquidity Measure (Amihud 2002).

2.1 Measures for Analysing the Size of the Company

The market capitalization expresses the company value as the multiplication of the number of issued shares (S_i) and their market price (P_i) (Benić and Franić 2008):

$$\text{Mcap}_i = S_i \times P_i \qquad (1)$$

Number of shares actually available on the market can be used for more precise liquidity measurement (Free Float).

2.2 Measures Representing the Volume (Quantity of Shares) per Time Unit

(a) The *Volume* represents the number of shares traded in a certain period of time—high volume withdraws higher market liquidity.
(b) *Turnover* is the multiplication of price (p_i) and the quantity of shares in the transaction (q_i) in a certain time interval (t) (Benić and Franić 2008):

$$T_n = \sum_{i=1}^{Nt} p_i \times q_i \qquad (2)$$

(c) *Turnover* is a more significant measure of volume because it allows comparison of more different shares. When turnover is analysed together with a market capitalization, the result is *Trade Turnover* that determines how many times securities have changed owners (Benić and Franić 2008):

$$\text{Trade Turnover} = T_n/\text{Mcap} \qquad (3)$$

(d) *Indicator of* Average *Daily Change in Value of the Market Index* shows volatility of the market. The lower value of this indicator (less price change) means higher liquidity.
(e) *The Ratio of the Average Daily Change of the Index and the Trade Turnover* shows the impact of turnover and market capitalization on the volatility of prices (Sarr 2002). The lower the ratio is, the higher is liquidity and market efficiency. If this indicator is low, the market depth is not satisfactory, or high-value transactions affect the price because there are not enough large and numerous orders with low price range.

2.3 Measures of Liquidity Associated with Time

Measures of liquidity associated with time show frequency of market transactions. High frequency of transaction execution and shorter time between transactions suggest that the market is liquid. The *number of orders* in a certain time period is also a measure of liquidity which belongs to this group of measures, which is important in comparing the situation in several capital markets.

2.4 Measures Associated with the Spread

Measures associated with the spread (the difference between bid and selling price) show amount of costs associated with trading. *Absolute or Quoted Spread* is the difference between the highest bid and the lowest selling price. This spread is always positive under the condition the trading is regular. The lower limit of the spread is minimal money unit permitted on the capital market. Market liquidity is higher as the measures of spread are lower (Sarr 2002).

2.5 Multidimensional Liquidity Measures

Multidimensional liquidity measures include two ratios: *Amivest Liquidity Ratio* (Amihud 2002) and *Amihud Illiquidity Measure* (Amihud 2002).

(a) *Amivest Liquidity Ratio* relates securities trading volume in certain period with the percentage of price change in absolute terms (Benić and Franić 2008):

$$\mathrm{LR1}_t = \frac{Tn_t}{Ir_t I} = \frac{\sum_{i=1}^{N} p_i \times q_i}{Ir_t I} \qquad (4)$$

Meaning: $\mathrm{LR1}_t$—liquidity ratio in time, r_t—percentage of price change (yield), expressed in absolute terms, Tn—trade, N—number of transactions in the time period t, p_i—price, q_i— quantity of securities in the transaction.

Higher ratio means that the market is possible to absorb a larger price change which means market is more liquid.

(b) *Amihud Illiquidity Measure* shows the percentage of price change in absolute terms and the trading volume (Amihud 2002):

$$\mathrm{ILLIQ}_t = \frac{1}{\mathrm{LR1}_t} = \frac{Ir_t I}{Tn} \qquad (5)$$

This indicator analyses several measures of liquidity, such as price change, trading volume, and the impact of trading volume on the price. It shows the influence of one convertible mark (or dollar) on the percentage of daily price change in the market. A lower value of measure indicates a higher market liquidity, and vice versa.

In analysing the liquidity of certain market, it is necessary to apply more measures in order to gain the right information of existence of liquidity and the degree of market illiquidity. Companies with more liquid shares traded on more regular basis have higher operating income, which is ultimately increasing company value. Furthermore, performances of the companies with liquid shares are growing by increasing the incentive effects of managerial contract founded on performance on more liquid markets.

3 The Overview of Previous Research on Market Liquidity

The effect of liquidity on the performances of the company is in the focus of causal theories based on agency costs. One of the most important representatives of these theories is Maug (1998), who believes that liquid markets support effective corporate governance. Market liquidity cannot be considered separately from trading with private information on the capital markets or from monitoring of companies by large investors in order to realize capital gains on shares. Liquid capital markets contribute to resolving the lack of information. In less liquid market, large investors will choose a smaller stake to diversify risk. According to Edmans (2009), the majority shareholders in the market behave as informed participants, not as control subjects, and their added value of majority shareholders should depend on liquidity. Reducing market liquidity and increasing the share of majority shareholders control imply that the stakes of large shareholders become less liquid. Although these two actions reduce the liquidity of large blocks of shares, they have the opposite effect on the monitoring—reducing market liquidity decreases monitoring (Maug 1998, p. 68). The growth of the required control stake forces the majority of shareholders to accumulate larger block of shares in order to maintain control, which means they need to take a higher level of monitoring in the future.

The expected profit increase of monitored companies is always included in the share price. The only source of profit from the monitoring for large investors arises from the uncertainty of the final payment. Profit comes from an increase in volatility, not from change in the refund amount. If capital markets are less liquid, large shareholders will be less engaged around monitoring. In order to avoid the obligation for monitoring, they will diversify their portfolio, that is, they will possess smaller stakes in several companies. Liquid share market leads to greater monitoring because it allows the investor to cover the costs of monitoring through trading based on relevant information. When a large shareholder can choose between monitoring and acquisition as various forms of intervention in companies that operate with loss, they will prefer less expensive method if the market is not liquid and more effective method if the capital market is liquid.

Liquid markets increase the possibility of successful corporate restructuring in two ways. First, liquid markets allow shareholders to realize gains from monitoring through informed trading, and second, they ensure application of the restructuring method because of its efficiency, not lower price (Maug 1998, p. 89). Rent which large shareholders draw from the company monitoring can be reduced if larger packages of voting rights are required, forcing large shareholders to concentrate their stakes (large stakes are therefore less liquid). Higher demands for majority control increase initial stakes, reduce rents, and enhance the tendency to monitoring.

In theory, there is strong evidence suggesting that market liquidity affects positively the performance and thus the value of the company. Since the shares are determinant which is crucial for determining cash flow and control rights, marketability of shares will undoubtedly have a decisive role in corporate governance, value appraisal, and performances of the company. Liquid markets allow purchase of a large or a control block of shares, reduce opportunism of managers, promote a more efficient system of managers remuneration, and stimulate trade between informed investors, thereby improving investment decisions through more informative share prices (Khanna and Sonti 2004).

Numerous papers have been supporting the claim that market liquidity has effect on the performances of the company. Highly liquid shares used to calculate the ratios such as market-to-book ratio show better performance. Market-to-book ratio is a very good starting indicator in calculating different measures of liquidity. Companies with shares quoted on liquid capital markets and generally with more liquid shares achieve higher returns on assets and have more equity in the capital structure. On the other hand, the price-to-operative earnings ratio is similar for liquid and for illiquid shares. These conclusions are valid in determining controlling stake for the industrial branch, the level of shareholder rights, risk, and the moment when return to shares is achieved (Fang et al. 2009, p. 151). Furthermore, exogenous shocks and changes in the environment in terms of liquidity indicate that major changes in the shares liquidity lead to major changes in the performances of the company.

Subrahmanyam and Titman (2001) in their study of the relationship between share prices and company's cash flow have showed that the positive effects of a liquid market on the performances of companies are greater for liquid shares with high business uncertainty (high volatility of operating income and intense investment in research and development). Liquid markets allow informed investors to expose private information and profit from them. With the higher inflow of such information, the results of greater liquidity are increasing gains from the use of compensation based on shares. However, liquidity does not increase or diminish the effects of performances on shareholder rights. The market liquidity positive effect on performances comes from improving the incentive effects of the compensation in shares and improving investment decisions of corporate insiders.

In an extensive study, Fang et al. (2009) have analysed the correlation between market liquidity and the performance of companies, measured by Tobin's Q indicator. They used the indicator of the effective range based on daily TAQ[1] data, which is considered to be one of the best shares liquidity representatives. To check indicators' power, they used three alternative measures of liquidity: adjusted measure of illiquidity (Amihud 2002), measure of liquidity based on a percentage of zero daily returns (Lesmond et al. 1999), and the relative quota range on TAQ data basis.

The indicators on Tobin's Q basis have been used as a measure of companies' performances. Tobin's Q is used in a number of similar studies and represents the ratio of the company's market value and the costs of replacing its assets. Indicator Q in Fang et al. (2009) expresses the quotient of the assets market value and assets book value of the company at the end of the fiscal year. In addition, there have been calculated earnings-to-price ratio as the value of the operating income after depreciation divided by the market value of common shares and financial leverage ratio as a proportion of equity in the market value of the company's assets. All measures have revealed similar results, proving that market liquidity positively affects the performances and value of the company.

4 Methodological Frameworks for Empirical Analysis

Illiquidity of the capital market and its impact on the performance and operating profitability of the companies and thereby on the value of the companies are the subject of a number of foreign studies, as well as few domestic analyses. Liquid markets allow informed investors to expose private information and profit from them. Results of other studies (Maug 1998; Subrahmanyam and Titman 2001; Khanna and Sonti 2004; Fang et al. 2009) compared with ours confirmed our hypothesis. Relevant information found on liquid capital market such as New York Stock Exchange proves that companies with more liquid shares have more success in corporate governance and higher operative business result. The main aim of this research is to confirm that liquidity of market and the marketability of shares (having in mind that cash flow and control rights are determined by shares) will be a decisive factor in corporate governance, assessing the value and performances of the company.

We used information obtained by interviewing 50 certified appraisers in Bosnia and Herzegovina, who owned the licence for evaluation. Most of the questions are of closed type: direct questions, questions with multiple choices, and intensity questions. Respondents highlighted the characteristics of market illiquidity, which they believed existing in the Republic of Srpska. Furthermore, respondents gave their opinion about the characteristics and intensity of market illiquidity and how that

---

[1] The Trade and Quote (TAQ) is a database that contains the daily trading and quotas of all securities listed on the New York Stock Exchange, American Stock Exchange, the NASDAQ national system of trading and securities of relatively small market capitalization (SmallCap issues). TAQ provides information about all securities quoted on the New York Stock Exchange since 1993.

affected their choice of methods and approaches they used performing their appraisal work. They answered the question about the correlation between the market liquidity and performance of the companies they evaluated. Also, respondents declare an effect of managerial contract on companies' performance on capital market in the Republic of Srpska.

The survey was limited to the examination of illiquidity of capital market in the Republic of Srpska. In the case of illiquid markets, the process of input determination for assessing the value is more complicated, and for reasons of lack of transparency, unavailability of information, and other inherent risks, the value of the company is less relevant than it would be in liquid capital markets. In illiquid markets, the level of importance attached to transaction prices is inevitably analysed, compared to other indicators of fair value. The level of transaction significance depends on the facts and circumstances, such as transaction volume, transaction temporal proximity to the measurement date, and transaction comparability with asset or liability whose fair value is measured.

We also used data from the Banja Luka Stock Exchange, Institute of Statistics of Republic of Srpska, as well as data from New York Stock Exchange, International Monetary Fund, World Bank, and studies of other relevant institutions and authors.

5 Results of Analysis and Discussion

Foremost, the research results show a high degree of agreement of respondents with the statement that the capital market in our country is illiquid. Ninety-four percent of total number of respondents believes that the capital market in the Republic of Srpska is not liquid, while 6% of the respondents did not answer the question. Of those interviewed, none has said that the capital market in our country is liquid (Fig. 1).

Respondents have agreed that all features of illiquid capital are characteristic of capital market in the Republic of Srpska; only the degrees of manifestation of certain features are different (Fig. 2).

Results indicate that 95% of respondents believe that there are small numbers of transactions for observed security or securities with similar characteristics on our capital market. Also, poor market liquidity and insufficient depth of the capital market (number and financial potential of buyers and sellers) are observed by 94 and 91% of surveyed appraisers, respectively. Likewise, the interviewees have found that the insufficient number of similar securities that are comparable with the observed one is a significant problem in our capital market (92%). Somewhat smaller numbers of respondents are convinced that they can find willing and informed buyers and sellers at any time (78%).

However, less than half of the respondents, that are 45%, think that information about the transactions is not reliable and available. The least marked characteristics of illiquid capital market are the high transaction costs (16%) and a significant variation of securities prices over time or between market participants (14%).

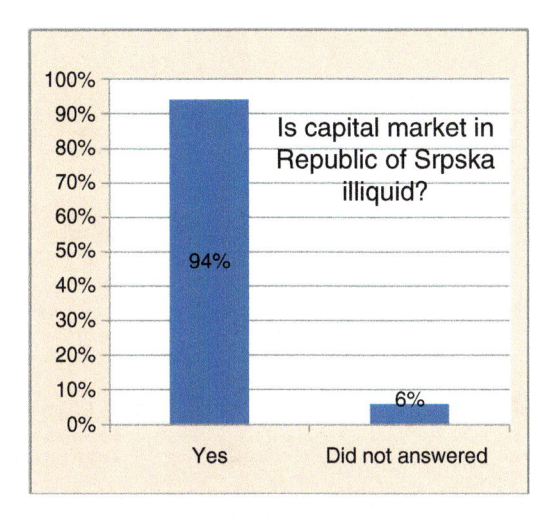

Fig. 1 Is capital market in the Republic of Srpska illiquid?

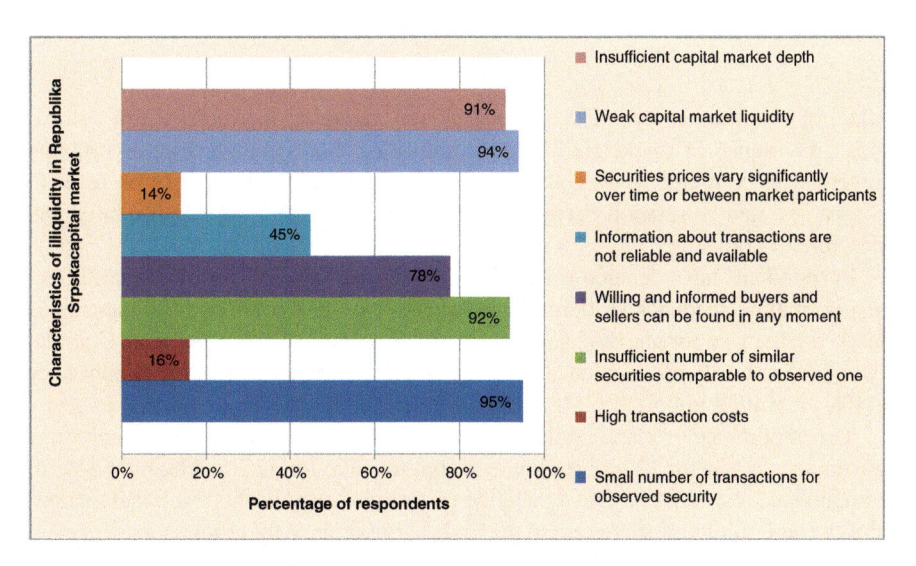

Fig. 2 Characteristics of illiquidity in the Republic of Srpska capital market

Obviously, the capital market in the Republic of Srpska is characterized as illiquid with all features of illiquidity at lower or higher extent.

The importance and the level of significance of market liquidity that respondents assigned to specific statements related to value and performance of companies are presented in Fig. 3.

Examinees marked theses related to market liquidity as not important (1), less important (2), medium important (3), and very important (4). Examined theses are

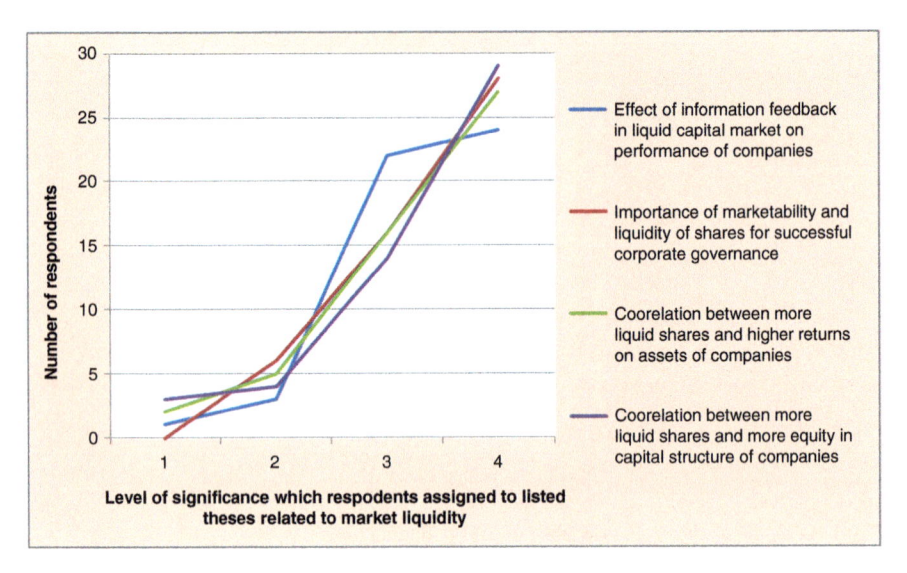

Fig. 3 Significance of capital market liquidity for performance, return on assets, and capital structure of companies

effect of information feedback in liquid capital market on performance of companies, importance of marketability and liquidity of shares for successful corporate governance, correlation between more liquid shares and higher return on asset of companies, and correlation between more liquid shares and more equity in capital structure of companies.

Respondents have decided if four listed theses are less or more important. Effect of information feedback in liquid capital market on performance of companies is marked as not important by 2% and less important by 6% of examinees. Cumulatively, the majority of examinees believe that information is of medium importance (44%) or of high importance (48%) for result and performance of companies.

The importance of marketability and liquidity of shares for successful corporate governance is low for 12% of respondents, but medium for 32% and high for 56% of respondents, respectively. Obviously, the majority of respondents think that marketability and liquidity of shares are of the highest importance for efficient management business.

The correlation between more liquid shares and higher return on asset of companies is very strong according to 54% of respondents and medium strong for 32% of them. Ten percent of respondents marked this correlation as less strong and only 4% of respondents see mentioned correlation as weak.

The correlation between more liquid shares and more equity in capital structure of companies is determined as medium strong by 28% of respondents and as very strong by 58% of them. Similar to the previous thesis, 6 and 8% of examinees think that this correlation is weak and less strong, respectively.

Table 1 Some of characteristics of liquid capital market

Liquid market enables	Percentage of respondents who agreed with statement (%)
Facilitating purchase of control or large block of shares	76
Decreasing opportunism of managers	67
More efficient system of rewarding managers	69
Stimulation of trading between informed market participants/investors	89
Improving investment decisions and corporate governance	72

Source: Author's survey

Conclusion following from all listed results is that in liquid capital market companies have higher returns, more equity in capital structure, better performance, as well as more successful management, due to increasing incentive effects of managerial contracts. Thus, liquid capital market leads to higher value of companies listed on that market. More equity in capital structure of companies listed on liquid markets is explained by more effective share issues and continuous and regular shares trading.

Table 1 presents results from analysis of some effects of liquid markets. Seventy-six percent of examinees consider that liquid market enables easier purchase of control or large blocks of shares. Decreasing opportunism of managers and more efficient system of rewarding managers are assigned as characteristics of liquid markets by 67% and 69% of respondents, respectively. Stimulation of trading between informed market participants/investors is enabled by liquid market according to 89% of examinees. Finally, liquid market enables improving investment decisions and corporate governance as it is concluded by 72% of respondents. This is also presented in Fig. 4.

The great majority of respondents agreed that a liquid capital market has a positive impact on many aspects of operating business. On the other hand, in the Republic of Srpska, capital market is illiquid which means that companies are faced with lower performances and more difficulties in gathering equity capital and achieving positive business results. The analysis showed that due to lack of liquidity in capital market in the Republic of Srpska, appraisals are limited in using some of the methods of appraisal, especially methods of market approach. When market is illiquid, market value as the most reliable concept of value does not correspond to conditions of appraisal, so other concepts such as fair value or special value have to be used. This means that illiquid capital market significantly restricts possibility of using certain appraisal approaches and concepts which results in less reliable and representative value of companies. The causal correlation between less relevant company value achieved in appraisals and lower performance on illiquid market is found to be existing in capital market of the Republic of Srpska.

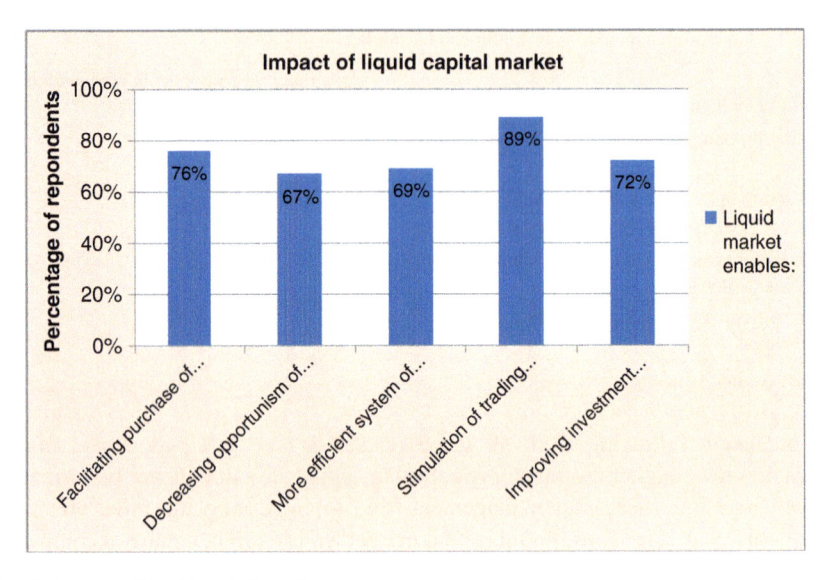

Fig. 4 Impact of liquid capital market

6 Conclusions

The market liquidity is based on the existence of a large number of buyers and sellers at any moment, the ability to perform the following transaction at the same price as the previous one, and the market capacity to absorb buying and selling larger amounts of securities without significantly affecting the price. The liquidity of capital markets is defined by four aspects: trading time, density, depth, and elasticity. Liquidity measures are classified into two categories: one-dimensional and multidimensional. One-dimensional measures include measures for analysing the size of the company, measures that represent the volume (quantity of shares) per time unit, measures associated with the spread, and measures of liquidity associated with time. Multidimensional measures are consisting of Amivest Liquidity Ratio and Amihud Illiquidity Measure, among others.

Results of the other authors' studies showed that the market liquidity positively affects the performance and operating profitability of the company. Causes of these results also have been examined, and there have been provided empirical support for models of share price as well as for the view that liquidity improves the value of management compensation linked to the results achievement. In order to identify the causal effects of market liquidity on performance, the effect of exogenous shocks on liquidity has been tested theoretically. Increasing liquidity in the months of exogenous shocks enhances performance by boosting operating income. Liquid share market leads to greater monitoring because it allows the investor to cover the costs of monitoring through trading based on relevant information. Liquid markets increase the possibility of successful corporate restructuring by allowing shareholders to realize gains from monitoring through informed trading and by ensuring application of the restructuring method based on efficiency not lower price. Market liquidity cannot be considered separately from trading with private information on the capital markets or from monitoring of companies by large investors in order to realize capital gains on shares.

In this chapter, we examined characteristics of market illiquidity existing in the Republic of Srpska, as well as intensity of market illiquidity, and how that affected choice of methods and approaches appraisers used performing their appraisal work. The subject of analysis was a correlation between the market liquidity and performance of the companies evaluated. Also, we analysed impact of market liquidity on (a) facilitating purchase of control block of shares, (b) decreasing opportunism of managers, (c) efficient system of rewarding managers, (d) stimulation of trading between informed market participants, and (e) investment decisions and corporate governance.

Empirical analysis that we conducted in our country evidences that all features of illiquid capital are characteristic of capital market in the Republic of Srpska; only the manifestation degrees of certain features are different. Significance of capital market liquidity for performance, return on assets, and capital structure of companies was also demonstrated. Finding following from all listed results is that in liquid capital market companies have higher returns, more equity in capital structure, better performance, as well as more successful management, due to increasing incentive effects of managerial contracts. Information feedback on the market price of shares which managers and other stakeholders are getting is responsible for the better performance of companies whose shares are quoted on the more liquid capital markets. Thus, liquid capital market leads to higher value of companies listed on that market.

More equity in capital structure of companies listed on liquid markets is explained by more effective share issues and continuous and regular shares trading. This means that illiquid capital market significantly restricts the possibility of using certain appraisal approaches and concepts which results in less reliable and representative value of companies. The causal correlation between less relevant company value achieved in appraisals and lower performance on illiquid market is found to be existing in capital market of the Republic of Srpska. We conclude that the market liquidity improves the performance of the company over the higher operating income, which finally increases the value of the company.

References

Amihud, Y. (2002). Illiquidity and stock returns: Cross-section and time-series effects. *Journal of Financial Markets, 5*(1), 31–56.
Amihud, Y., & Mendelson, H. (1986). Asset pricing and the bid-ask spread. *Journal of Financial Economics, 17*, 223–249.
Banja Luka Stock Exchange. (n.d.). Accessed July 01, 2015, from http://www.blberza.com
Benić, V., & Franić, I. (2008). Komparativna analiza likvidnosti tržište kapitala Hrvatske i zemalja regije. *Financijska teorija i praksa, 32*(4), 481–502.

Chordia, T., Sarkar, A., & Subrahmanyam, A. (2005). An empirical analysis of stock and bond market liquidity. *Review of Financial Studies, 18*(1), 85–129.

Edmans, A. (2009). Block holder trading, market efficiency and managerial myopia. *Journal of finance, 64*(6), 2481–2513.

Fang, V. W., Noe, T. H., & Tice, S. (2009). Stock market liquidity and firm value. *Journal of Financial Economics, 94*, 150–169.

International Monetary Fund. (n.d.). Accessed June 29, 2015, from http://www.imf.org

Khanna, N., & Sonti, R. (2004). Value creating stock manipulation: Feedback effect of stock prices on firm value. *Journal of Financial Markets, 7*, 237–270.

Lesmond, D. A. (2005). Liquidity of emerging markets. *Journal of Financial Economics, 77*, 411–452.

Lesmond, D. A., Ogden, J., & Trzcinka, C. (1999). A new estimate of transaction costs. *Review of Financial Studies, 12*, 1113–1141.

Levy Yeyati, E., Schmukler, S., & Van Horen, N. (2007). *Emerging market liquidity and crises*. Policy Research, Working Paper, 4445. The World Bank. Accessed June 29, 2015, from http://www-wds.worldbank.org/external/default/WDSContentServer/WDSP/IB/2007/12/13/000158349_20071213152426/Rendered/PDF/wps4445.pdf

Maug, E. (1998). Large shareholders as monitors: Is there a trade-off between liquidity and control? *Journal of Finance, 53*(1), 65–98.

New York Stock Exchange. (n.d.). Accessed June 30, 2015, from http://www.nyse.com

Pástor, L., & Stambaugh, R. (2003). Liquidity risk and expected stock returns. *Journal of Political Economy, 111*, 642–685.

Republic of Srpska, Institute of Statistics. (n.d.). Accessed June 30, 2015, from http://www.rzs.rs.ba

Sarr, L. (2002). *Measuring liquidity in financial markets* (IMF Working Paper WP/02/232). Accessed June 29, 2015, from http://www.imf.org/external/pubs/ft/wp/2002/wp02232.pdf

Subrahmanyam, A., & Titman, S. (2001). Feedback from stock prices to cash flows. *Journal of finance, 56*, 2389–2413.

Von Wyss, R. (2004). *Measuring and predicting liquidity in the stock market*. Doctoral dissertation. University of St. Gallen, St. Gallen.

World Bank. (n.d.). Accessed June 30, 2015, from http://www.worldbank.org

Assessing Entrepreneurial Intentions, Motivations and Barriers Amongst WBC Students Through Developing a Network of Co-Creative Centers–iDEA Labs

Petar Vrgović, Danijela Ćirić, and Vladimir Todorović

1 Introduction

Entrepreneurial learning and trainings that lead to business empowerment are gaining momentum in the last few decades around the world, with different success across the globe. This chapter investigates some aspects of this phenomenon in the context of Western Balkans region, trying to identify basis for entrepreneurial activation among young people. This region has some common problems in this area, most of which could be described with the following facts (OECD 2012; Todorovic et al. 2012; Radevic and Tinaj 2011; Karanassios et al. 2006):

- Small percentage of students is ready to start their own business after graduation.
- Majority of students report that during their studies they are only acquiring knowledge and skills useful to the public sector or to very big enterprises.
- Even when there is some form of entrepreneurial education, it is still academically driven.
- There are few students apart from those from economy and business studies that are engaged in entrepreneurial learning.
- Networking skills across the region and national boundaries are very limited.
- Knowledge about financial instruments of the equity and participation type is scarce.
- Companies are often isolated from higher education, thus not transferring their practical knowledge to active students.

And although it is found that individuals rely on their adaptive resources and entrepreneurial self-efficacy as they form entrepreneurial intentions (Tolentino et al. 2014), it is still necessary to offer organized support to young people in order to

P. Vrgović (✉) · D. Ćirić · V. Todorović
Faculty of Technical Sciences, University of Novi Sad, Novi Sad, Serbia
e-mail: vrgovic@uns.ac.rs

influence their career choices. There are different approaches on how to spark entrepreneurial learning in contexts that are lagging behind this type of learning, varying from immersing students in existing organizations to constructing hybrid spaces where business skills could be learned in parallel to creative idea development (Tekic et al. 2013; McPhee et al. 2012). Indeed, pre-incubators and incubators can be observed as enterprise teaching laboratories in which all main aspects of enterprise education can be undertaken (Kirby 2004). Students are found to highly benefit active means of learning about entrepreneurial activities, especially when they are let to run their own business in semi-controlled environment (Vincett and Farlow 2008).

In order to construct effective context for entrepreneurial learning, this chapter aims to identify students' potentials for the entrepreneurial and innovative activities. This will be achieved by summarizing answers given to a custom-made survey by student sample from the Western Balkans region. In the next step, this chapter will try to propose a model that describes teaching-and-working space within a university that could help students improve their knowledge and skills relative to business thinking and enterprise.

2 Research Method and Samples

Aiming to explore students' potentials for the entrepreneurial and innovative activities, a number of universities in the Western Balkans region were contacted, as well as other higher education institutions, which were observed as a dynamic context relevant for this project. Since most of the institutions did not have any data that could serve this purpose, it was necessary to assess students' potentials in a new research activity. Therefore, students were intended to be directly approached, so that a baseline for relevant activities could be set. The research question aimed to offer solution for the entire region, so the research activity had to cover as much of the population as possible, advocating for a diversified sample from multiple contexts. Nevertheless, the sample obtained in this study was appropriate, since there was no random access to students: research project partners were allowed to approach any student group they could agree with.

In order to explore structure and dynamic of students' entrepreneurial thinking and acting, as well as their ideation and innovation potentials, a questionnaire was designed, comprised of a number of thematic closed-ended questions (presented in Appendix).

Table 1 Students' intentions about career future

Descriptive Statistics: After you finish your current studies, how much are the following options appealing to you? (1–7 scale)		
	Mean	SD
To be employed in a government-owned organization	5.01	1.944
To continue with education	4.93	1.897
To start my own business	4.90	1.986
To be employed in a privately owned company	4.04	1.897

2.1 Data Collection and Sample Properties

The questionnaire was published in the form of a printed survey and distributed to three universities in Serbia, two in Bosnia & Herzegovina, and one in Montenegro in June and July of 2014.

The total sample of students has reached number of 1794. Students in the sample were mostly 18–25 years old. There were 52.7% of students identifying themselves as female and 47.3% as male. Current year of study is dominantly first (967 students) or a senior year (401 third year and 390 fourth year). The research wanted to cover especially students who are in their last year of study, but different studies vary between being 3 and 4 years long, hence two group of students from study years 3 and 4.

3 Data Analysis

The students were firstly asked about their preferences for their near future, after they finish their current studies. This question is important since it can describe current students' state-of-mind, which may stimulate or hinder them from developing their own business. As shown in Table 1, students give the highest mark to employment in public or government sector, which is closely followed by continuing their education and starting their own business; working in a privately owned company is the least appealing. Although the "own business" option is third in the ranking, the difference from the first option is quite small and not statistically significant, only 0.11 points on a 1–7 scale.

To shed more light on students' entrepreneurial intentions, answers to "start my own business" alternative were more closely observed on their own. It can be seen that a big number of students find starting their own business as much appealing as possible (31.3% students marked this option with the highest mark 7, Fig. 1). So, although the "employment in a government-owned organization" is marked as the most appealing option on average, there is still a big number of students who would be very happy working on their own. This gives hope to projects that nurture students' entrepreneurship education.

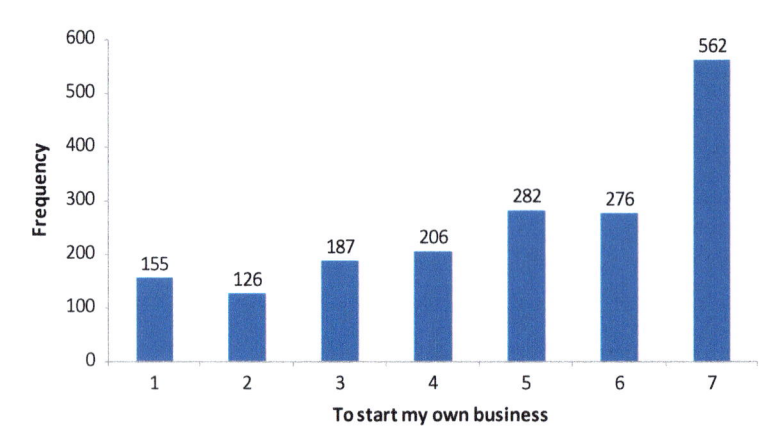

Fig. 1 Answer distribution to the "start my own business" alternative

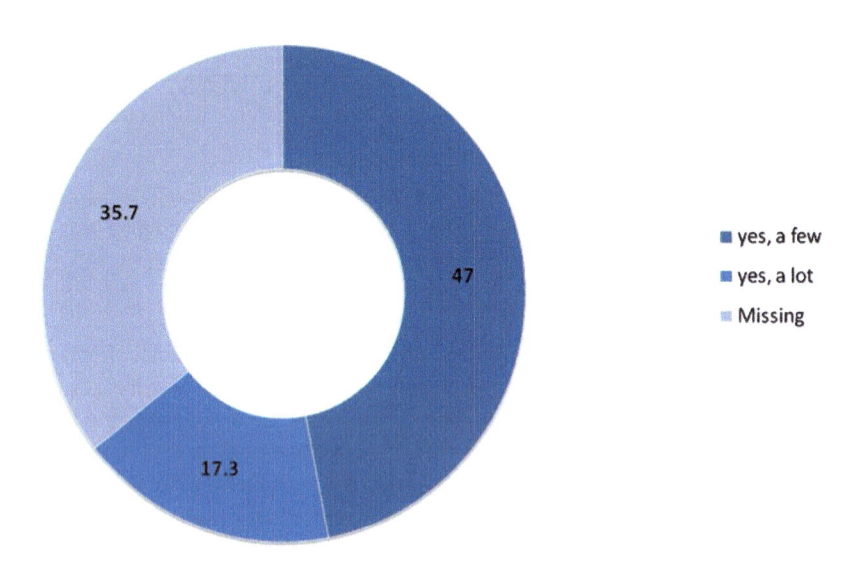

Fig. 2 Number of students who believe that they possess creative ideas or not

We can also observe that a big number of students from the sample have at least a few creative ideas that they believe could become business ideas. Furthermore, 18% of students believe they have a lot of creative ideas that they believe could become business ideas, which means almost one in five students could carry a big innovative potential (Fig. 2). This innovation potential is something that needs to be well taken care of and utilized for the benefit of both students and their universities.

id3 I would like to realize my creative ideas through some sort of entrepreneurial activity (% of total)

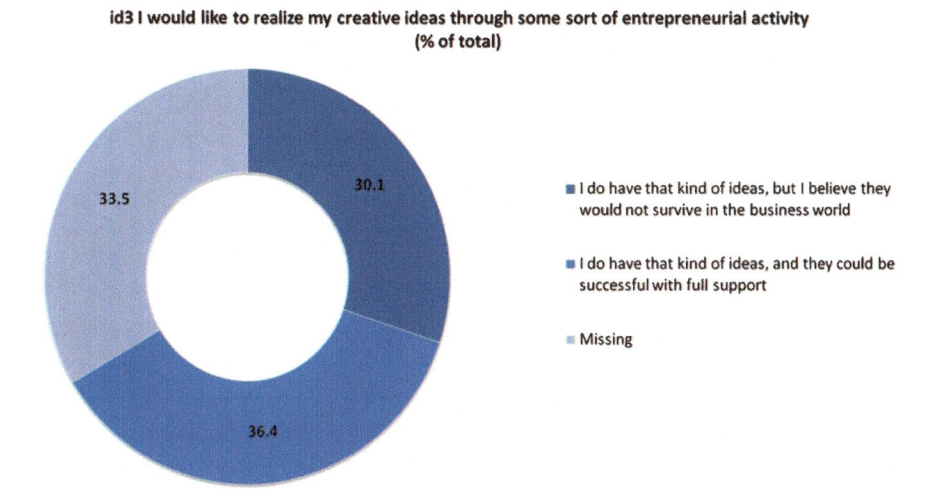

- I do have that kind of ideas, but I believe they would not survive in the business world: 36.4
- I do have that kind of ideas, and they could be successful with full support: 30.1
- Missing: 33.5

Fig. 3 Students' preferences about realizing their creative ideas

Students were then asked about their readiness to employ their ideas in some sort of entrepreneurial activity, with slightly more than 50% of those that stated they have some creative ideas (36.4% of the total sample) being optimistic about possible success of their creative ideas (Fig. 3). On the other hand, almost every other student that has some creative ideas is feeling pessimistic about those ideas, fearing that they would not survive in the business world. This finding suggests that we need to find means and ways to encourage students to work on realization of their ideas, without fear of failure.

The students were also asked about main obstacles that stand in their way when trying to realize their creative ideas. As shown in Fig. 4, the biggest obstacle is lack of working equipment, followed by lack of working space.

Students were next asked to mark their agreement with a number of statements relevant to this research, on a scale from 1 to 7. As shown in Fig. 5, the statement that students on average mostly identify with is the one that states that their University needs a place where students could develop their creative ideas. This finding is very relevant to this project, as it shows that students have this kind of need. Also, statements about students wanting to be involved in extracurricular activities and practical challenges are highly marked.

More than half of the students (62.6%) state that they would be interested in using some space organized for students' idea development, whether they may have their own ideas or not. While being aware of socially desirable responses that probably did inflate this percent, still there is enough space for optimistic plans with establishing idea labs (Fig. 6).

Finally, the students were asked about their curriculum and teachers' behavior as being growing factors for (a) students' creative ideas and creative problem solving and (b) for their team work with other students (Fig. 7). The results for both

The following factors are obstacles in realization of your creative ideas to what extent?

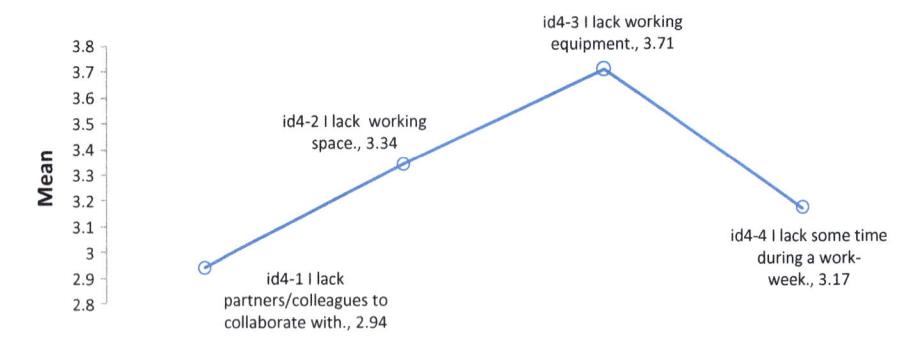

[Chart showing Mean values:
- id4-1 I lack partners/colleagues to collaborate with., 2.94
- id4-2 I lack working space., 3.34
- id4-3 I lack working equipment., 3.71
- id4-4 I lack some time during a work-week., 3.17]

Fig. 4 Severity of obstacles that students face when trying to realize their creative ideas

questions are quite similar and positively correlated (Spearman's rho 0.61, significant at 0.01 level), indicating that they share a common relation with curriculum and teachers. Since most of the curricula deals with subjects that are not creative by nature, it is acceptable to have this type of distribution to these questions, as we cannot expect every subject to develop creative thinking due to convergent problems found in many subjects. Still, the number of students who graded their curriculum and teachers' behavior as very simulative to their creative thinking is encouraging and shows a potential that could be harnessed.

4 Data Summary and Model Proposition

First of all, a significant number of students, 31.3% of the sample, have stated that starting their own business after their studies sounds highly appealing. This means that one in every three students has, at least, good motivation to start thinking in entrepreneurial mindset. This also means that promoting entrepreneurial goals, although highly beneficial, is not something that is primary since a good percentage of students is already inclined to this.

Two-thirds of students from the sample state that they have at least a few creative ideas that they believe could become business ideas, which is another finding that supports wide adoption of an idea lab among universities and other HEIs. However, every other student that has some creative ideas believes that his or her ideas would not survive in the business world. This is a big obstacle, as it may inhibit students' entrepreneurial intentions right from the start. In order to overcome this obstacle, universities need to help students to feel more safe and able to explore and experiment with their business ideas—their entrepreneurial intentions need encouragement. In

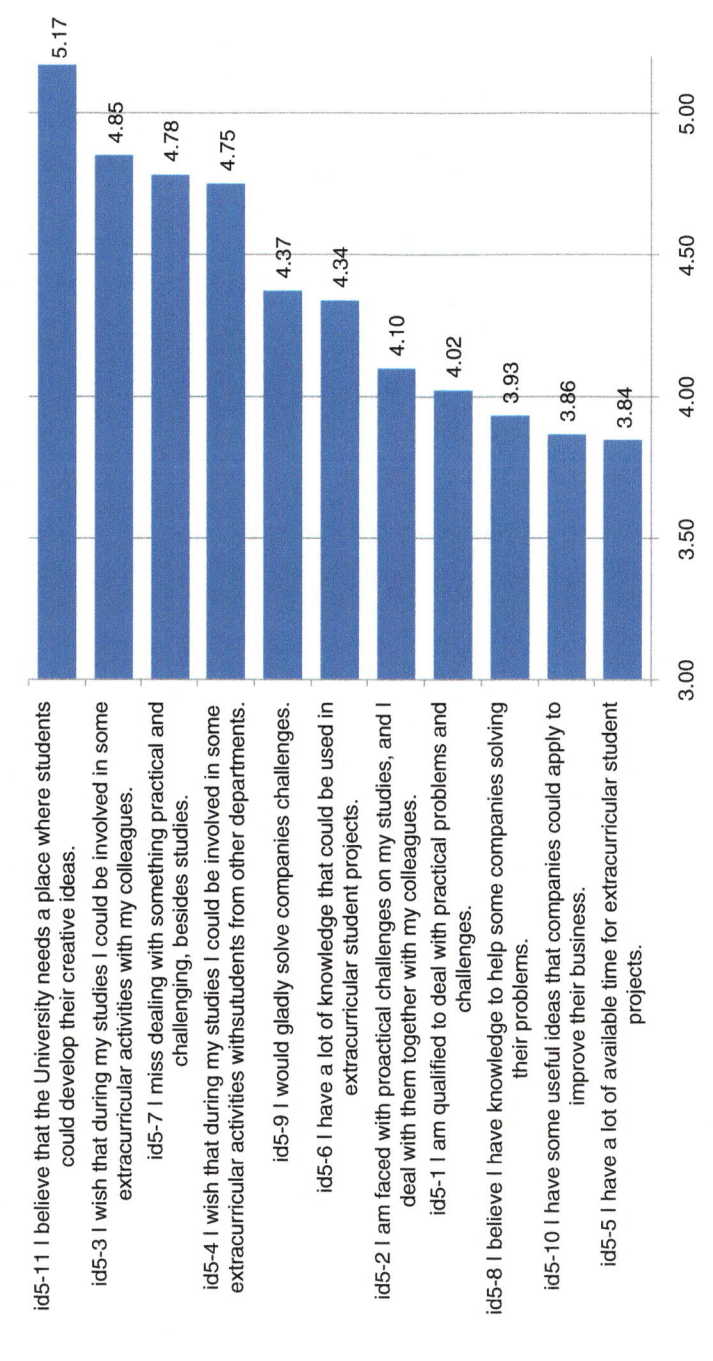

Fig. 5 Average agreement with a number of statements relevant to this research

- id5-11: I believe that the University needs a place where students could develop their creative ideas. — 5.17
- id5-3: I wish that during my studies I could be involved in some extracurricular activities with my colleagues. — 4.85
- id5-7: I miss dealing with something practical and challenging, besides studies. — 4.78
- id5-4: I wish that during my studies I could be involved in some extracurricular activities with sutudents from other departments. — 4.75
- id5-9: I would gladly solve companies challenges. — 4.37
- id5-6: I have a lot of knowledge that could be used in extracurricular student projects. — 4.34
- id5-2: I am faced with proactical challenges on my studies, and I deal with them together with my colleagues. — 4.10
- id5-1: I am qualified to deal with practical problems and challenges. — 4.02
- id5-8: I believe I have knowledge to help some companies solving their problems. — 3.93
- id5-10: I have some useful ideas that companies could apply to improve their business. — 3.86
- id5-5: I have a lot of available time for extracurricular student projects. — 3.84

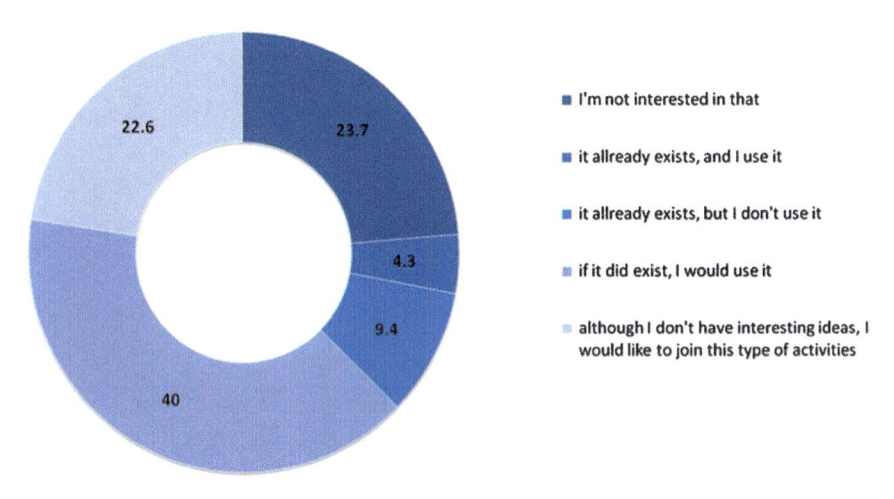

id6 If there was some organized space for students idea development, I would use it (% of total)

- I'm not interested in that
- it allready exists, and I use it
- it allready exists, but I don't use it
- if it did exist, I would use it
- although I don't have interesting ideas, I would like to join this type of activities

22.6　23.7　4.3　9.4　40

Fig. 6 Students' interest in organized space for idea development

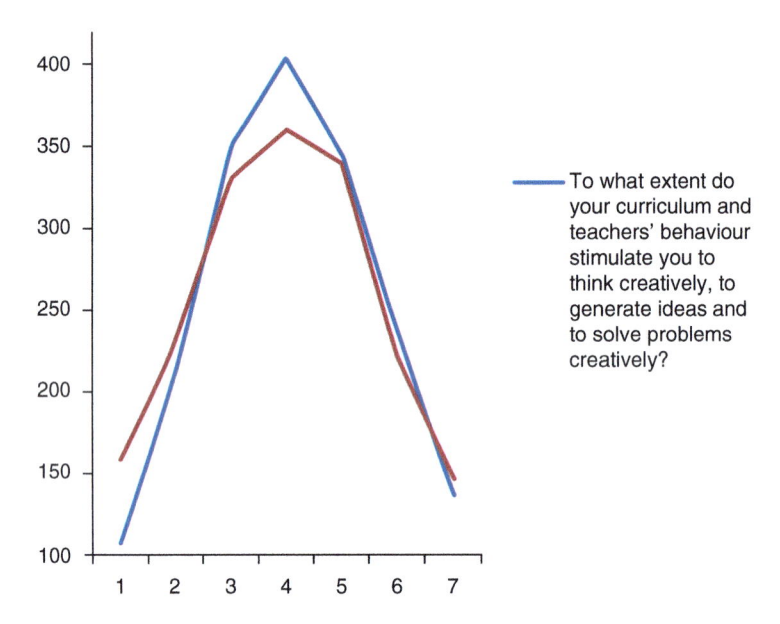

— To what extent do your curriculum and teachers' behaviour stimulate you to think creatively, to generate ideas and to solve problems creatively?

Fig. 7 Curriculum and teachers' influence on students' creative thinking, creative problem solving, and networking skills

other words, students need to be offered with some context that will help them to fail safely and to concentrate on progress instead of potential damage.

Students expressed interest in extracurricular, practical, and challenging activities, and also they are highly interested in collaborating with students from other departments. Both lack of working equipment and lack of working space are found to be significant obstacles to realization of students' creative ideas, which advocates for a specific place that could help students develop and realize their ideas, with financial support from the government institutions or international funds. Students have belief that this kind of place would be highly desirable, and they would like to be engaged in these extracurricular activities both with their colleagues and students from other departments. Almost two-thirds of the students stated that they would like to use that kind of place, whether they possess creative ideas or not.

On the basis of previously observed results, students' responses need to be combined into a coherent complex suggestion that will result in a model that can be a basis for successful entrepreneurial context for students. It is, therefore, interesting to develop a system that:

1. Embraces students with creative ideas with business potential.
2. Encourages students to realize their creative ideas in a context that frees them from fear of failure.
3. Supplies students with knowledge about business development, project managing, creative thinking, team work, networking skills.
4. Is spacially adequate and is supplied with relevant equipment.
5. Is oriented towards extracurricular, practical, and challenging activities.
6. Allows students from different departments to work together and create synergy.
7. Is organized enough to offer integral support for specific result-oriented activities.

This part of the research is intended to offer a model that could be constructed in order to answer students' needs in this area, while still being interesting to the universities and other stakeholders. The authors are proposing a model of an idea lab—a creative space that will allow university students to generate, develop, market, and commercialize their creative ideas into business concepts through entrepreneurial route (start-ups) or in collaboration with companies (open innovation). At the same time, this space would allow students to obtain usable knowledge and skills about entrepreneurial activities, both from other peers and experienced mentors. This idea lab is proposed as a hybrid between two concepts that are already familiar in this field, which target different aspects (Fig. 8). On the first side, classical living labs are intended as closed systems in which new technology concepts are put to the test in life-like situations. On the other side, pre-incubators are ment to serve as preparatory stations for business ideas.

Proposed idea lab combines these two concepts by allowing its users to test their ideas in business context, with integral support in all relevant aspects. Students, as idea lab users, will be systematically led, encouraged, and directed to develop their creativity towards business-oriented actions. Their talent, entrepreneurial skills, and abilities will be activated and improved with sets of trainings and mentorships organized by the lab. Besides starting their own business, students will be offered

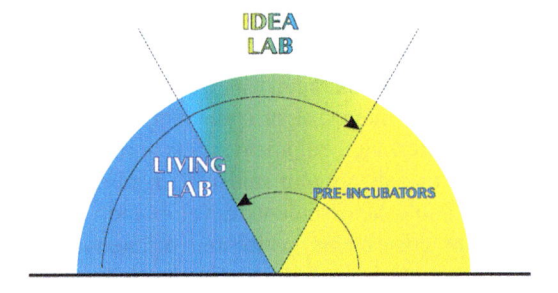

Fig. 8 A hybrid nature of proposed idea lab

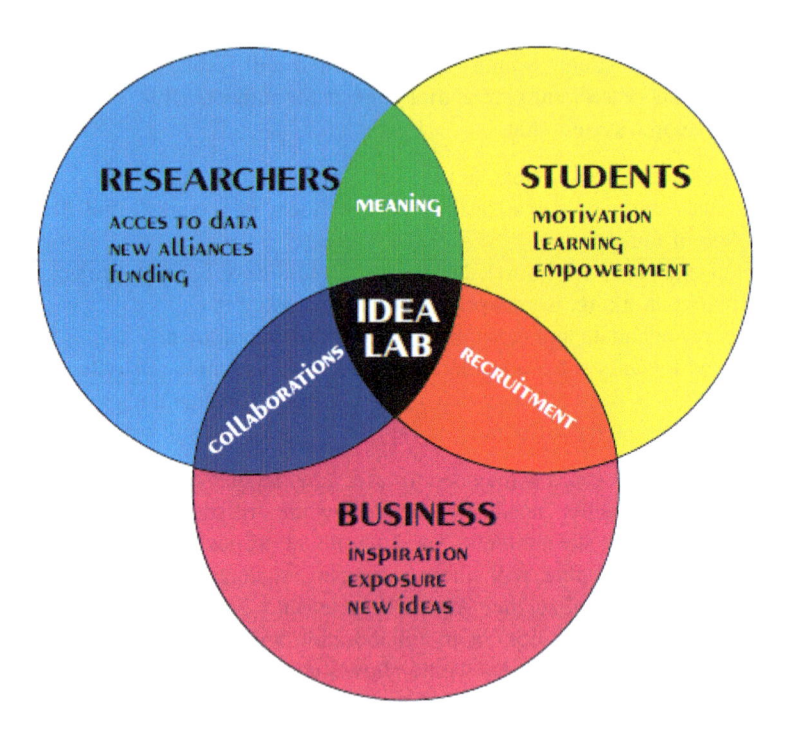

Fig. 9 Cross-section of stakeholders and their interests

engagement in solving problems and challenges from existing companies that will partner with the lab. This opportunity will be highly beneficial to the students, their university, and the involved companies, as it will allow practical knowledge, recognition in the business market, and direct contacts with the economy, as depicted in Fig. 9.

Besides proposing a single idea lab, it is relevant to construct a network of multiple idea labs that could be connected through a virtual platform for collaboration. In this way, students from different universities could benefit from contacts with peers from other institutions, exchanging knowledge, contacts, and ideas between themselves.

Virtual part of the iDEAlab should serve as a platform and a user tool that will enable students to review and develop their entrepreneurial ideas in a simple way, in a friendly environment and in cooperation with selected tutors, regardless of the current location.

The platform should support the whole innovation cycle, from intake and development of the ideas, launching and managing projects to releasing products/services to the market. Virtual platform should provide direct communication between individuals and teams, tutors, and teams in a friendly online environment, as well as connection with other iDEAlabs from the region and with partner institutions from the business sector.

Acknowledgement The authors of this chapter are very grateful to the TEMPUS project "iDEA LAB" (JPHES 544373-1-2013-1) for enabling and supporting participation at this event.

Appendix

Questionnaire for assessing students' innovative potentials and expectations
iD01 I have creative ideas that could become business ideas.

1. No	2. Yes, a few	3. Yes, a lot

iD02 I had some ideas about how to organize some things and make them happen

1. No	2. Yes, a few	3. Yes, a lot

iD03 I would like to realize my creative ideas through some sort of entrepreneurial activity.

1. I do have that kind of ideas, but I believe they would not survive in the business world
2. I do have that kind of ideas, and they could be successful with full support

iD04 To what extent are the following factors obstacles to realization of your creative ideas?

1. I lack partners/colleagues to collaborate with	1 2 3 4 5
2. I lack working space	1 2 3 4 5
3. I lack working equipment	1 2 3 4 5
4. I lack some time during a work week	1 2 3 4 5

iD05 Identify level to which the following statements relate to your studies.

1. I am qualified to deal with practical problems and challenges	1 2 3 4 5 6 7
2. I am faced with practical challenges on my studies, and I deal with them together with my colleagues	1 2 3 4 5 6 7
3. I wish that during my studies I could be involved in some extracurricular activities with my colleagues	1 2 3 4 5 6 7
4. I wish that during my studies I could be involved in some extracurricular activities with students from other departments	1 2 3 4 5 6 7
5. I have a lot of available time for extracurricular student projects	1 2 3 4 5 6 7
6. I have a lot of knowledge that could be used in extracurricular student projects	1 2 3 4 5 6 7
7. I miss dealing with something practical and challenging, besides studies	1 2 3 4 5 6 7
8. I believe I have knowledge to help some companies solving their problems	1 2 3 4 5 6 7
9. I would gladly solve companies' challenges	1 2 3 4 5 6 7
10. I have some useful ideas that companies could apply to improve their business	1 2 3 4 5 6 7
11. I believe that the University needs a place where students could develop their creative ideas	1 2 3 4 5 6 7

iD06 If there was some organized space for students idea development, I would use it.

1. I'm not interested in that
2. It already exists, and I use it
3. It already exists, but I don't use it
4. If it did exist, I would use it
5. Although I don't have interesting ideas, I would like to join this type of activities

References

Karanassios, M., Athianos, S., & Zlatintsi, P. (2006). Student entrepreneurship in the Balkan context. *Higher Education, 20*(2), 85–96.
Kirby, D. A. (2004). Entrepreneurship education and incubators: Pre incubators, incubators and science parks as enterprise laboratories. In *14th Annual IntEnt Conference*, University of Napoli Federico II, Italia.
McPhee, C., Westerlund, M., & Leminen, S. (2012). Editorial: Living labs. *Technology Innovation Management Review, 2*(9), 3–5.
OECD. (2012). SME Policy Index: Western Balkans and Turkey 2012. In *Progress in the Implementation of the Small Business Act for Europe*. OECD Publishing.
Radevic, D., & Tinaj, S. (2011). Entrepreneurial behaviour among students–case study of University of Donja Gorica, Podgorica, Montenegro. In *Proceedings of First REDETE Conference – Economic Development and Entrepreneurship in Transition Economies* (pp. 304–311).

Tekic, Z., Kovacevic, I., Vrgovic, P., Orcik, A., Todorovic, V., & Jovanovic, M. (2013). iDEA Lab: Empowering university – Industry collaboration through students' entrepreneurship and open innovation. In *International Conference on Technology Transfer 2013* (pp. 269–272).

Todorovic, V., Tekic, Z., & Pecujlija, M. (2012). Preduzetničke težnje studenata Fakulteta tehničkih nauka. In *Zbornik radova druge medjunarodne konferencije "Ucenje za preduzetnistvo"* (pp. 205–215).

Tolentino, L. R., Sedoglavich, V., Lu, V. N., Garcia, P. R. J. M., & Restubog, S. L. D. (2014). The role of career adaptability in predicting entrepreneurial intentions: A moderated mediation model. *Journal of Vocational Behavior, 85*(3), 403–412.

Vincett, P. S., & Farlow, S. (2008). "Start a Business": An experiment in education through entrepreneurship. *Journal of Small Business and Enterprise Development, 15*(2), 274–288. https://doi.org/10.1108/14626000810871673

Ethical Behavior in the Context of Managerial Decision Making and Satisfaction of Employees: Lessons from the Experience of the Post-Transition Country

Ivana Bulog, Dženan Kulović, and Ivan Grančić

1 Introduction

Different authors in different ways describe and define ethics as a term. What all authors and theoreticians who deal with ethics agree with is the fact that ethics is something good, moral, and positive for most people or for all interest groups.

There is no doubt that managers are facing a number of ethical challenges in their everyday activities, trying to respond better to all demands of all stakeholders they are directly and indirectly linked to. Today, the ethical behavior of managers is a strategic important term when it comes to decision making and successful business. This is one of the key elements that contribute to a more successful achievement of their competitive advantage. When making business decisions, the problem of ethics and ethical behavior of managers arises.

It is expected that it is important for employees how managers are behaving in decision making and do they behave ethically or unethically. As a result, their perception has a positive or negative impact on the motivation for work that eventually affects company's overall performance. The way employees perceive (consciously or unconsciously) managers and their ethics in business is largely reflected in their level of satisfaction at work. Only employees with high level of satisfaction are prerequisites for long-term successful business operations. Despite all this knowledge, modern business world convinces us that there are very unethical companies that ended their business years with huge profits. The question is why is it so? Ethics and business ethics are intertwined throughout the organization and enterprise. Every employee, from a regular worker to a manager, even to a

---

I. Bulog (✉) · I. Grančić
Faculty of Economics, University of Split, Split, Croatia
e-mail: ivana.bulog@efst.hr

D. Kulović
Faculty of Economics, University of Zenica, Zenica, Bosnia and Herzegovina

shareholder, has to think and act in an ethical way. Managers are most often the ones who, unfortunately, behave unethically because their primary goal is a good business result and huge profit.

This work will adequately explain all the negative and positive effects of the ethical behavior of managers, but also all relevant frameworks will be presented when it comes to ethics in decision making that affects employee satisfaction. The work will also mention what managers can learn to avoid ethically dangerous zones.

2 The Concept of Ethics and Ethical Behavior

The term ethics is derived from the Greek word "*ethos*" which means habit, significance, and morality. Today, in the modern world, ethics is viewed and defined as a special branch of philosophy that tries to logically develop a series of moral principles that would lead to the conclusion what is exactly ethical behavior. Still, it is necessary to go in the past to explain the dawning of this branch of philosophy.

Deliberation about ethics and ethical behavior began in fifth century BC in Athens and continues today. Socrates, the ancient Greek philosopher, is known as the founding father of ethics. Socrates was first in all of Greece, which was then considered as a cradle of civilization, who started thinking about nature of good and evil, what is good and what is evil, and also where they originate. The word ethics is made up of two Greek words, as claimed by Žugaj (1990): "ethos" which means custom, habit and "ethikos" which means morality. Ethics is often associated with the Greek philosopher Aristotle, who mentioned ethics in the context of man's character property. Today in our contemporary world, most people identify ethics either with morality or with conscience. *Ethical* would refer to a good behavior where *unethical* refers to something unlawful. One of the major problems is the fact that a large number of people do not even know what ethics is.

Ethics has been associated with religion since its inception, which is right, but today, ethics is defined as a science of morality or as behavior defined by moral principles. Ethical behavior is a very interesting concept for which it is difficult to give a correct, single definition. That could be the behavior that is consistent with all moral principles and standards of an individual or organization, as Buble (2006) believes. There is a problem again because every individual has their own standards of behavior. The only thing that many theorists agree with, and what Buble (2006) states, is the definition of moral norms, and it says that the norm or standard is ethical only if it takes into account the interests and situations of all other people affected by the decision. Many people identify concepts such as ethical, ethical standards, ethics, and morality; hence, it is necessary to mention the definitions of these terms that are very similar but again have their own characteristics. To behave ethically means to behave in accordance with ethical principles, which for most people means to behave in a good, honest, and truthful way, as claimed by Aleksić (2007). Aleksić (2007) also considers that ethical standards are actually principles or ideals of human behavior.

However, ethics as a term can be defined as a field of science, study of morality of human activities, so ethics could be the correct standard of these activities, as claimed by Aleksić (2007). He also claims that morality is our inner voice telling us whether our decision was correct or not, and whether our decision was in accordance with our ethical principles or not. In general, it can be said that ethical behavior is particularly a search for the truth and the motive for making the best possible decision from acquired knowledge. A man, as a living being, wants to know the truth about all things, especially the truth about those he is interested in or which are of great importance to him. Man wants to find out the correctness and misconduct of human behavior, but no matter how hard a man is working on, no matter how much he understands what it means to work ethically, and how much he knows how to distinguish what is good and what is bad, there is no guarantee that the same man will behave well and ethically. In human nature, there are two extremes, two ends of possible behavior, good and bad, ethical and unethical. Accepting and understanding the importance of ethical behavior will lead human decision making and behavior to the proper end.

3 The Importance of Ethics in Business

After explaining the concept of ethics and ethical behavior, the next question is why ethics is so closely related to business and why ethics is so important to modern business at all. The business processes are extremely complex. Many factors have influenced them, which are simply impossible to control. Ethics of a company is also very complex. This complexity stems from the fact that ethics actually consists of several different subtypes of ethics. The general concept of ethics is often identified with managerial ethics, and managerial ethics, according to Perić (2011), has determinants such as individual ethics, business ethics, organizational ethics, social ethics, personal ethics, and professional ethics. Each of these terms, in a certain way, affects the company's overall ethics.

In order to make the business easier for managers, when it comes to determinants, there is an ethical codex created on the initiative of manager or business owner or even shareholders. The ethical codex is a type of document that seeks to ensure ethical behavior and decision making, according to Buble (2006). In codex, organization summarizes the most important values that it wants to act and the standards of acceptable and unacceptable behavior and action at all. It is common for the codex to be available for the public. The goals of the ethics codex are setting up a framework for ethical behavior, helping employees if they are in dilemma what is ethical and what is not, strengthening moral and community in organization, motivating employees, creating consumer and investor confidence, providing better service, and even strengthening corporate image.

Numerous studies have been conducted to find out what ethical behavior means for managers. Thus, Messick et al. (2006) indicate that most managers, up to 50%, said that ethics and ethical behavior implied their own feelings telling them what is right. Twenty-five percent of them argued that it represented a behavior that is in line with their religious beliefs. Eighteen percent of managers answered that such behavior should be in accordance with the golden rule, while others argued that it is a behavior that is good for most people or that is common behavior in society. Next study also mentioned by Messick et al. (2006) was conducted with 121 managers, leading to worrying facts, and that is, those who behave unethically have little tendency to change their behavior.

Experts tried to justify it by the pressure that superiors have made on the managers or by the distored moral principles of the superiors. There is no ethical behavioral measurement; therefore, managers by themselves assess what is ethical and what is not, what decisions and conclusions will be made about those decisions. Another problem for managers is that it is not enough to make a decision when they are convinced that decision is ethical to their own principles or organization principles. Before making such a decision, managers should take into account all customers, suppliers, interest groups, shareholders, the state, and the public completely. Importance of ethics and ethical business is primarily due to the fact that customers and consumers, long ago, began to divide companies on the ethical and unethical. This fact is more than enough for companies to turn on or start with ethical business.

Nowadays, ethics has become one of the key factors for distinguishing successful from unsuccessful companies. In fact, ethics has become a powerful means of differentiation. Ethical business means doing business by letter of law, executing all obligations on time, and putting consumers and clients in the first place. In addition, it is necessary to emphasize the transparency of business. Those companies which provide public access to some data create a positive image of them and remove the suspicion of acting unethically. Of course, certain information can be business secret, and such information is not available for the public. In business world, it is also worth to say "good news travels fast." It is important to emphasize that ethical thinking and decision making should be used in every situation, without exceptions, said by Messick et al. (2006), all to remain consistent with their own principles and to build awareness of the importance of ethics.

To conduct and do ethical business means to think about others, to think about future. Such companies that do business in an ethical manner have predetermined long-term goals and plans. Ethical business gives some kind of security and gives the future for development. Ethical companies are the ones that will give up short-term profit for long-term positive image in the public eyes. By doing business so, the company creates positive atmosphere, growing trust, overall employee satisfaction, increasing possibility of steady progress, and the company where such an atmosphere dominates and which gains long-term trust by its customers is at an advantage in front of companies which are operating in unethical way. Their business situation is contrastive. They will have short-term profits acquired in various ways, and in the long run, such companies can't compete with ethical companies.

4 Ethical Business Management

Ethics and ethical behavior as segments of successful business are very difficult, almost impossible to measure in a reliable way. Due to its complexity and dependence on numerous factors, the relationship between its importance and its complexity is always emphasized. The measurement of ethics is especially problematic because it is something inexhaustible as, Aleksić claims (2007), there is no device or measuring unit for its measurement. But what can be ethical for somebody, for others can be completely unethical. The same thing can be said on the state level.

Still, it was necessary to develop some ethical principles that would show us whether we are acting ethically. Such ethical management or business ethics leads us to the conclusion that there are some components and guidelines that will help us. One of them is the value of company that includes statements about company goals, company attitudes, and beliefs, as claimed by Aleksić (2007). Such statements of companies outline their course of action in terms of ethics and set the company's ethical goals. The next component is the earlier mentioned ethical codex that represents rules of a desirable behavior that are based on the fundamental values, principles, and rules of responsible business and behavior of an organization, but it should not represent strict rules of conduct in virtually every situation. The next component is the reporting and counseling line that has the purpose of early identification of ethical problems and timely reaction, as stated by Aleksić (2007).

Furthermore, ethical managers, employees, and committees are part of an organization that regulates business ethics. Their duty is manifested in developing strategies and management that will ensure that ethical standards of organizations are implemented and in the communication with everyone in the organization. Larger organizations can also establish ethical committees or commissions that provide ethical supervision and control. Ethical consultants represent consultants specializing in the field of business ethics. They offer their consulting services to small organizations which find using these services more profitable than developing them within their own organization. Ethical education and training have the purpose of introducing everyone with the importance of ethics and its application, the development of ethical tools, and the development of awareness of the importance of a quality business ethics management system. Reporting, accounting, and auditing have a purpose in some way to control the business but also an attempt to measure the effect of ethics. It is also worth mentioning the modern concept of managing business ethics, which is the concept of corporate social responsibility. Social responsibility has become a business imperative. Every organization, including its management, is aware that planning of organizational plans must take into account the welfare of society as a whole. Social responsibility has become the responsibility of management, who is forced to valorize every important decision based on economic effects and on social impacts.

5 Avoiding Ethical Dangerous Zones

Ethical decision making is conditioned by numerous facts and factors that decision makers should in some way take into account when deciding. In the business world, it is easy to lose and move away from ethics even when it is thought that the decision is ethical. It is, therefore, necessary to create a framework to improve ethical behavior. For this reason and for this purpose in the opinion of Messick et al. (2006), managers were focused on three key areas: quality, breadth, and fairness or honesty. As far as quality is concerned, there are three fundamental principles that affect the quality of decision, namely, ethnocentrism, stereotype, and wrong pattern perception.

Ethnocentrism is the attitude that "our" way of doing things is better and more appropriate and that other approaches are somewhat inferior. In the ethnocentric view, our group view and values become something against which others take measures. Managers practicing ethnocentrism are more at risk of having their decisions discriminating and ethically sound. In ethnocentrism, managers are unconsciously under the influence of stereotypes that pose additional threats by assuring managers that their prejudices to others are factual. Stereotypical managers do not use facts, and there is a higher likelihood that their decisions will not comply with the law. Sometimes managers will point to experience as proof of these beliefs, but they forget that even this experience can lead them in the wrong direction. Using quantitative processes, managers can easily avoid areas where wrong beliefs could affect their decisions. In most cases, quantitative approaches have the same result as qualitative, but the quantitative approach is less subjective to others. Businesses must accept proactive strategies and make it clear to their employees that they will not tolerate prejudices. Therefore, the potential dangers that may arise with quality include ethnocentrism, stereotypes, and wrong perceptions of the cause, and avoiding dangerous zones within the quality can be utilized by quantitative processes, having explicit corporate policies and seeking more details in all segments to find out the real root of the problem.

Another key area is the breadth that requires taking into account all potential stakeholder groups. Managers need to make extra effort and imagine other possible implications for all interest groups. Managers should keep open even those things that are not considered, which are considered as irrelevant. Sometimes it is avoided to deal with worrying risks if it is believed to have a good potential for significant profits. Long-term consequences can be catastrophic. Managers and decision makers should always take into account the society as a whole. Before they make a decision, they should consider the possible reaction of the public and the reasons for such reaction. If the public is worried about the manager's reaction, they should reexamine their own decision. An additional risk is when the decision maker tries to hide something from the public because today's IT technologies are more developed than ever, so it is easy to discover hidden facts or data. Not to lead themselves to the situation of having to hide something from the public or to simplify the consequences, it is necessary for the managers to prioritize a list of interest groups. Managers who do not take into account long-term goals can be found under accusations of taking advantage of the current state at the expense of the future. Each company should have its short-term but long-term goals as well. Although the short term seems to be more important, long-term view brings numerous benefits. So potential dangers in the breadth are ignoring unlikely events, ignoring the possibility of the public finding out the truth and discount the future. Dangerous zones can be avoided by compiling a list of all potential stakeholder groups, assessments from stakeholder perspectives, appropriate transparency, and quality consideration of future consequences.

The third key area is honesty and sincerity. This area should occupy a central place in all aspects of business including decision making. Some problems that can be mentioned here can, in a conscious or unconscious way, affect the integrity of decisions. Trust, intelligence, and moral strength allow managers to make difficult choices and successfully overcome the fact that because of such decisions they lose their popularity among others. People can learn to reconsider their own court, learn to calculate the risk, and test their intentions in evaluating others. It is necessary to ask yourself whether the decision will be made on the basis of reliable, current, and relevant information. The next problem in this context is too much self-confidence. Excessive confidence can cause the manager to avoid collecting additional information about the problem before making a final decision. To prevent too much self-confidence, managers can use their conscience to test if their decision is ethical or not. Sometimes a good quality solution to this problem is the idea of what kind of reaction would be for the decision or activity to end on the cover of some famous newspapers. The segment that is also worth mentioning here is human memory. Human memory is unreliable and can endanger the ethical and moral decision. It is important for managers to understand the shortcomings of human memory and to solve this problem by conducting detailed records. Thus, the potential dangers presented here are too much self-confidence, self-deception, and unreliable human memory. To avoid dangerous zones, managers need to follow their conscience, try to beat their assumptions, challenge whatever they think they know, and keep detailed records and performance measurements.

6 The Concept and Definition of Decision Making

Every man in conscious or unconscious way makes some decisions about important and less important segments of life. Decision making occurs every day throughout our lives. The notion of decision making is the concept of very broad meaning and use. Decisions can be made on a daily basis in countless situations concerning personal life, family, work, decision making in organization, society, at the state level, etc. However, business decision making should be emphasized as a special example of decision making. It is special because a lot of time has been spent on exploring segments and factors connected with this term. For this reason, there is no single explanation for notion of decision making, but a large number of scientists, linguists, and theorists have their own version of the term. On one fact the majority agree: decision making is closely related to management, it is the foundation of management.

Mescon et al. (1985) consider that decision making is a very broad term that marks the simplest choice such as choosing clothing for every day but also making important decisions such as choosing a partner for marriage. When it comes to definition, there are plenty of them, but they are very similar. Koontz and Weihrich (1990) consider that decision making could be defined as a choice of direction or mode of action between multiple versions. For Gordon et al. (1990), decision making is the process of creating and evaluating the versions as well as the process of choice between multiple versions. Daft (1992) defines decision making more widely, as a problem identification process and as process of solving problems. Perko-Šeparović (1975) speaks about decision making in a narrower and wider sense. By decision making in the narrow sense, he speaks about the choice between two or more versions, and by decision making in broader term, he implies the whole process of solving problems. If we summarize all definitions, we can conclude that decision making is the process that lasts for shorter or longer period and ends with adoption of decision, i.e., its application and control.

Decision making is therefore a choice between at least two or more options to solve the problem for which it is deciding for. As far as business decision making is concerned, it is about any decision making that is not related to privacy. It is also about choosing between two or more versions but in business situations. There is no distinction between private and business decision making when it comes to decision-making phases or the factors influencing decision making. The difference is only in question who the subject of decision making is, whether it is a man as a private person or a man as the representative of a legal person.

7 Decision Making and Ethics

Decision making and ethics have been continually linked since ancient times, and they are constantly mentioned in various aspects. Today, in the business world, the link between ethics and decision making has been questioned more than ever. One without other simply cannot exist. There are numerous ways and styles of decision making. The process of decision making is extremely complex, but whatever style or mode is in use, regardless of the weight of the process itself, ethics is intertwined in all segments. Thus, ethics should act as a kind of link between the whole decision-making process if it is in the interest of management and the whole enterprise.

Those managers and companies that behave ethically in every decision-making situation, whether it is important or not, gain many benefits in comparison to the companies which do not apply them. In the long run, business ethics should be a component that requires a lot of material resources because its importance is unquestionable. Managers must realize that ethical thinking must be rooted in all aspects of business. Every decision-making process must be linked with ethics in whole, and both the top of enterprise and its bottom should be thought in an ethical way. There will be many ethical principles that differ between people and states, but they should essentially lead to the same, which is generally good, socially responsible behavior. Quality, breadth, and honesty are concepts that should lead company to optimum results.

Prior to action and decision making, it is necessary to consider the implications and effects again, and to harmonize that decision with ethical principles of all interest groups in order to make the satisfaction at the general level. It is almost sure that certain problems will arise at each decision-making process. Sometimes managers find it easier and more effective to avoid the ethical mode of action. Sometimes their personal interest exceeds, but one thing is sure, the consequences of unethical decision making will be discovered sooner or later. Therefore, the problems that an enterprise faces in business ethics should not make the enterprise and its management to abandon ethical behavior. In fact, they should encourage them to find a quality and ethical solution for the benefit of the whole society, in a creative and reliable way.

Once again, it is extremely important to emphasize that ethical decisions, business ethics, and ethical thinking should be used in all situations, without exceptions, as only way for achieving the ultimate goal. Good reputation of the business is worth more than any short-term profit, so creating a quality image of own business has become the priority of all managers that will be accomplished only by doing business ethically.

8 The Concept and Definition of Satisfaction

Satisfaction as a term has been present since our existence. Reasons for that lie in the fact that every individual by human nature thrives to be satisfied. Satisfaction aspiration of a human being has always been an interesting topic for literates as well as for scientists. Satisfaction term has been viewed at from different aspects and compared to many different parameters. Every individual has their own desires and own motives and tendencies for satisfaction. Various things, circumstances, and events make a certain individual satisfied.

Regarding the employee satisfaction, there are two terms which are similar but different enough. Those are job satisfaction and satisfaction at workplace. Job satisfaction would primarily mean that employee is satisfied with the nature of the job he does, while satisfaction at workplace includes numerous factors that are very important when it comes to satisfaction of an employee. Some of crucial factors are salary, coworkers, superiors, working conditions, etc. In this particular case, for the requirements of this study, satisfaction at workplace will be observed because of its impact on the employee's behavior.

Analyzing various studies we concluded that there are different versions of authors' personal perceptions when it comes to definition of satisfaction at the workplace. Most of the available definitions are mainly the same, but on the other hand they are somewhat different, which makes them independent and unique. Only few of these definitions will be mentioned, those which are understandable to everyone, and professional to include everything authors consider to be important for the understanding of this term. Davis and Newstrom (1989) define satisfaction at workplace as a group of positive and negative feelings which employees feel toward their own job. Marušić (1990) states how satisfaction at workplace is often defined as a state of mind of an individual regarding its working environment. Leap and Crino (1993) state something similar but more profound in their definition. They define satisfaction at workplace as employee's attitude toward job he is performing, rewards he is given for his performance, and the social, organizational, and physical characteristics of the environment in which he performs. Similarly, Black and Steers (1994) define satisfaction at workplace as pleasant positive emotional state linked to the job they perform. Satisfaction at the workplace comes from perception an employee has regarding his workplace and what he receives for the job he is performing. Spector (1997), however, states that satisfaction at workplace is a level which shows how much people actually like their jobs. Very interesting definition comes from Daft and Marcic (2001); they state that satisfaction at workplace is an attitude workers have when their needs and interests are balanced out, when working conditions and rewards are satisfying, and when they are pleased to work with their coworkers. When taking into consideration all of the above stated definitions, conclusion can be made that every definition has one inner and common fact which is that satisfaction at workplace is a positive emotional state which relates to a job an individual is performing. It is also clear that certain authors define satisfaction as a core feeling and they do not divide it into separate components, while others state different factors which are more or less influential and in that manner define the level of satisfaction on the workplace. When mentioning different factors which with different authors influence the dissatisfaction at workplace, it is important to mention that some authors, like Furnham (1997), define satisfaction at workplace through the following mathematical formula:

$$ZnaR = f(IK^* \ KP^* \ PI\&P^* \ G);$$

where ZnaR = satisfaction at workplace, IK = individual characteristics of a worker, KP = job characteristics, PI&P = individual characteristics and job characteristics overlapping, G = error.

From abovementioned formula, it is visible that satisfaction at the workplace is a very complex term which depends on different factors which should be observed independently. This is exactly why this term is so complicated and why numerous researches have been dedicated to it.

There are few reasons why the term of job satisfaction has been given a great importance. First reason derives from human nature where each individual yearns for satisfaction and deserves to be treated justly which guarantees job satisfaction. Satisfaction at workplace is an indicator of emotional pleasure and psychological wealth. Hence, there are many factors influencing satisfaction at workplace:

company's current state, salary, the nature of job, coworkers, superiors, conditions, job safety, the possibility for promotion, etc. Next important thing to mention is the efficiency aspect because satisfaction at work determines worker's behavior which directly affects company's effectiveness, its profitability, and its image.

Job satisfaction is an aspect which every serious company will take into consideration on a regular basis. There are many advantages of researching and conducting employee satisfaction surveys in companies, and some of them are creating an image about general level of satisfaction within a company, establishing fields of satisfaction or dissatisfaction, and always appreciating interpersonal communications from top to bottom, where any employee can express his thoughts, while on the other side satisfied employees get the feeling that management cares for them. Next advantage is that job satisfaction surveys can help you detect the need for additional employee training and another positive factor is that it can help you recognize the problem before it is too late.

Every company would like to have satisfied employees which are key factors to the company's success. Employees having a high level of job satisfaction love their job, they have a sense of belonging and righteousness, and they consider that job brings happiness to their lives. Offering employees different options and possibilities, and positive aspects, company will secure hardworking, creative, loyal employees which will always give their best for the company. Satisfied employees will sometimes dedicate their private time to their jobs because they often know that they will also benefit from it. Regular communication is always needed for the smooth and impeccable efficiency and understanding between superiors and their subordinates. Satisfied employees are loyal and willing to improve and succeed which at the same time secures the company's future. Employee satisfaction is the key aspect of the company's long-term success, and that is why it should be dedicated a plenty of time. Its trends should be regularly followed by management that will also constantly create the environment for its advance and prosperity in order to avoid any possible dissatisfactory effects which always hurt company in a particular manner.

9 Factors Affecting Job Satisfaction

A long time ago managers realized that employee satisfaction is one of the key factors to company's long-term success. Considering this, managers are interested in all factors that might affect the employees' satisfaction. Noticing, recognizing, and inspecting factors affecting the job satisfaction or dissatisfaction is a long and complex process which every top-level company caring about their employees and future plans should take into consideration. Method of approaching job satisfaction factors individually at the workplace is used when we try to specifically establish the factors influencing and affecting satisfaction or dissatisfaction of an employee. Factors can differentiate depending on the company's size and number of employees. According to Mullins (1999), there are five different factor groups: individual, social, cultural organizational, and environmental factors. Spector (1997), however, groups factors into only two categories. First one relates to working environment and job itself, while the other one relates to individual characteristics of an employee. Third interesting classification is stated by Baron and Greenberg (1990). They distinguish three factor groups that influence the satisfaction: organizational factors, dimensions linked to job, and employees' individual characteristics.

Factors affecting the employees' job satisfaction would be job characteristics, room for improvement, career development, coworkers, superiors, salary, stimulations, working place, job conditions, balance between job and private life, stress, workload, and job safety, as stated by Bakotić (2009). Every aforementioned factor more or less influences and affects job satisfaction, depending on company, employees' performance, and eventually the company itself.

10 Job (dis)Satisfaction Effects

When speaking of job dissatisfaction and satisfaction, it is important to mention that in this case, different authors state different segments and variables. Variables most commonly taken into consideration in this context according to Bakotić (2009) are individual performances, absenteeism, fluctuation, physical and mental wealth, counterproductive behavior, life satisfaction, civil duty, and similar.

It is logical to assume that satisfied workers will be more productive than the not satisfied ones. Satisfied worker is also a happy and motivated worker who will do his best for the sake of the company. In contrast to the logical and simple assumption, there are researches that indicate that there is no connection between the job satisfaction and productivity or performance. One of the reasons is the fact that many jobs require a certain degree of technological equipment. Technology disables workers to directly affect their job efficiency. Another reason is reward that is directly linked to employees' performance. Salary depends on this connection. Employee's perception is very important regarding the salary and how it is distributed. In this context, in the positive correlation of job satisfaction and individual performances it is important to mention that this correlation increases as the job complexity increases, because more complex jobs require a certain level of autonomy and a sense of importance which directly affects satisfaction. Positive correlation also increases as the role of an employee within company increases. This correlation is much higher in more successful and influential companies. Likert (1961) points out that difference and interest but also the requirements of a job affect the job satisfaction and individual performances relation because boring and repetitive jobs do not affect motivating factors. Cadwell and O'Reilly (1990) accentuate that there is a reverse effect, meaning that individual performances affect the job satisfaction. This thesis is justified in the context of self-actualizing of an individual, meaning that an individual who reached his potential and who improved his skills will be happy and satisfied with the job and will serve as a good example to others.

Absenteeism can be defined as absence from work. There are various reasons why this happens, but whatever they might be, consequences of absenteeism are always negative. By being absent from work, there is the lack of workforce on a particular position which automatically influences efficiency of the company. Employees' absence means that company has to find a proper substitute to fill in his position which requires additional cost. At the same time, company most often pays employees' day off and his substitute. Absenteeism greatly influences company's cost, and at the same time, it affects the working environment and environment within the department in which absent employee works.

Fluctuation, however, is defined as one of the key factors directly influencing job satisfaction. Workers that are extremely dissatisfied with the job will most likely seek out higher level of satisfaction, meaning they will look for a new job. Fluctuation as a factor should be divided into evitable and inevitable. Evitable fluctuation includes job abandoning by their own decisions and desire basis or because of the organizational needs. Inevitable fluctuation includes job leaving because of retirement or death. Companies can greatly influence evitable fluctuation, while on the other hand they cannot influence inevitable fluctuation. Bahtijarević-Šiber (1999) points out that fluctuation is often an expression of dissatisfaction, while its high rate and tendency are a result of dissatisfactory state within the company. Meaning, if organizational and individual factors are strong and influential enough to directly affect the job dissatisfaction or simply decrease satisfaction, then there might be the need for employee to leave. Having that intention, individual will start seeking a new job. If opportunity for an alternative job arises, fluctuation is unlikely. By employee's departure, company has to find a proper substitute on a short notice. Companies have to be ready and prepared for situations like these. It is required to act positively in company's working environment and to care about the satisfaction of the current employees, but at the same time HR management has to plan ahead situations like these and have a strategy for future hirings so that the consequences of potential fluctuations would be lower. Mainly, the cost of potential fluctuation falls under departure costs, acquiring costs, selection costs, and training costs.

Counterproductive behavior as a consequence of job dissatisfaction is also important segment that has to be noticed on time and prevented accordingly. Counterproductive behavior is a serious issue because employees willingly damage the company they are working for. That damage can occur through disobedience, disturbing others while working, aggressive behavior toward coworkers and subordinates, damaging the company's goods and estate, and even sabotage and theft. Companies have to be aware that behaviors like these are a reality and that there is no guarantee that something like this will not happen within a particular company. The only thing companies can do in this situation is to positively influence the satisfaction of the employees and regularly check the satisfaction level.

Satisfaction with one's own private life is also a segment that is in correlation to job satisfaction. Job satisfaction definitely affects the mental state of an individual and like that it pours into private life satisfaction. As much as an individual tries to balance out and separate private life from the work, its mental state from one segment will most definitely affect the other. Managers have to be aware that non-satisfied worker will be less happy in his private life and that there is anxiety and depression whose consequences are much more extensive than the potential employees' departure from the company.

Some of the ways of showing dissatisfaction at job are being late to work, theft, etc. Tardiness can relate to a couple of minutes up to a couple of hours. It can be a direct consequence of dissatisfaction. That exact same tardiness affects the timely task execution and relationship between coworkers and others that have to make for that individual. If tardiness occurs often, management should consider that as one of the signals that there is a certain degree of dissatisfaction within the company and that something has to be done in that regard. Theft on the workplace is also one of the bad ways of showing dissatisfaction and can have long-term consequences on future hirings of an individual. Reason why theft occurs can be a desire for additional material means, targeted damage (purpose), or dissatisfactory consequence with the compensation package for own work. Theft as a felony is a tough way of showing dissatisfaction. If company notices the theft, then symptoms of a huge dissatisfaction will be revealed too. After noticing the theft, it is needed to find the core issue and gradually solve it for the sake of long-term satisfaction for both parties.

11 Manager Ethical Behavior in the Context of Croatian Companies: Analysis of the Current State and Directions for Improvement

Ignoring the ethics in a contemporary business world is surely something that usually has the long-term negative consequences. Besides neglecting ethics and ethic behavior completely, in all segments of business, the problems are also exceptional situations where ethics is put aside in making big decisions.

We are witnesses that in the Republic of Croatia, there are a large number of enterprises whose high ranked employees are not familiar with the terms such as ethics, ethic behavior, and ethical decision making. Business managers are definitely those who have the greatest responsibility when it comes to business ethics. They are the ones who make crucial decisions their enterprise depends on. Primarily their acquaintance with ethical principles and ethical framework is introduction to Ethical Behavior in Decision Making.

Talking about management of business ethics in the Republic of Croatia, we come to defeating data. Croatia is definitely way behind the developed world states in the matter of business ethics. If you compare Croatia's business activities with the level of ethics, we are among the top nations of business insecurity. We are talking about mid-sized enterprises which have bad or not at all developed business ethics control system. Maybe the reason to that lies in the fact that our people give small significance to ethics when business is in question, because profit comes first to those people, short-term goals are more important than long-term goals, and they practically do not choose how to achieve them; what matters the most is that they are achieved.

Perhaps we need higher level of knowledge about ethics and importance of ethical behavior. It is important to get people acquainted with ethics, and the way it functions as a term, and give them reasons to act in the future in accordance with ethics. There are also special organizations that hold lectures on ethics and help implement ethics in business, but this does not work for our small businesses because it requires certain financial resources and it takes away all of our precious time.

In this way of thinking, as a state, we will find ourselves in various problems. Unlike already aforementioned small and mid-sized enterprise, large enterprises have realized the importance of ethical behavior and they invest more time and money into quality ethical management and handling training. They are aware of the fact that only this way they will achieve their long-term goals and create a quality picture of their enterprises in the eyes of the observers. Croatia has tried its best throughout the years to get better ethic-wise; growth is imminent, but considering all the possibilities in relation to other nations, we are lagging behind. Problems are more complex, and a series of issues should be handled in that regard especially corruption and bribe. Corruption is one of the main issues leaving Croatia unable to prosper ethic-wise. Legislative system fronts in this particular issue. Solutions are existent, but structural changes are required. Mentality and the way people perceive things should be changed which is not an easy task. Even though, if it lasts for quite some time, it is important for corruption to cease, for the sake of future generations and for the sake of our country. Maybe one of the potential solutions is privatization that brings foreign investors who think and do business in an ethical manner. They might be the ones to bring and pass on the importance of business ethics and the importance of socially responsible behavior.

In a business world, it is easy to stray away from ethics and then when decision is thought to be the ethical one. Therefore, it is necessary to create an ethical framework within an organization. Ethical frameworks are the product of ethical codex of the organization. With the existence of ethical framework within an organization, managers, in a great deal of situations, would know if some of the problem-solving facts fall under ethical framework, therefore acting ethically. If there is a decreased application of ethical behavior in the organization, it would probably have consequences on employee's morale. Managers are the ones who with their example and behavior present themselves as role models to others. Being a good example, managers in particular companies can surely influence on employee satisfaction, who will consequently be more efficient and effective in their job performance. Managers consciously or unconsciously influence the employee satisfaction, through qualities such as trust, loyalty, pride, arrangement, working environment, organizational atmosphere, strengthening employees, organizational activities awareness, and taking part in decision making.

Managers need to be active in creating positive surroundings and conditions for success, transparency, and responsibility. To make their employees satisfied, managers need to pay attention to their motivation, factors of their motivation, needs and wishes, and their active involvement in decision making. Thus, managers have to be given attention on building up the capacity of their own followers for the purpose of creating the sustainability. That would mean existence of tendency of scouting and developing the best and most talented employees. That is the exact moral imperative that will help leadership in adding the additional value to the organization. Managers' ethical behavior will positively affect the quality of decision-making process. By acting ethically, managers will simply learn the principle of making the optimal decision for their companies. They will learn how to view all the relevant facts and make the right call in acceptable amount of time. Quality of decision making itself will not be questioned. Managers will have the right information at the right time and when they are guided by their ethical principles, the process of making the right decision somehow will become habitual because in the organization where ethical behavior awareness is developed, work quality is not questionable.

Likewise, manager's ethical behavior will affect positively on employees' satisfaction in one of the key factors of long-term companies' success. Managers, by acting ethically, thinking about the overall good of all the employees, the whole company, let the employees know they care for them and that they will always try to make the optimal decision for all the interest groups. Understanding the importance of employee satisfaction, managers will often initiate investment into improvement of satisfaction, accordingly. In such environment, loaded with trust, employees will surely be happy and satisfied. They will pass on that satisfaction consciously and unconsciously to their work which will in the end reflect onto business success. Satisfied employee is a prerequisite to an efficient worker and company's success. Hence, in an enterprise where ethical management is present, decisions will be made in a quality manner. Such decisions will be beneficial for whole company and all employees; trusting environment will result in employee's satisfaction which eventually leads to long-term company success. It's about one causative-consequential circle which needs to be understood. It is necessary to invest in proper resources so that in the end, all the interest groups can be satisfied, and the company can reach its success.

12 Empirical Research

The empirical research of this chapter was focused on two levels of observation. The first level of observation was decision makers' ethics, while the second was the employee's satisfaction. The selected company is a Croatian public city company located in Split. By using a questionnaire filled out by the employees of this company, the ethics of the decision makers were analyzed, as well as the satisfaction

Table 1 Cronbach's alpha test

	Cronbach's alpha	No. of items
E1 Respecting organizational rules	0.988	6
E2 Importance of Personal Interest	0.991	7
E3 Quality of relationship with other people	0.988	7
E4 Personality of the decision maker	0.981	4

of the employees with ethical behavior of all major decision makers in the company. The following hypotheses were tested:

H1 The ethical behavior of decision makers positively affects the quality of the business decision-making process.

H2 The ethical behavior of decision makers positively affects the employee satisfaction.

Thirty employees were involved in the research: 76.6% of male and 23.33% of women. For the analysis of main variable—ethical behavior of decision makers—four variables of the total of 24 statements were used to test hypotheses: *E1. Respecting organizational rules; E2 Importance of Personal Interest; E3. Quality of relationship with other people; E4. Personality of the decision maker.*

In order to confirm relevance of formed variables, the Cronbach's alpha test was performed. Since values were greater than 0.6, it could be claimed that these variables are consistent (Table 1).

This research was based on the following assumptions. If decision makers are familiar with business ethics, then the process of making such decisions is not so complex. Namely, decision makers can learn to avoid ethically dangerous zones and thus avoid any more complicated situations. Knowing the ethical principles and codes, having already experience in ethical situations, the decision-making process will be faster, decisions will be less reconsidered, and the same decision will be positive in the eyes of employees and the public.

Each decision that had been made has an influence on the enterprise performance but at the same time has influence on the employees of that enterprise. Most often, this activity reflects the satisfaction of employees. By acting ethically in all situations without exception, decision makers gain the confidence of employees. Behaving ethically also means occasionally holding meetings with employees and discussing some issues that bother them. In this way, the relationships between managers and employees will be satisfactory, which will result in a positive working atmosphere which is the one of the factors for successful business.

The results of the testing settled hypothesis are shown in Table 2. As can be seen from the table, the results of the tests have shown that there is significant interdependence between observed variables. The results showed that the ethical behavior of managers has a positive effect on the quality of the decision-making process. By acting ethically, managers will simply learn the principle of making optimal business decisions. They will learn how to look at all the relevant facts in an acceptable time and make the right decision. The quality of the decision-making process in this way will not come into question. Managers will have the right

Table 2 Ethical behavior of decision makers, quality of decision making, and employees' satisfaction

Spearman's rho Correlation coefficient; Sig. (2-tailed); $N = 30$	DMQ	ES
MS1	0.932**	0.903**
	0.000	0.000
MS2	0.896**	0.900**
	0.000	0.000
MS3	0.902**	0.897**
	0.000	0.000
MS4	0.876**	0.879**
	0.000	0.000

Source: Research results
**$p < 0.01$

information at the right time, and guided by their ethical principles, the process of making the right decisions becomes a bit routine because in a company where awareness of ethical behavior is developed, quality of work is not questionable. According to the results, the first hypothesis was accepted meaning that ethical behavior of the managers positively affects the quality of the business decision-making process.

By testing the second hypothesis, it can be concluded that the ethical behavior of decision makers positively affects the satisfaction of employees who are ultimately one of the key factors of long-term business success. As it can been seen from the table below, there is a statistically significant interdependence between ethical behavior of decision makers (MS1; MS2; MS3; MS4) and employees' satisfaction (ES). Decision makers, who are acting ethically, will consider the benefit of all employees and the whole enterprise when making decisions.

Realizing the importance of employee satisfaction, managers will regularly initiate adequate investment in improving the satisfaction segments. This satisfaction will be consciously and unconsciously transmitted to their own work that will ultimately affect the company's business success. Satisfied worker is a prerequisite for an efficient worker, and accordingly, the business of the company will be efficient and therefore result in profit. Looking at the results obtained with the second hypothesis, it is concluded that there is a strong and positive link between managerial ethics and overall employee satisfaction. Accordingly, another hypothesis is confirmed in the work, which is that the ethical behavior of the managers will positively affect the total satisfaction of the employees.

13 Conclusion

Ethics is definitely a term which is greatly neglected in today's business world but also a term whose importance rises. Its importance is unquestionable. Only questionable thing is, at what level ethics is applied in internal decision-making processes. Organizations in today's environment have responsibility, not just for their own interest, but they have to act in accordance with the social demands and circumstances. A condition is being laid out in front of the socially responsible behaving companies which is based on ethic principles. Those ethic principles have to be embedded in every organization's structure, primarily through ethical standards of the organization itself that are manifested in ethic codex, ethical boards, and training, thus becoming the crucial part of the organizational culture. Managers are those who should take care of ethical harmony rules in the company. Ethical managers are the ones being called out for being unethical during the decision-making process.

For ethical decision making, it is important that throughout the whole process, ethic is always in the first place. It is also important that ethic spreads out through the whole decision-making process. Successful manager is the one who creates such environment that enables his subordinates and superiors to develop independence and responsibility in decision making. Socially responsible behavior enables organizations a prominent image. Acting in accordance with ethical standards, it attracts new employees, motivates and keeps previously hired employees, and develops an image of organization as a law-abiding citizen. Employee satisfaction is closely linked to manager's ethics. By acting ethically, managers directly affect employee's satisfaction. Satisfied worker will be more efficient. Investing and maintaining employee satisfaction elements, managers achieve the double benefit. Only the companies that realize in time the importance of ethics and satisfaction will continuously invest in improvement of previously mentioned factors. Only companies like these can achieve their long-term profits and goals and deal with their business efficiency. In spite of great importance of ethics in the business world, overall employee satisfaction, the necessity for the promotion of social values, and responsibility, business practice in Croatia is on many levels behind the developed countries in the world. That lack of expertise is visible in small and mid-sized companies where ethical management skills are less developed. They lack regular investment in satisfaction elements, unlike the bigger companies of Croatian economy which accepted world trends.

Ahead of all companies and ahead of all nations, and so Croatian, is the future that holds many opportunities and troubles. Only those companies doing business in an ethical manner, those who have present ethical thinking when making decision, those who judge discrimination, and those who base their every move on the ethical thinking have their doors wide open in the world and gain satisfaction of all interest groups. We will see what will happen in the future, but one thing is certain and that is the fact that manager's ethics and job satisfaction will become the key segment of company's success.

References

Aleksić, A. (2007). Poslovna etika – elementi uspješnog poslovanja, Zbornik ekonomskog fakulteta u Zagrebu (str. 420–428).

Bahtijarević-Šiber, F. (1999). *Management ljudskih potencijala* (str. 939–941). Zagreb: Golden Marketing.

Bakotić, D. (2009) *Međuovisnost zadovoljstva na radu radnika znanja i organizacijskih performansi*. Doktorska disertacija, Split (str. 46–89).

Baron, R. A., & Greenberg, J. (1990). *Behaviour in organizations: Understanding and managing the human side of work* (p. 165). Boston: Allyn & Bacon.

Black, S. J., & Steers, R. M. (1994). *Organizational behaviour* (p. 87). New York: Harper Collins College Publishers.

Buble, M. (2006). *Osnove managementa* (str. 60–63). Zagreb: Sinergija nakladništvo.

Cadwell, D. F., & O'Reilly, C. A. (1990). Measuring person-job fit with a profile-comparison process. *Journal of Applied Psychology, 75*, 648–657.

Daft, R. L. (1992). *Organization theory and design* (4th ed.p. 346). St. Paul: West Publishing.

Daft, R. L., & Marcic, D. (2001). *Understanding management* (p. 358). Mason, OH: South Western Thomas Learning.

Davis, K., & Newstrom, J. W. (1989). *Human behaviour at work* (p. 176). New York: McGraw-Hill.

Furnham, A. (1997). *The psychology of behaviour at work. The individual in the organization* (p. 896). London: Taylor & Francis.

Gordon, J. R., Mondy, R. W., Sharplin, A., & Premeaux, S. R. (1990). *Management and organizational behaviour* (p. 173). Boston: Allyn and Bacon.

Koontz, H., & Weihrich, H. (1990). *Essentials of management* (5th ed.p. 108). New York: McGraw-Hill.

Leap, T. L., & Crino, M. D. (1993). *Personnel/human resource management* (p. 61). New York: Macmillan Publishing Company.

Likert, R. (1961). *New patterns of management*. New York: McGraw-Hill (Preuzeo od: Katz, D., Kahn, R. L. (1967). The social psychology of organizations).

Marušić, S. (1990). *Motivacija za rad i profesionalni razvoj* (str. 22). Zagreb: Ekonomski institut Zagreb.

Mescon, M., Albert, M., & Khedouri, F. (1985). *Management* (p. 169). New York: Harper and Row.

Messick, D. M., Bazerman, M. H., & Stewart, L. (2006). *Avoiding ethical danger zones* (pp. 4–16). Business Roundtable Institute for Corporate Ethics.

Mullins, L. J. (1999). *Management and organizational behaviour* (p. 631). London: Financial Times, Pitman Publishing.

Perić, J. (2011). Poslovna etika. Dostupno na: http://www.efos.unios.hr/arhiva/dokumenti/PE1_Poslovna%20etika_Uvod_25042012.pdf (Pristupljeno 24.08.2016).

Perko-Šeparović, I. (1975). *Teorije organizacije* (str. 134). Zagreb: Školska knjiga.

Spector, P. E. (1997). *Job satisfaction, application, assessment, causes and consequences* (p. 30). London: ATOB.

Žugaj, M. (1990). Znanstveno-istraživački rad mladih, Zbornik radova, Fakultet organizacije i informatike, Varaždin (str. 288).

Printed by Printforce, the Netherlands